Theology in the Public Sphere

Theology in the Public Sphere

Sebastian C. H. Kim

scm press

Published in 2011 by SCM Press
Editorial office
13–17 Long Lane,
London, EC1A 9PN, UK

SCM Press is an imprint of Hymns Ancient & Modern Ltd
(a registered charity)
13a Hellesdon Park Road
Norwich NR6 5DR, UK

www.scm-canterburypress.co.uk

British Library Cataloguing in Publication data

A catalogue record for this book is available
from the British Library

978-0-334-04377-5

Typeset by Regent Typesetting, London
Printed and bound by
CPI Group (UK) Ltd, Croydon, CR0 4YY

Contents

Preface

'The time has come. The moment of truth has arrived!' says the Kairos Document. At the height of the Apartheid oppression in South Africa, the Kairos Document was signed by 156 church leaders and theologians in the town of Soweto in September 1985. This is a highly significant document that challenged not only the Apartheid regime but also the churches in South Africa. The signatories questioned what they called 'state theology', which endorsed the status quo. Instead, they advocated 'prophetic theology', which urged Christians to act to bring hope for the nation. The legacy of this 'Kairos' movement continued when the post-Apartheid South African government set up the Truth and Reconciliation Commission led by Archbishop Desmond Tutu, which made a significant contribution to healing the wounds of the nation.

During the 1970s and 1980s, South Korea went through a time of crisis as the vast majority of company workers were exploited by the *jaebul* – family-run mega-companies. Minjung theologians challenged the modern capitalist market economy of the *jaebul* and the unjust operation of the military-backed government. Minjung theologians captured people's imagination and brought the issue of poverty and injustice into the Church. They also encouraged the workers by showing that they should not be the objects of exploitation and that their protest was a legitimate one. Minjung theology made a vital contribution to modern Korean history by bringing the biblical concept of justice into the Korean political arena and by standing side by side with the people who are suffering.

On 2 July 2005 in Edinburgh, against the background of the Castle and Mound, Princes Street was thronged with people wearing white T-shirts and holding placards with slogans as they participated in the Make Poverty History campaign. Indeed, it was the largest demonstration Scotland had ever witnessed; an estimated 225,000 people from all over Britain. The Jubilee 2000 campaign and later the Make Poverty History campaign were, by and large, initiated and carried out by Christian churches and organizations. Christians took one of the most pertinent (and yet perhaps least implemented) symbols of justice from the Hebrew Bible and applied it to the contemporary context of global injustice. The campaign influenced political leaders to listen to the voice of people. It is indeed the demonstration of a mature society, where people are concerned not only for their immediate family, relatives or friends but for those of other continents, nations and cultures.

The above examples are some well-known cases of how Christian theology has shaped and challenged the course of societies in various ways, and illustrate how the Church can be involved in socio-political and economic life.

Public theology is not a new concept; Christian theology has always tried to be relevant to the context and society. Now, with the privatization of Christian faith, public theology has emerged in theological discourse. As the South African theologian John de Gruchy points out, theologians tend to fall into one of two extremes: either believing that theology makes more of a contribution and a difference than it actually does, or underestimating the significance of its public role.[1] This is due to the fact that the language and audience of Christian theology has been largely confined within church circles. Public theology is to do with seeking to engage in dialogue with those outside Christian circles on various issues and urging Christians to participate in the public domain. It seeks to converse with citizens on issues wider than religious matters.

Kenneth S. Latourette, in his monumental work *A History of the Expansion of Christianity*, explained the way he interpreted the expansion of Christianity in three perspectives: geographical expansion (according to the numbers of Christians and churches); the vigour of Christianity in any given era (according to new movements and denominations); and the effect of Christianity upon humankind.[2] Most studies – even, I would say, Latourette's work itself – are done from the first two perspectives, and the last perspective is very difficult to assess indeed, if not impossible. However, the question of how we assess Christianity in a given context needs to include more than its numerical strength and the study of the ways and means of its expansion. I will argue that evaluating the strength of Christianity in any society has more to do with the *integrity* of the Christian Church, and this has to be constantly reassessed, however difficult it may be.

In plural societies, Christians do not have a monopoly on public space – they may even be a small minority – but this does not necessar-

---

1 John de Gruchy, 'From Political to Public Theologies: The Role of Theology in Public Life in South Africa', in William Storrar and Andrew Morton (eds), *Public Theology for the 21st Century* (London and New York: T & T Clark, 2004), pp. 45–62.

2 Kenneth S. Latourette, *A History of the Expansion of Christianity*, vol. 7 (New York: Harper & Row, 1971), pp. 416–18.

ily diminish the public significance of the Christian message. When we discuss the situation of the Church in a particular region, nation or continent, people often talk about the numbers of churches or Christians as if that is the measurement of the public significance of Christianity there. Yes, statistics may give a general picture of the situation, but they don't provide an accurate understanding of the role and impact of the Christian gospel on that society. As I have argued elsewhere,[3] many churches around the world, in spite of their small numbers, have made significant contributions to the society and nation, not just protecting their own immediate concerns or those about the numbers of congregations, but seeking the public good.

There are three main arguments in this book. First, that in the contexts of postmodern and pluralist societies, for reasons of justice, the Church should oppose any monopoly on power – political, economic, social and religious – and support the creation of a public sphere with open access and public debate. Second, that the Church should actively engage in the public sphere, and so needs to develop a 'public theology' in order to play an appropriate and prophetic role in the wider society. This endeavour is not in order to formulate a set methodology but rather utilizes a variety of theological approaches to deal with complex issues. And third, doing public theology should be the outcome of interaction in the hermeneutical circle of theory and practice so that the task involves the whole Christian community – theologians, church leaders and ordinary congregations – by actively interacting with other religious communities, NGOs and the wider society.

According to Harold Breitenberg, there are three types of literature on public theology: writings about particular 'public theologians' and what they understand public theology to be; discussion of what public theology is and how it should be carried out; and the 'constructive public theology', which means 'theologically grounded and informed interpretations of and guidance for institutions, interactions, events, circumstances, policies, and practices, both within and outside the church'.[4] The first two are more to do with developing public theology as a discourse, whereas the last category is to do with the practical application of theology in the public square. I would place this monograph in the last category of constructive public theology.

Because the practical application of theology is always contextual, instead of presenting a systematic and comprehensive account of public theology 'from above' as a worked-out programme applicable to every

---

3 Sebastian C. H. Kim and Kirsteen Kim, *Christianity as a World Religion* (London: Continuum, 2008).

4 E. Harold Breitenberg, 'To tell the Truth: Will the Real Public Theology Please Stand Up?', *Journal of the Society of Christian Ethics* 23/2 (2003), pp. 55–96 at 64.

situation, I will provide selected historical and contemporary examples of doing public theology so that readers will appreciate the public issues faced by Christian communities in various contexts and the different theological approaches they have developed to deal with them. I have deliberately included cases from global contexts partly because they are less well known to wider theological circles and also to show that there are many creative public theological explorations taking place. Towards the end of each chapter, I will draw out some methodological points pertinent to other contexts and common to the public engagement of theology in contemporary societies. In other words, I will work 'from below', using concrete examples, to distinguish public theology as a theological approach while also recognizing its diversity on the ground.

In Part 1, I will first give a brief survey of the development, rationale and methodologies of public theology. I shall then examine how the Bible has been utilized in forming various distinctive Christian perspectives, and more importantly how the various interpretations helped Christian communities to meet challenging situations. I will also discuss different approaches to constructing eco-theology as an example of doing public theology in ways that reinterpret traditional theology to meet the contemporary ecological crisis. In Part 2, I shall discuss four different public theological discourses in the global contexts of India, Korea, Latin America, the UK and the USA. These deal respectively with the issues of the relationship between the Christian community and wider communities, socio-political reconciliation, global inequalities and peace-building. The chapters in this Part will demonstrate some of the critical challenges churches have faced and their theological and practical responses to them. They demonstrate that Christians have not shied away from the difficulties but have actively participated, risking their security and moving out from their comfort zones. The chapters in Part 3 focus on issues in contemporary Europe – Archbishop Rowan Williams' lecture on sharia law, the Danish cartoons controversy, and the UK Racial and Religious Hatred Bill – in order to demonstrate some of the challenges faced in Europe. These are identified as the role of secular values and religious faiths in legal systems, freedom of expression and respect for faith, and identity and critical dialogue for a healthy engagement of religious communities in the modern, postmodern, and supposedly secular societies of Europe.

With the growth of civil society and the increase in secularism, there is both an invitation and also an urgent need for Christian theology to be actively engaged in conversation on public issues. Of course, Christian theology does not have all the answers to these issues but, among other voices, it can put forward moral, ethical and spiritual insights that make a vital contribution to addressing problems and promoting the common good in modern societies.

I would like to express my appreciation to the various people who have made valuable contributions and have supported me in this project: Dr Natalie Watson and her team at SCM Press, my colleagues at the Faculty of Education and Theology at York St John University, the members of the Global Network for Public Theology, the Editorial Board members of the *International Journal of Public Theology*, and to my family, Kirsteen, Jonathan and Lydia.

PART 1

Exploring Public Theology

I

Introduction:
Theology and the Public Sphere

As the theology of God's kingdom, theology has to be *public* theology: public, critical and prophetic complaint to God – public, critical and prophetic hope in God.[1]

Public theology is Christians engaging in dialogue with those outside church circles on various issues of common interest. It involves urging Christians to take the opportunity to participate in the public domain in modern secular democracies and to converse with other citizens on issues wider than religious matters. There is an urgent need for Christian theology to be actively engaged in conversation on public issues with the understanding that it can offer complementary or supplementary approaches, and even alternative solutions, to the very complex issues facing society today. The key word for public theology is public *conversation*, contributing to the formation of personal decisions and collective policy-making in economic, political, religious and social realms. In many ways public theology shares some characteristics of different theological discourses such as political theology, social ethics and liberation theology but, as I will show, it has also established its own distinctive ways to engage in public issues.

The development of public theology

The term 'public theology' was introduced by Martin Marty in his attempt to distinguish it from the 'civil religion' discussed by Robert Bellah in commenting on American public life in the 1960s.[2] While both concepts overlap considerably, civil religion emphasizes the place

---

1 Jürgen Moltmann, *God for a Secular Society: The Public Relevance of Theology* (London: SCM Press, 1999), p. 5.

2 Martin Marty, 'Reinhold Niebuhr: Public Theology and the American Experience', *The Journal of Religion* 54/4 (October 1974). See also Martin Marty, *Public Church: Main-line–Evangelical–Catholic* (New York: Crossroad, 1981). Robert Bellah, 'Public Philosophy and Public Theology', in Leroy Rouner (ed.), *Civil Religion and Political Theology* (Notre Dame, IN: Notre Dame University Press, 1986), pp. 79–97.

and role of religion (and Christianity in particular) in relation to the nation and its people in their public life and social responsibilities, whereas public theology starts from the religious community and considers its contributions to the society and nation. Discussions of the difference between civil religion and public theology, and the marginalization of Christian theology in the context of America, were ongoing in the 1970s and 1980s in theological circles in the USA, led by John Courtney Murray,[3] David Hollenbach,[4] David Tracy,[5] Richard John Neuhaus,[6] Max Stackhouse,[7] Linell Cady[8] and Ronald F. Thiemann,[9] among others.

In his discussion of mainline Protestant, Evangelical and Catholic churches in the USA, Martin Marty suggested that together they form a 'public Church', which holds distinctive resources to respond to the challenge of what he identified as a 'crisis of morale and mission'.[10] He defines the 'public Church' as 'a family of apostolic churches with Jesus Christ at the centre', which are especially sensitive to the *'res publica*, the public order that surrounds and includes people of faith'. Since it is made up of several different confessions, he also describes 'the public Church' as 'a communion of communions', distinctive and yet sharing 'a common Christian vocation'.[11] Marty contrasts his vision of the public Church with other ways in which religions organize themselves: totalist (a theocratic approach); tribalist (exclusive and self-interested approaches); and privatist (an individualistic approach).[12] He derives the word 'public' from the 'public religion' described by Benjamin Franklin, which he thinks 'fits the American pluralist pattern better' than Jean-Jacques Rousseau's 'civil religion'. This suggests that these three churches can contribute out of their particular resources to

---

3 John Courtney Murray, *We Hold These Truths: Catholic Reflections on the American Proposition* (New York: Sheed & Ward, 1960).

4 David Hollenbach, 'Public Theology in America: Some Questions for Catholicism after John Courtney Murray', *Theological Studies* 37/2 (June 1976); David Hollenbach, *The Global Face of Public Faith: Politics, Human Rights, and Christian Ethics* (Washington, DC: Georgetown University Press, 2003).

5 David Tracy, *The Analogical Imagination: Christian Theology and the Culture of Pluralism* (New York: Crossroad, 1981).

6 Richard John Neuhaus, *The Naked Public Square: Religion and Democracy in America*, 2nd edn (Grand Rapids, MI: Eerdmans, 1986).

7 Max Stackhouse, *Public Theology and Political Economy: Christian Stewardship in Modern Society* (Lanham, MD: University Press of America, 1991).

8 Linell E. Cady, *Religion, Theology and American Public Life* (New York: State University of New York Press, 1993).

9 Ronald F. Thiemann, *Constructing a Public Theology: The Church in a Pluralistic Culture* (Louisville, KY: John Knox Press, 1991).

10 Marty, *Public Church*, pp. ix–xii.

11 Marty, *Public Church*, pp. 3 and 170.

12 Marty, *Public Church*, pp. 6–8.

'public virtue and the common weal'. Public theology then becomes, in Marty's view, 'an effort to interpret the life of a people in the light of a transcendent reference'.[13] Doing public theology or being public Church is to exhibit 'commitment to relate private faith to public order'.[14] The public Church recognizes that it 'shares traditions, reasons, aspects of Enlightenment, civic purpose, and transecting philosophies with many of the constituents and collegia in the larger civic order', but 'adapting does not mean letting all moorings go'. Although the public Church is in some respects also a political church, and will be seen by some as compromising and unfaithful, it cannot be so or its very existence must be questioned. The public Church contributes to public discourse out of its own particular revelation and the principles it has developed.[15]

Although he tends to be over-optimistic about the role of the Church in American public life, Marty's idea of the public Church and its relationship with politics and society is very helpful and has certainly made a significant impact on the discussion of public theology. He argues historically that each of the three traditions – mainline Protestant, Evangelical and Catholic churches – have inherently public theologies which have influenced US society over several centuries. Although the term was not used explicitly, it has been present in the USA from the time of the Pilgrim Fathers. Public theology was prominent especially in the Evangelical revivals and in the social gospel movement. Since the 1960s especially, public theologies that have been influential globally include Catholic social teaching, statements on social and political issues by the ecumenical movement, and the black theology of the civil rights movement. It has also been prevalent in discussion of religious pluralism, and in the black and feminist theologies of recent years.[16] In the 1980s, the publication of the two pastoral letters from the US Conference of Bishops, *The Challenge of Peace: God's Promise and Our Response* (1983) and *Economic Justice for All* (1986), triggered much discussion within the Church and in the academy on the issues of 'civil discourse' and the ways and means to engage in public life.[17] The dominant themes of public theology in the USA in this period were the role of religion in a democratic polity, Christian social vision and political liberalism, the significance of church-related social institutions and the relationship of theological resources to the global economy.[18]

---

13 Marty, *Public Church*, pp. 9–22.

14 Marty, *Public Church*, pp. 98–9.

15 Marty, *Public Church*, pp. 164–6.

16 Steven M. Tipton, 'Public Theology', in Robert Wuthnow (ed.), *The Encyclopedia of Politics and Religion* (Washington, DC: Congressional Quarterly Inc., 1998), pp. 624–5.

17 See W. D. Lindsey, 'Public Theology as Civil Discourse: What are We Talking About?', *Horizons* 19/1 (1992), pp. 44–69.

18 J. Bryan Hehir, 'Forum', *Religion and American Culture* 10/1 (2000), p. 20.

In the last decade, there have been relatively fewer writings published in the USA on public theology and instead initiatives have been coming from Europe, South Africa and Australia particularly. Unlike the US situation where individual scholars are leading discussions on the topic, elsewhere centres for public theology have been established within universities and denominations. This development has produced a new vitality in discussing public theology and, as a result, the Global Network for Public Theology (GNPT), with a membership of 25 centres and institutions worldwide, was launched in Edinburgh in 2006 and formally established in Princeton in its second consultation in May 2007. Its aim is to conduct interdisciplinary research in theology and public issues in global and local contexts. At the second consultation, the *International Journal of Public Theology* (*IJPT*) was launched to provide a 'platform for original interdisciplinary research in the field of public theology' in dialogue with different academic disciplines such as politics, economics, cultural studies and religious studies, as well as with spirituality, globalization and society in general.[19] Within the Network, some major research centres are the Centre for Theology and Public Issues (CTPI) of the University of Edinburgh, the Beyers Naudé Centre for Public Theology, University of Stellenbosch, South Africa, the Public and Contextual Theology Strategic Research Centre, Charles Sturt University, Australia, the Manchester Centre for Public Theology, and Dietrich Bonhoeffer Research Centre for Public Theology, University of Bamberg, Germany. These centres of the Global Network are based in universities and their main concerns are to address particular issues in their local and national contexts, but they are increasingly interested in wider issues such as globalization, climate change, poverty, civil society, human rights, gender and racial equality.

In the UK in recent years, in addition to those mentioned above, a number of other centres have been established within universities and churches: the Institute for Religion and Public Life in the University of Leeds, the Network for Religion and Public Life in the University of Exeter, the McDonald Centre for Theology, Ethics and Public Life in the University of Oxford; the Heythrop Institute for Religion, Ethics and Public Life; the Chair in Theology and Public Life in York St John University; and the Centre for Faiths and Public Policy, University of Chester. There are also independent and church-based centres: Theos: Public Theology Think Tank; the Kirby Laing Institute for Christian Ethics; Jubilee Centre; the prominent 'public theology' wing of the ministry of the Evangelical Alliance; and the Board of Mission and Public Affairs of the Church of England. These centres have, by and large,

---

19 http://www.brill.nl/ijpt (accessed 23 Dec. 2010).

been interested in practical socio-cultural, political and economic issues in their own contexts and have engaged in developing various distinctive approaches and programmes to meet the challenges. In most cases, they work with churches and local communities and disseminate their research findings through them.

It seems the idea of 'public theology' or 'theology in the public sphere' is quite commonly accepted in theological departments and churches, but the understanding of what it means differs from one to another. In fact, activities and research done by Christian groups on socio-political issues overlap with the work of the institutions mentioned above. So what do we mean by doing theology in the public sphere? How can theology – seemingly the subjective understanding of God, humans and society developed in the Christian community – be applicable to the wider, secular and pluralistic society?

A rationale for doing public theology

Jürgen Moltmann, in his book, *God for a Secular Society: The Public Relevance of Theology*, asserts that theology must publicly maintain the universal concerns of God's coming kingdom because 'there is no Christian identity without public relevance, and no public relevance without theology's Christian identity', and 'as the theology of God's kingdom, theology has to be *public* theology' in the mode of 'public, critical and prophetic complaint to God – public, critical and prophetic hope in God'.[20] Theology, he insists, should exhibit 'general concern in the light of hope in Christ for the kingdom of God' by becoming 'political in the name of the poor and the marginalized in a given society', by thinking 'critically about the religious and moral values of the societies in which it exists', and by presenting 'its reflections as a reasoned position'. In addition to this, public theology 'refuses to fall into the modern trap of pluralism, where it is supposed to be reduced to its particular sphere and limited to its own religious society'. For Moltmann, public theology is critical, prophetic, reflective and reasoned engagement of theology in society for the sake of the poor and marginalized to bring the kingdom of God.

Ronald F. Thiemann, in his more pragmatic approach, defines public theology as 'faith seeking to understand the relation between Christian convictions and the broader social and cultural context within which the Christian community lives'.[21] In his emphasis on comparative

---

20 Moltmann, *God for a Secular Society*, pp. 5–23.
21 Thiemann, *Constructing a Public Theology*.

studies in doing public theology, the goal is not an overarching theory connecting God, Church and the world, but rather 'to identify the particular places where Christian convictions intersect with the practices that characterize contemporary public life', such as liberal democracy, a capitalist economy, and a secularized consumer society. He envisages mutual critique between the public and the Church, saying that 'the goal should not be the simple recommendation of one form of life over the other, but a careful and critical analysis of the variety of ways'. He insists that theology should be communal and a public activity, and that theology should 'regain its status as a significant critical inquiry' in various contexts, since he believes that 'critical inquiry emerging out of deeply held religious convictions can greatly enrich the cultural, intellectual, and spiritual life of our society'.

Similarly, in addressing the question of the acceptance of the discipline of theology in wider public discussion, Linell E. Cady defines public theology as seeking 'to overcome the cultural marginalization so highly characteristic of contemporary theology' and 'to contribute to the upbuilding and critical transformation of our public life'. To achieve this, Cady argues that theology should not only address itself to the wider social and political issues, but it must 'appropriate a form of argumentation that is genuinely public'. She further argues that to achieve a public form of argumentation, theologians must make changes on two fronts: on the one hand they must 'unmask the impossible pretensions to neutrality and universality that underlie the Enlightenment understanding of public, and the public exercise of reason', while on the other hand respecting 'the Enlightenment distinction between open inquiry and dogmatic citation, and work to combat the authoritarian traces that linger on in contemporary theology'. Drawing on feminist theology, she further argues that public theology should challenge the dichotomy of public and private in modern society:

> The problem of a public theology ... is not simply securing a greater public role for religion. That way of construing the matter, besides failing to distinguish adequately between religion and theology, takes at face value the prevailing typography of public and private life, and attempts to move religion from the private to the public realm. For both methodological and substantive reasons, theology must resist appropriating the current mapping of public and private. Hence in its endeavour to secure a larger, more appropriate public role, theology should simultaneously work for the reconfiguration of the public realm.[22]

---

22 Cady, *Religion, Theology and American Public Life*, p. 147.

E. Harold Breitenberg, in his article surveying public theology, finds there are various different understandings among scholars.[23] He identifies civil religion (or public religion) and public theology as sharing similarities in that both are concerned with relationship between political authority, government and society, on the one hand, and God and the sacred, on the other. But he also distinguishes the two. In its starting point, civil religion's main concern is with the nation and its people whereas public theology begins from religious faith and practice. Civil religion emphasizes public life and the social responsibilities of people; in particular, public religion is closely related to civil government and contains both religious and secular proponents. Whereas public theology represents the perspectives of religious communities and particular faith traditions and deals with the 'public import and explication of theological concepts', which gives rise to theological reflections often critical of government policies. In this sense, it is similar to political theology, but public theology is dealing not only with politics but with the wider area of public life.

Breitenberg defines public theology as 'religiously informed discourse that intends to be intelligible and convincing to adherents within its own religious tradition while at the same time being comprehensible and possibly persuasive to those outside it'. It addresses issues that are of concern to a religious community as well as to the larger society, and furthermore, its resources, language and methods of argument are 'open to all'. It is 'theologically informed public discourse about public issues', addressed to religious communities as well as the general public, 'argued in ways that can be evaluated and judged by, and possibly be persuasive to, society at large'. Public theology, for him, is about 'how Christian belief and practices bear ... on public life and the common good' and 'in so doing possibly persuade and move to action both Christians and non-Christians'.[24]

Reflecting on the arguments presented by those who are interested in public theology,[25] I would like to draw out the following points for a rationale for doing public theology. First, theology is inherently public. In other words, the enquiry and findings are applicable to a wider audience beyond the Christian community because of the evaluative

---

23 Breitenberg, 'To tell the Truth: Will the Real Public Theology Please Stand Up?', *Journal of the Society of Christian Ethics* 23/2 (2003), pp. 55–96.

24 Breitenberg, 'To Tell the Truth', pp. 64–7.

25 See William Storrar and Andrew Morton (eds), *Public Theology for the 21st Century* (London and New York: T & T Clark, 2004); John Atherton, *Public Theology for Changing Times* (London: SPCK, 2000); Michael J. Himes and Kenneth R. Himes, *Fullness of Faith: The Public Significance of Theology* (New York: Paulist Press, 1993); Benjamin Valentin, *Mapping Public Theology: Beyond Culture, Identity, and Difference* (London: Continuum, 2002).

and critical nature of theology and also because its context is not confined to the Church but relates to the kingdom of God. Indeed, as Duncan Forrester comments, 'to withdraw ... from public debate would result in [theology's] serious impoverishment'.[26] Second, the fact that theology is not 'neutral' does not disqualify it from participation in public discussion; on the contrary, because of its distinctive perspective, theological findings can make an effective contribution to public issues. Third, the dichotomy of 'public' and 'private' is not helpful in defining public theology. Public theology should not be understood as interested only in public issues in contrast to domestic or private matters. 'Public' does not refer to the place of doing theology but to the openness of theology for any party to engage in debate: it is to do with universal access and open debate for all the members of the society. Fourth, in order to establish a healthy development of public theology, theologians need to convince the Christian community of the public relevance of theology and, at the same time, persuade the general public of the necessity of utilizing theological insights in public discussion. Fifth, for the authentic and sustainable engagement of the Church in the public sphere, the Church needs to guard against the temptation to take pragmatic approaches and to measure the result of ministries in numbers or external appearances, and to develop a public theology suited to the issues and relevant to the context.

Doing public theology

If we agree with some of the above rationale for doing theology in the public sphere, the natural question should follow: how does theology engage in public issues in an appropriate manner? In order to answer this, I would like to examine the nature of the public sphere, the method of public theology, and compare public theology with political theology and liberation theology.

The nature of the public sphere

The idea of the 'public sphere' was first articulated by Jürgen Habermas in his classic, *The Structural Transformation of the Public Sphere*.[27] Habermas regarded the 'public sphere' as an open forum that emerged in modern western societies in the situation where the state and the

---

26 Duncan B. Forrester, *On Human Worth: A Christian Vindication of Equality* (London: SCM Press, 2001), pp. 72–4.

27 Jürgen Habermas, *The Structural Transformation of the Public Sphere: An Inquiry into a Category of Bourgeois Society*, trans. Thomas Burger (Cambridge: Polity Press, 1989; original publication in German in 1962).

market economy predominated in daily life. It evolved in the 'field between state and society',[28] protecting individuals and their families from both tyranny by the state and from the predations of the market. The public sphere was created by the recognition of three sets of rights: first, the right of radical–critical debate and political representation – freedom of speech and opinion, the free press, freedom of assembly, and so on; second, the right to personal freedom and the inviolability of the home; and third, the right of private ownership, which required equality before the law. The public sphere depended on the principle of universal access, without which it could not be public.[29] Habermas's initial theoretical framework was based on emerging male bourgeois societies, and was therefore heavily criticized by feminist theorists, and many of his ideas need to be revised to meet the demand of the contemporary complex situation of plural societies.[30] In view of the dichotomy between the public and domestic spheres in patriarchal societies, the term 'public' could be problematic, but in so far as his theory of the 'public sphere' can be characterized as upholding the principles of universal access and open debate, it is very significant for our discussion.

Taking account of proposals put forward by the above scholars, we can identify some of the main players in the public sphere: the state, the market, the media, the academy, civil society and religious communities. Although there is a danger of oversimplification of the complexity of the public sphere, Figure 1 on page 13 will help us to visualize the public sphere for our study.

The state includes local and central governments, the Parliament, judiciary, military and public sector. The main functions include policy-making, the maintenance of law and order and providing for the socio-political security and welfare of the people within its boundary. The academic disciplines of political science and law relate to this area. The market involves the economic activities of business, companies, banks, the local and global economy and the unions. The main function of the market is to provide material security and prosperity to members and wider society. The subjects of economics, management, business studies and others look at these activities. Along with state and market economy, the media has become a key player in a democratic society. It includes the broadcast media, publishing, the internet and other forms of mediating popular and traditional culture. The media serve the functions of reporting and critiquing the activities of individual and

---

28 Habermas, *The Structural Transformation of the Public Sphere*, p. 141.

29 Habermas, *The Structural Transformation of the Public Sphere*, pp. 83–5.

30 See Craig Calhoun (ed.), *Habermas and the Public Sphere* (Cambridge, MA: MIT Press, 1992); Nick Crossley and John Michael Roberts (eds), *After Habermas: New Perspectives on the Public Sphere* (Oxford: Blackwell, 2004).

corporate bodies in the public sphere, and enhancing the exchange of information and entertainment. Various subjects of arts and humanities and media studies are particularly helpful in this area.

Among the other players in the public sphere, the academies include universities and other higher education institutions, research centres and schools, which provide research findings, knowledge transfer and training for members of other bodies. All the academic disciplines are formulated and shaped here; also the practical applications in other parts of public life will in turn feed into the formations of academic disciplines. Civil society involves all NGOs, local communities, various interest groups and movements for advocacy and campaigning for particular causes. The main function of civil society is to enhance or challenge the contribution of these groups in the public sphere. Religious communities are largely formed into institutionalized religions and religious orders but also include a large number of those who hold various forms of personal spirituality. One of the main contributions of this player to the public sphere is to provide spiritual, moral and ethical frameworks for people's daily lives as well as contributing to social care and the welfare of the people both within and outside their own communities.

These six categories (see Figure 1) are common to all modern societies but the relative power of each and the interrelations between them may vary from one society to another. For example, in non-democratic countries the state tends to control the media and in communist countries the state exercises a high level of control over the economy. In some Islamic states the leaders of religious communities exercise considerable control over the state. For healthy interaction in the public sphere, a plurality of voices is needed. In the modern and postmodern contexts, the state (politics), the market (economy) and the broadcast media tend to dominate public life and monopolize the mode of engagement. The various forms of broadcast media provide a forum for the public, and this is the strength of liberal democracy, which relies on free and fair access to information and debate through the media. However, in recent events in the West the media have often played the role of judge, asserting their own verdict rather than allowing the public to engage in a healthy debate, or they have been driven by the self-interests of profit-making. For healthy debate, the provision of a forum for a critical dialogue is vital, but the powerful bodies of the state, the market and the broadcast media tend to incorporate a secular ideology and reject anything to do with religion. In response to this tendency, Bhikhu Parekh, scholar of political science and a member of the House of Lords, argues convincingly that the secularist's notion of the strict separation of religion and politics on the grounds that political

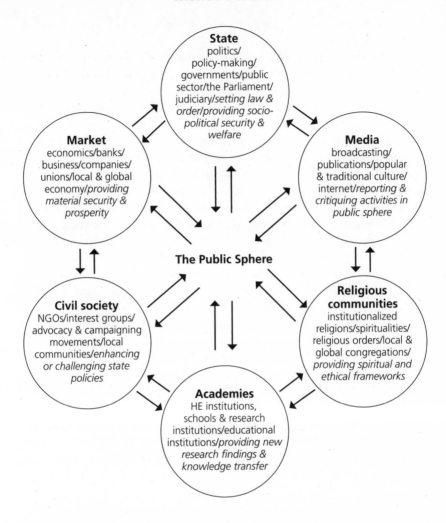

Figure 1: Main bodies engaged in the public sphere.

debate and deliberation should be conducted in terms of secular reason alone is problematic because secular reason is not 'politically and culturally neutral'.[31] Reasons, Parekh continues, are public 'not because their grounds are or can be shared by all, as the secularist argues, but because they are open to inspection and can be intellectually discussed by all'. He further argues that, in spite of its many weaknesses, religion provides a 'valuable counterweight to the state', offers 'an alternative

---

31 Bhikhu Parekh, *Rethinking Multiculturalism: Cultural Diversity and Political Theory* (New York: Palgrave, 2000), p. 323.

source of morality and allegiance', and reminds us that 'human beings are more than citizens'.[32]

Theology is situated both in the academy (mainly in universities and seminaries) and in religious communities (in the case of Christian theology, the Church) for its theological resources and method. Public theology, while maintaining its connections with religious communities, deliberately expands its sources, audience and applications in the public sphere in association with the other four players, depending on issues. To do so is not a new approach since various such theological discourses have been developed in more recent years. Political theology and liberation theologies (which deal primarily with economics) are two obvious examples, which we will look at shortly, but also the number of scholars working on the other areas of civil society and media in relation to theology is growing in different global contexts. Social ethics is another such form of engagement, and many public theologians are in Christian ethics departments. However, a major difficulty of these interactions has been that the audiences and sources of theological interaction have been one-sided in that, while theology utilizes the findings from other bodies and academic disciplines, other disciplines and bodies do not engage with the findings of theology. An expression of this is that the place of theology in contemporary secular universities is often in question. The protagonists of public theology try to overcome this problem by developing methodologies for dialogical public engagement with all the players concerned, and try to identify meeting-points while keeping their own distinctive mode of inquiry in order to preserve their unique contribution to other bodies in the public sphere.

The methodology of public theology – by whom and in what way?

The question of the appropriate method for engaging in the public sphere is not an easy one, and the variety of forms taken by public theology suggests there are a number of legitimate ways of doing it. This is not only because the theologians who are seeking to apply theology to public life come from a variety of sub-disciplines, such as theology, religious studies and social ethics. It is also because public theology is done in a variety of different social and political contexts that both constrain and shape its methods. In some of the chapters that follow we shall see how this is the case.

---

32 Parekh, *Rethinking Multiculturalism*, p. 328.

Critics of public theology have raised suspicion that it relies on 'alien and corruptive sources' or that it could be seen as functionalist or instrumentalist. They have also raised the question of to 'what extent it is a form of theology that remains faithful to Christian source and tradition'.[33] The question of methodology here is twofold: first, the question of who should be doing public theology; and second, whether it should employ sources of insight that are not exclusively or distinctively Christian in order to give interpretation of and guidance to society and 'present [it] in a way intelligible and potentially persuasive to both inside and outside the church'[34] or continue to maintain Christian distinctiveness but apply the findings in different situations and contexts.

It seems that there is general consensus among public theologians that the main driving force of public theology is the Christian community, and theologians should play the role of catalysts only. Public theology is not purely an academic endeavour to be developed in academia and then conveyed to the wider public, but rather this type of theology is a public activity. Therefore it has to be accessible to all and enable the participation of the whole Christian community. Public theology is done in interaction with churches, faith communities and the wider society and, in turn, informs academia of its findings. Therefore, for forming a healthy public theology, the Christian community in which theology is based – the Church – is vital. Jürgen Moltmann, along with Johann Baptist Metz, suggests that theology should contain three elements: context, *kairos* and community. Moltmann sees the social, political and religious communities as the core 'location' of any theologizing process.[35] Furthermore, public theology needs to relate both to the Christian community (or any religious community) and to the wider communities in society. The Indian theologian Stanley Samartha advocated the concept of a 'community-of-communities' in which Christians do not form an isolated group but an open community that, while preserving its Christian values and faith, deliberately moves out into other communities.[36]

For exploring the praxis of public theology, John de Gruchy recommends seven theses, which I accept in my own work on public theology and warmly commend, especially because he emphasizes the importance of both addressing the public and developing the life of the Church. Good public theological praxis:

---

33 Breitenberg, 'To Tell the Truth', p. 89.

34 Breitenberg, 'To Tell the Truth', p. 67.

35 Jürgen Moltmann, 'Public Theology in Germany after Auschwitz', in Storrar and Morton (eds), *Public Theology for the 21st Century*, pp. 37–43.

36 Stanley Samartha, *Courage for Dialogue: Ecumenical Issues in Inter-Religious Relationships* (Geneva: World Council of Churches, 1981).

1 does not seek to give preference to Christianity but to witness to values that Christians believe are important for the common good;

2 requires the development of a language that is accessible to people outside the Christian tradition, and is convincing in its own right; but it also needs to address Christian congregations in a language whereby public debates are related to the traditions of faith;

3 requires an informed knowledge of public policy and issues, grasping the implications of what is at stake, and subjecting this to sharp analytical evaluation and theological critique;

4 requires doing theology in a way that is interdisciplinary in character and uses a methodology in which content and process are intertwined;

5 gives priority to the perspectives of victims and survivors, and to the restoration of justice; it sides with the powerless against the powerful, and seeks to speak truth to power drawing its inspiration from the prophetic trajectory in the Bible;

6 requires congregations that are consciously nurtured and informed by biblical and theological reflection and a rich life of worship in relation to the context within which they are situated, both locally and more widely;

7 requires a spirituality that enables a lived experience of God, with people and with creation, fed by a longing for justice and wholeness and a resistance to all that thwarts well-being.[37]

The second question of whether to develop a particular methodology based on Christian theology or to create a common forum in which all the concerned bodies can share is more complicated than the first. One of the early theologians who identified common ground for public theology was John Courtney Murray. In his widely read book *We Hold These Truths* (1960), Murray presented a Catholic defence of American constitutionalism and argued that the Catholic community could participate fully in American public life with religious integrity. His argument can be summarized thus. First, he argued that the 'American consensus' recognizes the sovereignty of God over nations as well as over individual people. It is based on the tradition of natural law and the principle of consent so that the 'people are governed because they consent to be governed'. He further pointed out that the state is distinct from society and limited in its offices towards society and that the freedom of the people is not libertarianism but a 'moral and spiritual enterprise', the freedom to do what is right.[38] Second, because Murray

---

37 John de Gruchy, 'Public Theology as Christian Witness: Exploring the Genre', *International Journal of Public Theology* 1/1 (2007).

38 Murray, *We Hold These Truths*, pp. 28–36.

worried that this 'political freedom is endangered in its foundations as soon as the universal moral values ... are no longer vigorous enough to retrain the passions and shatter the selfish inertia of men',[39] he emphasized the need for strengthening the 'public philosophy' already present in the Declaration of Independence, which is the foundation of American public life. He regarded this as already compatible with Catholic faith, but in view of tendencies to the 'philosophical error of pragmatism' he argued the need for the Church to work with society to establish a 'new moral act of purpose and a new act of intellectual affirmation'.[40]

In his essay 'Civil Unity and Religious Integrity', Murray discussed 'theologies of the First Amendment', that is, the first two articles: 'Congress shall make no law respecting an establishment of religion, or prohibiting the free exercise thereof.' He argued that these were 'articles of peace' rather than 'articles of faith' and therefore it was not possible to oppose them 'because they are law and good law'.[41] He justified his argument on the basis of three 'American experiences': that political unity and stability are possible without uniformity of religious belief and practice and without government restriction on any religion; that stable political unity and the pursuit of the common good of the people can be strengthened by exclusion of religious differences; and that the Church has benefited through the policy of the separation between Church and state. He encouraged Catholics not to 'believe' in the first two clauses of the Amendment as articles of faith, which would be to make an ideological idol out of them, but rather to make a 'moral commitment to them as an article of peace in a pluralist society'.[42] Murray's contribution in paving the way for Catholic engagement in American public life is very significant. By identifying and strengthening what he believed to be the public philosophy that was at its foundation, and showing that it was in accordance with natural law, he laid the groundwork for Catholics to participate in politics without fear of compromising the integrity of their faith.

However, more recently the idea that there is a 'public philosophy' common to all Americans has been challenged in view of the history of aggressive secularism in the formation of the US Constitution's 'American consensus'. This aggressive secularism is more apparent now than it was in the 1950s and 1960s, and Catholic social teaching seems increasingly to clash with federal law, for example in the cases of abortion, contraception, divorce, euthanasia, pornography, sexuality

39 Murray, *We Hold These Truths*, p. 37.
40 Murray, *We Hold These Truths*, pp. 79–87.
41 Murray, *We Hold These Truths*, p. 49.
42 Murray, *We Hold These Truths*, pp. 72–8.

and conscientious objection. Furthermore, critics see a deterioration in the civility of the public sphere and the level of public discourse, and little sense remaining of the common good.[43] This is a reminder that the relation of the churches to the public sphere is constantly being renegotiated as the society around them changes.

In his discussion of religion and politics in the USA, David Hollenbach redefines the task of public theology in the context of global interdependence and pluralism as a vision of 'good human life'. He points out the dilemma for philosophers, theologians and political theorists that, in the presence of pluralism, there is 'by definition ... no agreement on the meaning of the good life', and yet, in view of globalization, there is a greater necessity than ever for 'a clearer vision of the common good of the whole human race'. Against John Rawls' argument that religion has no place in public reasoning, Hollenbach favours José Casanova's analysis of the public presence of religion in the contemporary world and agrees with Casanova that religion must be differentiated from the other spheres of public life. To do otherwise, he writes, would mean that 'religious efforts to identify and pursue the public good will amount to attempts to negate the achievements of modernity' in the realms of religious and personal freedom. This means there is an urgent need for Christians to rethink the way they relate their faith to public life but that this cannot only be done on the basis of European experience alone in view of the fact that Christianity is a world religion.[44]

Dealing with the Catholic Church particularly, Hollenbach insists that it is no longer appropriate to universalize the Roman model of a social ethic as the Church has done for centuries. Instead he suggests a 'dialogic universalism', which he sees as incipient in the Second Vatican Council's stress on respect for the other. This combines 'fidelity to the particularistic vision of the human good rooted in the gospel with a commitment to discerning the common morality needed in a pluralistic but interdependent world'. In the context of the free exercise of religion, religious communities have the right to seek to influence policies and laws and the public culture, while recognizing that others can do the same. So that persuasion through reasonable discourse is the proper mode of public participation.[45] He further argues that religion, which is about the ultimate good of the whole of human life, should be encouraged to play a role in public life[46] and urges the Church to

---

43 M. J. Baxter, 'John Courtney Murray', in Peter Scott and William T. Cavanaugh (eds), *The Blackwell Companion to Political Theology* (Oxford: Blackwell, 2004), pp. 150–64.

44 Hollenbach, *The Global Face of Public Faith*, pp. 3–6.

45 Hollenbach, *The Global Face of Public Faith*, pp. 10–14.

46 Hollenbach, *The Global Face of Public Faith*, p. 118.

articulate a 'public theology' that 'attempts to illuminate the urgent moral questions of our time through explicit use of the great symbols and doctrines of the Christian faith'.[47]

When it comes to the issue of employing Christian concepts and values in doing public theology, Ronald Thiemann and others assert the need to be distinctively based on the Christian faith while 'genuinely addressing issues of public significance' in order that the distinctive substance of Christianity and its prophetic voice will be manifested.[48] On the one hand, by emphasizing too much the need to meet the public and facilitate a common language, public theology may lose its Christian distinctiveness and contribution, but on the other hand, by prioritizing Christian values and understanding, it may not enter the common platform for discussion on complex issues in society. While I do appreciate the notion of Christian distinctiveness in public theology, I would see that an important part of authentic public theology has to be finding concepts that are acceptable to and understandable by the general public and specific academic disciplines, otherwise the findings may be limited to a Christian audience, and this would defeat the aim of public theology. The lack of any widely acceptable basis for appropriate concepts and values in public issues – especially in the context of postmodernity[49] – means this is a difficult and ongoing project. Furthermore, the ability of Christian theology to relate to a wider audience is not only a matter of its distinctively Christian content. There is also a danger that public theology that is done in academic circles exclusively, discussing the why and how of public theology, can easily be limited to an academic exercise and not impact the daily lives even of Christians. This has been the main self-criticism of public theology done in the USA: that it was conducted inside universities out of academic interests[50] and failed to bridge between theologians and ordinary congregations, and theory and practice.[51]

In more recent writings, it has been pointed out that there is not just one public to which public theology relates but several different publics, requiring different approaches to address each of them. These have been conceptualized in several ways. Max Stackhouse sees four publics – religious, political, academic and economic[52] – whereas Dirkie

---

47 Hollenbach, 'Public Theology in America', p. 299.

48 Thiemann, *Constructing a Public Theology*.

49 Duncan Forrester, *Christian Justice and Public Policy* (Cambridge: Cambridge University Press, 1997), pp. 9–10.

50 William Dean, 'Forum', *Religion and American Culture* 10/1 (2000), pp. 1–8.

51 Mark Noll, 'Forum', *Religion and American Culture* 10/1 (2000), p. 11.

52 Max Stackhouse, 'Public Theology and Ethical Judgement', *Theology Today* 54/2 (1997), pp. 165–79. Robert Benne adds law as another public – see *The Paradoxical Vision: A Public Theology for the Twenty-First Century* (Minneapolis: Fortress Press, 1995).

Smit sees the political sphere, the economic sphere, civil society and public opinion as four distinctive discourses in public theology.[53] For the application of theology in these spheres, Alison Elliot examines how public theology can draw strength from practice. In particular she looks at the characteristics of three different publics with which theology engages – an institutional public, a constructed public and a personal public – each drawing on distinctive theological assumptions about Church and faith. Although these distinctions help us to examine the different publics and to develop relevant methodology to meet these criteria, I agree with David Tracy that there cannot be a single methodology that is accepted in doing public theology. At the same time, I am concerned about the danger in isolating different social realities, resulting in the lack of a comprehensive or coherent approach to issues that involve two or three types of public.

Political theology, liberation theology and public theology

The third item of discussion in this section is to make some observations on the different approaches of political, liberation and public theologies. There have been several attempts to do this. In Peter Scott and William Cavanaugh's comprehensive *Blackwell Companion to Political Theology*, Daniel M. Bell and Marsha Aileen Hewitt have tried to compare and differentiate them.[54] In his discussion on state and civil society, Bell correctly identifies political theology as envisioning the Church as an institution of 'critical freedom' on the basis of the eschatological future, thus challenging the status quo. Political theology sees the state and civil society as the principal agents of social and political change, embraces secularization and the rise of the nation-state as positive aspects of modernity, and seeks the association of religious ideals with political realities. He regards liberation theology as firmly grounded in the revolutionary vision of its challenge to the current political and economic order. Like political theology, liberation theologians realize that modernity's freedoms have not yet been fully realized and also use the methods of statecraft to achieve their aims. Regarding public theology, he sees the early North American public theologians as emphasizing a moral consensus 'necessary to sustain the health and vitality of Western liberal society' along with the idea of 'public philosophy'. They understand that Christianity is essentially a matter of

53 Dirkie Smit in Nico Koopman, 'Some Comments on Public Theology Today', *Journal of Theology for Southern Africa* 117 (Nov. 2003), pp. 3–19 at 9.

54 Daniel M. Bell, 'State and Civil Society', in Scott and Cavanaugh (eds), *The Blackwell Companion to Political Theology*, pp. 423–38; Marsha Aileen Hewitt, 'Critical Theory', in Scott and Cavanaugh (eds), *The Blackwell Companion to Political Theology*, pp. 455–70.

values and world-views and that the 'publicness' of public theology is in recognizing that 'Christianity's value-system or vision is necessary for the enduring viability of modern liberal social order'. However, Bell's descriptions are rather distorted by his desire to show that not only public theology but also more surprisingly political and liberation theologies unquestioningly accept the legitimacy of the nation-state and use its methods of statecraft to achieve their aims. This argument is in the interests of promoting a radical orthodoxy view of 'the Church as the true politics', which despises the modern state. The political agenda of radical orthodoxy with regard to existing states remains unclear but it appears as a theological exercise to reinstate the hegemony of the Church with little regard to the views of the wider society.

While Bell does at least identify the key concerns and methodologies of political theology, liberation theology and public theology, Hewitt's argument is dismissive of all three forms of theology, asserting the importance of her notion of 'critical theory' rather uncritically. Through her critique on Jürgen Habermas, David Tracy and Charles Davis, she accuses public theologians of insisting on 'the universal validity of Christian values and truth claims in their efforts to privilege Christian sensibility and political values in public, political life' and argues that, unlike critical theory, 'political theology and liberation theologies could not sustain or develop their critical impact, especially in complex pluralistic, modern societies'.[55] In my view, this is a rather unsubstantiated criticism of these theologies in general and of public theology in particular. Public theology includes a wider range of understandings of the term 'public' and more methodologies than she chooses to dwell on in her discussion, and it has moved on from earlier discussions. Public theology does not require the privileging of Christianity in public life and its theologians do not necessarily see their work as superseding the other two theologies. Public theology takes its place in the different contexts of plural and secular societies as a complementary approach alongside many other theologies and philosophies.

Gaspar Martinez provides some more convincing comparisons between the three theologies in his study on Johann Baptist Metz, Gustavo Gutiérrez and David Tracy. In his assessment, political theology is responding to the privatization of religion, the challenges of the Enlightenment, the complicity of Christians in the Second World War and the danger of Christianity being co-opted by modernity. It aims to rescue theology from its loss of identity in a society that has 'colonized reason and separated it from its own history'. He regards liberation theology as representing a radically new theological perspective that

---

55 Bell, 'State and Civil Society', pp. 465–68.

tries to 'interpret Christianity in a way that is relevant to people's liberation from all kinds of exclusion, dependencies, and exploitations'.[56] And he sees public theology as trying to make Christian claims public to the postmodern society with the liberating and critical resources of the Christian tradition. He summarizes his argument thus:

> Whereas Metz wants to rescue and to find a firm foundation for the dead and forgotten of history and Gutiérrez seeks to liberate and to find hope for the poor and all those who suffer innocently, Tracy is looking for ways to affirm and give hope to every 'other,' especially to the repressed 'others.'[57]

Taking account of the above discussions, I would argue that liberation and political theologies, in spite of their differences, share many common features in contrast to public theology (see Tables 1 and 2 below). Public theology has a different emphasis from the other theologies. First, public theologians, as I have argued in the previous section, try to create common ground and methodologies for engaging in public issues with various conversation partners in the public sphere. This does not mean losing a Christian identity or distinctiveness, but rather, while keeping them, actively searching for a shared solution so that theological insights will not be excluded in public conversation. Second, the theological concerns and emphases are in pursuing the publicness of theology – the public meaning of theology and theology of public life.[58] It works with the 'Church–academy–society' dynamics, seeking the implications of the kingdom of God in contemporary society as it exists, and promoting a theology of public engagement. Third, the attitude towards existing systems is not that they are necessarily evil or entirely wrong. Public theology takes a reforming position rather than a revolutionary one. But it challenges any kind of monopoly in public life and seeks for a more fair and open society by employing advocacy, critical dialogue and debate. For this reason, public theology requires a certain degree of democratic development in society such that there is a reasonable level of engagement with critical inquiry and open debate in the public. In particular, public theology, along with religious communities, closely works with civil society for its articulation of theology as well as the implementation of its findings. The Jubilee 2000 and Make Poverty History campaigns are a good example of this aspect of public

---

56 Gaspar Martinez, *Confronting the Mystery of God: Political, Liberation, and Public Theologies* (London: Continuum, 2001), p. 217.

57 Martinez, *Confronting the Mystery of God*, p. 251.

58 Charles T. Mathewes, *A Theology of Public Life* (Cambridge: Cambridge University Press, 2007).

Table 1: Liberation theologies and public theology

	Latin American Liberation Theology	Feminist theology	Black theology	Minjung theology	Dalit theology	Political theology	Public theology
Context	Latin America	N. America/Europe/Asia/Africa	N. America/South Africa	South Korea	India	Post-war Germany	N. America/Europe/South Africa/Australia
Main theologians	Gustavo Gutiérrez, Leonardo Boff, Juan Luis Segundo, José Miguez-Bonino	Elisabeth Fiorenza, Rosemary Ruether, Kwok Pui-Lan, Mercy Amba Oduyoye	James Cone, Dwight Hopkins, Allan Boesak	Suh Nam-Dong, Ahn Byeung-Mu, Kim Young-Bock, David Kwang-sun Suh	A. P. Nirmal, Nirmal Minz, Sathianathan Clarke	Johann Baptist Metz, Jürgen Moltmann	Reinhold Niebuhr, David Tracy, John Courtney Murray, Duncan Forrester, M. M. Thomas, GNPT members
Issues	poverty/injustice/state & Church/revolution	inequality/injustice/church hierarchy/eco-feminism/domestic violence/human trafficking	slavery/apartheid/injustice	capitalist market/injustice/exploitation of workers and farmers/military-backed governments	caste system/discrimination/dignity/injustice/conversion	suffering/religious faiths and politics/political involvement	inequality, policy-making/privatization of religions/monopoly of states, market, media/globalization/civil society
Theological themes	praxis/liberation/option for the poor/liberation of theology/Exodus/the Nazareth manifesto	hermeneutical rereading of the Bible/feminist God/feminist reading	black consciousness/black power	han/minjung as subject of history/Jesus as minjung & minjung as Jesus	dalit consciousness/Jesus as dalit/Jesus broken, crushed & torn/dalitness of the divinity	critical theory/theology of hope/crucified Christ	publicness of theology/church–academy–society/kingdom of God/theology of public engagement
Methodology	hermeneutical circle/hermeneutic of suspicion/text and context/priority of praxis	critical evaluation of the Scripture/feminist interpretation of the Scripture/challenge male hierarchy in the Church and society	restoration of black dignity through challenging white supremacy	critique of capitalist market/seeking to bring reconciliation between two Koreas/utilizing poems, arts, music, storytelling	conscientization of dalits/challenge the rationale for caste system/structural change	engagement of political theories/critique of political systems and misuse of state power	multi-disciplinary engagement of subject concerned/critical enquiry and open debate/methodology of social ethics and consensus politics
Aim	just society for the poor and oppressed	women's full participation of society/female-male equality	black liberation/black dignity	justice for minjung and reconciliation of two Koreas	abolition of discrimination against dalits	just political system	fair society for all for/critical inquiry and open debate
Limitations/criticisms	lack of spirituality/Pentecostal options for the poor/address to less democratic contexts/Often takes radical approach	theological imperative vs cultural diversity/issue based/lack of engagement of systematic theology	appeal to black audience/changing contexts in the USA and South Africa	theology for minjung and not of minjung/lack of support from general Church members/changing context of Korean economic and political situation	exclusive to dalits/less open to critique by outsiders/lack of shared identity among dalits	focus on politics and structures/political left/close association with Marxist interpretation	meaning of 'public'/concerned issues are too broad/lack expertise and focused approach/lack of consistent methodology/lack of clear stance on justice issues for the poor and marginalized

Table 2: Liberation theologies and public theology

	Liberation theologies	Public theology
Characteristics	revolutionary	reforming
Prophetic voice	challenge socio-political & economic status quo	challenge monopoly of any kind
View of existing system	system is evil or wrong	system is not necessarily evil or entirely wrong
Course of action	radical change of system	gradual reformation through advocacy & debate
Starting position	side with the poor & marginalized	negotiating between opposing parties
Aim for society	just & equal society	fair & open society
Expectation of Church	tool for raising prophetic voice & protesting against injustice	tool for advocacy & civil engagement
Working with	workers, marginalized & oppressed	civil societies & other religious groups
Political process	conscientization & mobilization of the poor & marginalized	advocate for reforming & re-visioning of systems or attitudes
Methodology	critical rereading of the Scriptures, current systems, contexts & history	critical enquiry & open debate/social ethics & consensus politics
Theological emphasis	liberation, justice, Jesus' life & teaching/God (Christ) as poor, marginalized, black, dalit, minjung & female/salvation as liberation	Kingdom of God/God in the midst of history/God in human wisdom and systems/
Tools for social analysis	Marxist & socialist analysis/ black & feminist critique	Christian social ethics/political philosophy
Conversation with other academic disciples	economics/politics/sociology/ cultural studies	philosophy/politics/economics/ peace studies/environmental studies/governance

theology. Fourth, major issues for public theology are inequality, the privatization or marginalization of religions in public life, the dominance of the state, the market or the media in the public sphere. For the purpose of challenging the main bodies of the public sphere regarding these concerns, public theology is actively involved in policy-making both within and outside of local and central governments. Public theology takes the role of the prophet within the existing system.

Perceived major limitations, criticisms and areas for future exploration of public theology are:

- the lack of a clear and concrete meaning of 'public';
- that the issues concerned are too broad and therefore it lacks the necessary expertise and a focused approach;
- the lack of a consistent theological methodology;
- the lack of a clear stance on justice for the poor and marginalized;
- and, as we discussed above, the struggle between the tension of keeping Christian distinctiveness and creating a shared platform for a common conversation.

Although these criticisms and concerns are valid and should not be dismissed too readily, public theology can offer a significant contribution to the quest for meaningful engagement of Christians in general and theologians in particular in the public sphere. This should be a place where no particular bodies dominate, but rather all the individuals and co-operative bodies are given an inclusive forum for debate in order to negotiate with each other in the pursuit of a fair and open society.

Conclusion: the purpose of public theology

During the controversy caused by the Archbishop's lecture on sharia law (see Chapter 8), questions were raised about whether the Archbishop, a religious leader, should discuss matters related to the realm of the legal system of the country, and whether it is appropriate for a Christian leader to discuss a matter that does not concern his own constituency and speak on behalf of Muslims. In response to this, the Archbishop gave a strong defence during his presidential speech at the General Synod a few days later, convincingly arguing that it is entirely appropriate for a bishop of the Church of England 'to address issues around the perceived concerns of other religious communities, and to try and bring them into better public focus'.[59] I believe this firm conviction

---

59 Rowan Williams, 'Presidential Address', *Church Times*, 15 February 2008.

comes from an understanding of the public nature of theology. Theology should not be confined within a narrowly defined community identity but should embrace the transcendent nature of Christian values and the concern for others inherent in Christian ethics. Daniel Hardy's comment on the task of theology is helpful here:

> The task of theology, then, is to begin from common practice and examine its quality in open trial by the use of natural reason in order to discover the truth of this practice, by a truth-directed reason; and the fulfilment of this purpose requires reference to the author of practice and practical reason. And the outcome of the trial should be an agreement on the proper organisation of common life which would actually promote the practice of society. It is notable that throughout the concern is *public*, theology mediated in public practice, the use of public reason, open trial of the truth and the achievement of truly social existence.[60]

It is indeed the task of any faith community to attend to the 'proper organisation of common life' and to contribute to the betterment of the wider society.

---

60 Daniel Hardy, 'Theology through Philosophy', in David Ford (ed.), *The Modern Theologians: An Introduction to Christian Theology in the Twentieth Century*, vol. 2 (Oxford, Blackwell, 1989), p. 33.

2

The Bible as a Public Book: Perspectives from Global Christianity

Looking at Southern Christianity gives a surprising new perspective on some other things that might seem to be very familiar. Perhaps the most striking example is how the newer churches can read the Bible in a way that makes Christianity look like a wholly different religion from the faith of prosperous advanced societies of Europe or North America.[1]

In his book *The Next Christendom*, Philip Jenkins points out the significance of the Bible in the rise of Christianity in Africa, Latin America and in Asia. Indeed, not only has the Bible been a significant catalyst for transforming societies in Asia, Africa and Latin America, but additionally the theologies and Christian commitments shown through the way these Christians have accepted and applied the Bible into their own contexts reveal new aspects of Christian faith and practice. The engagement of Christian churches in the public sphere is enriched by looking at the different ways in which the publics of different cultures and societies have engaged with the Bible.

The Bible is not a book that is only read and interpreted within the Christian community. It is a public book that speaks to people of different faiths and in many different social contexts. It is a key authority and inspiration for doing public theology.

Scripture and the formation of distinctive contextual Christianity

Because of its power and centrality to Christian faith, the translation and distribution of the Bible was a vital concern for Protestant missionaries in the nineteenth century. Stephen Neill commented that 'the first principle of Protestant missions has been that Christians should have

---

1 Philip Jenkins, *The Next Christendom: The Coming of Global Christianity* (Oxford: Oxford University Press, 2002), p. 217.

the Bible in their hands in their own language at the earliest possible date', whereas he pointed out that Catholic missionaries were engaged in translating mostly catechisms and books of devotion.[2] As the Protestant missionary enterprise grew rapidly in the nineteenth and twentieth centuries, so the translation and distribution of the Bible was of great importance in many parts of the world. The British and Foreign Bible Society (BFBS) and other Bible societies, and more recently the Wycliffe Bible Translators, played key roles in this. Eric Fenn of the BFBS even asserted that the missionary work of the Church has been essentially 'Bible-centred' in three ways: the Bible has been the source of inspiration for the missionaries, the basis of the worship of the Church and a means of evangelism in itself.[3]

However, R. S. Sugirtharajah, in his recent publication *The Bible and the Third World*, rightly points out that the Bible was introduced into Asia and Africa by Catholic missionaries before the colonization of these continents. In this period, the Bible did not play a significant role in the lives of the believers and was only known through oral transmission, mainly through the liturgy and sermons, so 'non-textual means came to be regarded as the prime media of God's revelation and presence'.[4] Furthermore, prior to the arrival of the Protestant missions, there were no translations available in the languages of Asia and Africa. The Bible was regarded as one among many sacred books, and Christians did not try to subsume or surpass the religious texts of the other religions. In contrast to this, Sugirtharajah criticizes Protestants of a dogmatic attitude of 'acknowledgement of the sufficiency of scripture, assertion of its authority over tradition, [and] treating it as the incorruptible Word against human error'.[5] As a result, the pattern of Protestant mission has been one of 'the denunciation of the natives' idolatrous practices' and 'preaching accompanied by the presentation and dissemination of the Bible as the answer to their miserable state'. He then went further, calling the work of the Bible Society 'scriptural imperialism':

Scriptural imperialism had its roots in the image the [Bible] Society invented for itself. It saw its mission in millennial terms and projected itself as the chosen agent of God to whose care the onerous task of transmitting God's Word had been entrusted. The oracles of God,

2 Stephen Neill, *A History of Christian Mission* (London: Penguin, 1963), p. 209.

3 Eric Fenn, 'The Bible and the Missionary', in S. L. Greenslade (ed.), *The Cambridge History of the Bible* (Cambridge: Cambridge University Press, 1963), p. 383.

4 R. S. Sugirtharajah, *The Bible and the Third World* (Cambridge: Cambridge University Press, 2001), p. 37.

5 Sugirtharajah, *The Bible and the Third World*, p. 52.

which were first given into the custody of God's chosen, the Jews, had now been passed on to the Christians, especially the British.[6]

In particular, Sugirtharajah found that the work of the BFBS was modelled on the administration of the British Empire. This is not an uncommon criticism of the mission organizations of the colonial period, but when Sugirtharajah criticizes the intentions of these societies and those who are involved in the translation and distribution of the Bible as part of 'scriptural imperialism', I find it necessary to raise some questions. Sugirtharajah writes:

> The Society's intention of providing the Bible in the vernacular was another mark of scriptural imperialism. In colonialism's cultural conquest, vernacular Bibles, enabling the natives to read the Word of God in their own languages, could be seen as the sympathetic and acceptable face of its civilizing mission: it appeared to be a noble cause. But behind this noble claim, one came across constant complaints by the Society's translators who found that the indigenous languages not only had no suitable vocabulary but also lacked concepts to convey the ideas of the gospel.[7]

In addition,

> Scriptural imperialism was furthered by the Society's ambition to print the Bible at affordable prices and place it within the reach of all people; it was also prepared to print and distribute Bibles at a loss. Its aim was to make the Bible the 'cheapest book' that had been published.[8]

Here, Sugirtharajah dismisses the efforts of the organizations and missionaries by giving a few odd examples of people complaining about their difficulties in finding a suitable vocabulary for their translation as evidencing an imperial attitude, and the Society's efforts to distribute the scriptures as widely as possible as an imperial agenda. Sugirtharajah's argument is that the Bible was used as a key part of colonial discourse and that the western imperial powers, especially the British, used the Bible not only as the chief means to penetrate the people but also to control the people. What are absent from Sugirtharajah's argument are accounts of the testimonies of the people who received the scriptures and those local people who were engaged in the translation work. Were

---

6 Sugirtharajah, *The Bible and the Third World*, p. 56.
7 Sugirtharajah, *The Bible and the Third World*, pp. 57–8.
8 Sugirtharajah, *The Bible and the Third World*, p. 60.

they simply serving the grand purpose of their colonial masters? Or do they have something to say to us? Were they just passive participants who were ignorant of their own traditions and accepted the scripture without any value judgement on it?

I would argue first that, though translation of the scriptures was mainly initiated by missionaries and often funded by foreign organizations, the local Christians were not just passive recipients or even simply collaborators with them, but rather they were actively involved in the work; moreover, the way they interacted with the Bible resulted in the particular characteristics of Christianity in that context. In this sense, the Bible played a key role in shaping the life of Christians and the shape of Christianity itself. It was therefore highly significant for guiding Christians in their public involvement in the wider society. Furthermore, the Bible, once translated, was accessible to the whole society and Christians interpreted it in dialogue with the wider community.

The Bible as authenticating African Christianity

Though it is quite difficult to talk about Africa as a whole, and also the situation is more complicated when it comes to the written scriptures since the vast majority of African cultures are based on 'oral' tradition, nevertheless, no other continent shows more clearly the impact of the vernacular Bible on society. Even John Mbiti, who is very critical of Christian mission, saw the translation of the Bible as of crucial importance to African Christianity: 'the Bible in the local language becomes the most directly influential single factor in shaping the life of the church in Africa.' He continues:

> The scriptures have therefore provided African Christians with indispensable guidance at a crucial period at which they would otherwise have been inarticulate. So began the demand of African society for spiritual independence from the religious imperialism of Western extra-biblical ideas.[9]

This is particularly so in the case of African Independent (Initiated or Instituted) Churches. In fact, there is a strong relationship between the translation of the scriptures (or a portion of the scriptures) and the rise

---

9 John Mbiti, *Bible and Theology in African Christianity* (Oxford: Oxford University Press, 1986), pp. 28–9. See also Aloo Osotsi Mojola, 'How the Bible is Received in Communities: A Brief Overview with Particular Reference to East Africa', in Philip L. Wickeri (ed.), *Scripture, Community, and Mission* (Hong Kong: Christian Conference of Asia, 2002), pp. 46–69.

of the first African Initiated Churches. Looking at Akurinu Churches in Kenya, Nahashon Ndung'u concludes that the availability of the Bible was the key instrument for forming the church.

> Since the rise of the Akurinu movement, the Bible has been a major factor in shaping the life of this Church. Since they did not want to imitate the practices of the mission Churches, they turned to the Bible. From where they identified the teachings and practices which are observed to the present ... Several events in their history reveal their deep sense of identity with and even a zeal to emulate biblical experiences. Among such events was the giving of the Law on Mount Kenya.[10]

Not only the application of the teachings from the Bible, but the Bible itself is treated as a sacred book. For example, the Bible is often accepted as having power, so in the time of faith healing, the Bible is placed on the patient's body in addition to prayer for them as 'the Bible is more than a text, it is a religio-magical symbol of God's presence and power'.[11] This attitude to the book was also characteristic of leaders of the African Initiated Churches, of whom the most well known was William Wadé Harris (1860–1929) in Ivory Coast. In his evangelistic journey, he always carried a cross, water, a calabash (African drum) and the Bible, which he placed on people's heads to draw out evil spirits.

But the most interesting aspect of Africans' reading of the Bible is the intense identification with the characters and events in the Bible, particularly in the Old Testament. They see a close relationship between the African and Israelite traditions, for example regarding ancestors: 'While the Israelites approached God through the gods of their progenitors, their spiritual patrons, the Africans did so through the ancestors.'[12] The stories of the Bible are loved by people not only for lessons to draw from the stories, but because also people are experiencing the life exhibited by the characters in the stories. This is particularly so since many stories in the Old Testament mention the people and places of Africa, which gives African Christians a sense of identity with and participation in biblical history.[13] Allan Anderson shares a similar opinion, in his study

---

10 Nahashon W. Ndung'u, 'The Role of the Bible in the Rise of African Instituted Churches: The Case of the Akurinu Churches in Kenya', in Gerald O. West and Musa W. Dube (eds), *The Bible in Africa: Transactions, Trajectories, and Trends* (Boston: Brill, 2000), p. 241.

11 Ndung'u, 'The Role of the Bible', p. 243.

12 Mafico, in West and Dube (eds), *The Bible in Africa*, p. 488.

13 Holter, in West and Dube (eds), *The Bible in Africa*, p. 579.

of the Pentecost and Zion churches in South Africa, as he observes the vital importance of the Bible to preachers, church leaders and the congregations in these churches. He insists that the characteristic of African hermeneutics is the 'enlarging' of the meaning of the text being interpreted, because it is 'meaningless to discuss the interpretation of the text by itself' since most of the members rely on oral rather than a literate understanding of the Bible. This is based on their belief that 'God is speaking' directly to them through the Bible and that the Bible has to relate to their daily experience.[14]

What are the African contributions to the reading of the scriptures? The African intense integration of the scriptures with African contexts will enrich our reading of the scriptures as Mbiti passionately insisted:

> As Christianity deepens its presence in Africa, two features among many stand out prominently to exert a strong impact in that process. These are the use of the Bible, especially in African languages, and the integration of the African world (with its culture, world-view, mentality, spiritual awareness, creativity and modern challenges). These two features cannot be removed from the new African Christianity. One provides the dimension of freshness, newness, otherness, and of universal and ecumenical outreach. The other supplies the base, the roots, the stronghold, the depth of culture and history. The two features meet and enjoy a high degree of commonality which makes them enter into each other. So this interpenetration of biblical and African worlds is strongly represented and visible in African Christianity. It is a major source of strength, whatever issues it may precipitate as side effects.[15]

Whether we can ignore these 'side effects' is in the hands of African Christians themselves to decide. The inculturation of biblical accounts in the African world has been characteristic of African Christianity. However, going further than this two-way inculturation model, Justin Ukpong suggests that there have been three stages of hermeneutical approaches in African Christianity. The first stage (1930s–70s), characterized as 'reactive and apologetic', focused on legitimizing African religion and culture, dominated by the comparative method. This attempt has provided a 'preparatory' place in African culture for the Christian message. The second stage (1970s–90s) was 'reactive-proactive': the use of the African context as a resource for biblical

---

14 Allan Anderson, *Zion and Pentecost: The Spirituality and Experience of Pentecostal and Zionist/Apostolic Churches in South Africa* (Pretoria: University of South Africa Press, 2000), pp. 133–4.

15 Mbiti, *Bible and Theology in African Christianity*, p. 228.

interpretation, dominated by the inculturation-evaluative method and liberation hermeneutics (black theology), making Christianity relevant to the African religio-cultural context. But the main contribution of African interpretation, according to Ukpong, is the third and recent approach of recognizing both the important role of the ordinary readers and the African context as the subjects of biblical interpretation.

> In this way the people's context becomes the subject of interpretation of the biblical text. The goal of interpretation is the actualization of the theological meaning of the text in today's context so as to forge integration between faith and life, and engender commitment to personal and societal transformation ... The basic hermeneutic theory at work is that the *meaning of a text is a function of the interaction between the text in its context and the reader in his/her context*. Thus, there is no one absolute meaning of a text to be recovered through historical analysis alone. Also there are not two processes, consisting of recovery of the meaning of a text through historical analysis and then applying it to the present context, but one process of a reader who is critically aware of his/her context interacting with the text analysed in its context.[16]

This integration of interpretation certainly has great potential, and would contribute to a reading of the scriptures further in wider contexts, but there will be some difficulties with this method. This reading could be subjective, depending on one's context, and may not be able to be shared with people in a different context. Furthermore, taking biblical passages literally often leads to fundamentalist tendencies, as we observe in some of the churches in Africa – indeed this is not limited to Africa. The issue of discernment between the biblical notion of spiritual gifts and power and African traditional religious practice is an ongoing struggle for African Christianity. Even more importantly, who is deciding this could be a vital issue? Reading the work of theologians and biblical scholars on this issue, they seem to have neatly worked out how these interactions should work, but the reality on the ground may be remote from what is discussed in academic writings. This question of authority is important to address because often in an African context, elders and ancestors (through vision and dreams), and even more significantly the charismatic leaders of the churches, hold an ultimate authority.[17]

---

16 Justin Ukpong, 'Developments in Biblical Interpretation in Africa', in West and Dube (eds), *The Bible in Africa*, p. 24.

17 See Anderson, *Zion and Pentecost*, pp. 133, 136–7.

Indian Christianity and the Bible as śruti

Indian approaches to the Bible have not so much concentrated on studying the text itself, but rather on the interpretation of the scriptures, the application of the text, or on comparing it with other Hindu scriptures. Indian Christianity has a rich tradition of developing an Indian hermeneutics following the Hindu tradition of reading their scriptures, and this approach in turn has shaped Christianity in India. Robin Boyd, in his classic book *The Introduction to Indian Theology*, endorses the idea of Appasamy and asserts that the task of Christian theology in India has been settling the 'sources of authority', and that this source has been always the Christian scriptures. However, the scriptures for Indians are not necessarily what is written but rather what is heard and seen. He continues:

> [T]he conception of *śruti* itself is a valuable one, which represents a positive contribution of Indian theology to the world Church. The word ... has the double meaning of 'Scripture' and 'revelation', both of which, according to the Indian conception, have their origin in hearing, *śruti* being derived from a root *śru* meaning 'to hear'.[18]

In addition to the sources of authority in Hindu tradition, there are various hermeneutical tools in interpreting the texts. According to Sugirtharajah, the Hindu approach of *dhvani* has been used as an alternative to western literary and historical methods in illuminating the biblical texts. '*Dhvani* is a reflective and exegetical method used by Indian grammarians and in Sanskrit poetics'; 'like rhetorical criticism, it emphasizes the beauty and the aesthetic sense of the passage'.[19] This understanding encourages Indian Christians to use the scriptures creatively in various art and literature forms. More significantly, it tends to enhance Indian attempts to interpret the scriptures in ways relevant to the Indian culture and society, and these approaches have long been accepted and used in the Indian church tradition.

Here I would like to discuss two approaches to the scriptures in Indian Christianity. First, is the approach of articulating Indian Christology by interpreting the life of Jesus in the Gospels. The concept of God-man is a very familiar one in Indian religious tradition. Jesus Christ is widely recognized as being in this category, and so the life and words of Jesus are admired by both Christians and Hindus. For example, Jesus was very early regarded as 'guru' (by Mazoomdar) or

---

18 Robin Boyd, *An Introduction to Indian Theology* (Delhi: ISPCK, 1975), p. 229.

19 R. S. Sugirtharajah and Cecil Hargreaves (eds), *Readings in Indian Christian Theology I* (Delhi: ISPCK, 1993), p. 200.

'*avatar*' (by Appasamy and Upadhyay). Indian theologians tend to see the person and teachings of Jesus as authoritative over against the systematization of the text and the Christian doctrines. Indian Christian thinkers and theologians have been constantly struggling to reread the life and teaching of Jesus and trying to revise the doctrines developed by the western churches in this light. Second, Indian Christians have always been engaged in inculturating the text into Indian culture and Hindu philosophies. They have concentrated on the issue of bridging the Christian text with Indian contexts and making the text meaningful in such a diverse culture. Indian Christians have been wrestling with interpreting or reinterpreting the text into their own context so that the meaning of the text might be relevant to them. Developing Indian Christology based on the life story of Jesus is a method that can be found in most of the writings of Indian theologians. Among the sources of the story of Jesus, the Gospel of John is most popular in India because of its mystical nature, which appeals to Indian concepts of spirituality. Abhishiktananda even described the Gospel as 'the Johannine Upanishad' because of its resemblance to Hindu scriptures. Contemporary theologians from a variety of traditions use the Fourth Gospel more than the Synoptics in their theologizing.[20]

One of the earliest attempts at Indian Christology can be found in the work of Ram Mohan Roy. As a young Bengali Brahman, Roy was influenced by Islam and saw the need of reforming Hinduism. He openly criticized orthodox Hinduism for the practice of idolatry, which he saw as a corruption of Hindu philosophy.[21] Roy had a monotheistic faith in the unity of God grounded in *Vedanta*.[22] He believed that reason should merely serve to purify religion.[23] He was so attracted to Christian teaching[24] that he made a great effort to learn Greek and Hebrew and showed a remarkable ability to handle the biblical languages in his writings. In 1820 he published *The Precepts of Jesus: The Guide to Peace and Happiness*, which was a collection of the selected

---

20 Kirsteen Kim, 'India', in John Parratt (ed.), *An Introduction to Third World Theologies* (Cambridge: Cambridge University Press, 2004), pp. 44–73.

21 In 1804, Roy published a Persian tract, *Tohfat al-Muwahhiddin* (A Gift to Deists) criticizing idolatry and polytheism: Kenneth W. Jones, *The New Cambridge History of India, III.1: Socio-Religious Reform Movements in British India* (Cambridge: Cambridge University Press, 1989), p. 30. Also E. Daniel Potts, *British Baptist Missionaries in India, 1793–1837: The History of Serampore and Its Missions* (Cambridge: Cambridge University Press, 1967), p. 229. Potts points out that Roy's monotheistic concept was very 'Islamic'.

22 Kalidas Nag and Debajyoti Burman (eds), *The English Works of Raja Rammohun Roy*, Part II (Calcutta: Sadharan Brahmo Samaj, 1945), pp. 60–1.

23 M. M. Thomas, *The Acknowledged Christ of the Indian Renaissance*, 3rd edn (Madras: The Senate of Serampore College, 1991), p. 3.

24 Sophia D. Collet, *The Life and Letters of Raja Rammohun Roy* (Calcutta: Sadharan Brahmo Samaj, 1900), p. 109.

teachings of Jesus, mainly taken from the Gospel of John, excluding his miracles, death and resurrection. For Roy, accepting the atoning death of Christ was not necessary for a true disciple of Jesus, and following Jesus need not involve embracing exclusive Christian doctrines. In assessing Roy's attempt, M. M. Thomas pointed out that Roy separated the teaching of Jesus Christ from the historical events of his life, death and resurrection and their biblical interpretation.[25] For Roy, 'knowledge of the moral law had it in its own power to reconcile men to God and empower them to lead the moral life'.[26] Thus Roy's approach was, for Thomas, the prototype of 'the struggle of modern India to define the truth and meaning of Jesus Christ in terms relevant to its life and thought', and was significant 'in part as the church's witness to its faith in dialogue with a segment of the Indian mind'.[27]

Indian readings of the Christian scriptures have been creative interpretations of the text, and rich theological work has been produced from this subcontinent. This attitude towards the scripture comes quite evidently from the Hindu hermeneutical traditions of *śruti* and *dhvani*, and therefore it makes sense to the Indian hearers.[28] This is not to say that Indian Christians are not interested in the text, but rather, they are more concerned with the image of Jesus Christ which comes through the text, particularly of the Gospel of John, into the Indian living culture. The historical meaning of a particular text and the context in which it was written are not of the same importance as the interpretation of it into the contemporary Indian context. It is the living manifestation of the scriptures in experiencing Jesus Christ by hearing and seeing the gospel in their lives that matters most to Indians. This approach has resulted in a very lively and interactive form of Christianity in which

---

25 See Sunand Sumithra, *Christian Theology from an Indian Perspective* (Bangalore: Theological Book Trust, 1990), p. 41.

26 Thomas, *The Acknowledged Christ*, pp. 10–14. Thomas pointed out that Roy was moving from metaphysical Hinduism to ethical Christianity. What attracted him to the Gospel was its ethics, and therefore, for him and many Hindus like him, 'the communication of the Gospel of salvation has to be in terms of the nature and fulfilment of the moral life'. Thomas argued that it is not an 'uncommon development for a Hindu to go through the moral ideal of Jesus to the secret of his personality and his work of salvation'.

27 Thomas, *The Acknowledged Christ*, pp. 30–2. Thomas further challenged Christians with a pertinent question: 'Is there not a path to understand and encounter Jesus Christ as the ground and salvation of reason and morality within a secular framework without a return to traditional religiosity?'

28 Furthermore Indian tradition, inducting Indian Christian tradition, does indeed give an honoured place to revelation by sight, the unveiling signified by the etymology of the English word (*re-velare*), as for example in Sundar Singh's *darśanas* of the risen Christ, and indeed the word *darśana*, or 'vision' of God, has deep religious significance in India. Boyd, *An Introduction to Indian Theology*, p. 229.

this broad possibility of expression naturally leads to a more creative interpretation of the Christian scriptures.

However, this approach may have caused Indian theology to have a tendency to apply the text too quickly to the context without careful examination of the context from which the text emerged. The dismissal of the Christian traditions and doctrines and also the radical incultura-tion of the text may have weakened the confidence of Christians who may not yet have grasped the text itself. Furthermore, the selective usage of Christian scripture might lead to a limited perspective on Christian faith. A lack of interest in the Old Testament is quite noticeable in Indian biblical tradition, perhaps due to the Hindu rejection of Semitic tradition, reflecting the tension with Islam. There is also a tendency to treat the Hindu tradition as the substitute for Old Testament tradition. As Boyd warned, there is an urgent need for Indian theologians to give attention to the Christian scriptures as a whole.[29]

Korean Christianity as 'Bible Christianity'

The early Korean Protestant Christians were eager to read the Bible in Korean, and there is no doubt that this contributed to the growth of the Korean churches even when the missionaries were not allowed to enter the peninsula. Of course, the growth of the Korean church has to be understood in the light of the socio-political circumstances of the Korean peninsula in the second half of the nineteenth century, and not just the availability of the Bible. However, it is clear that Bible studies contributed to the characteristics of the Korean church and its revival.[30]

> Poor though Korea is, and afflicted with much economic distress, the country shows wonderful spiritual life in many places. It is the conviction of competent observers that the remarkable growth and development of the Korean church is due to the systematic teach-ing of the Bible, which has been one of the characteristic features of foreign mission work in this land ... Country [Bible] classes are held in various districts and people may have walked 50 to 150 miles, with the temperature below zero, in order to attend, and others have

---

29 Boyd, *An Introduction to Indian Theology*, p. 229.

30 The Institute of Korean Church History Studies, *A History of Korean Church* I (Seoul: Korean Literature Press, 1989), pp. 142–8. Lak-Geoon George Paik, *The History of Protestant Missions in Korea: 1832–1910* (Seoul: Yonsei University Press, 1929), pp. 148–53. Min Kyoung Bae, *History of the Christian Church in Korea* (Seoul, Christian Literature Society of Korea, 1982), pp. 147–8; Yi Mahn-Yol, *Korean Christianity and the Unification Movement* (Seoul: Institute of Korean Church History, 2001), pp. 175–211; *A Study of the History of the Reception of Christianity in Korea* (Seoul: Durae Sidae, 1998), pp. 60–94.

carried their supply of grain on their backs, being too poor to pay the necessary charges for their board.[31]

Similarly, William Blair and Bruce Hunt, reporting the revival movement of Korea, gave credit to the place of the Bible study classes:

> The Bible-study class system is a special feature of the Korean work. Each Church appoints a week or longer some time during the year for Bible study. All work is laid aside. Just as the Jews kept the Passover, the Korean Christians keep these days sacred to prayer and the study of God's Word.[32]

In fact, the tradition of Bible study was so much the hallmark of early Korean Christianity that one missionary called it 'Bible Christianity':

> The Christianity being developed in this land is pre-eminently a Bible Christianity. It is the Scripture that the evangelist takes in his hand when he goes forth to preach. It is the word of God that is being believed, and by which men are being saved. It is the Bible that is the daily food of the Korean Christians – his spiritual meat and drink. In a way that is difficult for one to understand who lives in a land of daily newspapers, magazines, and books coming from the press in a constantly increasing stream, the Bible holds the chief place in the mental or spiritual nourishment of a multitude of people in this land.[33]

The distinctiveness of Korean Christianity as Bible Christianity is due to the fact that the Korean education system was heavily influenced by the Confucian traditional method of teaching and learning. Confucian learning was highly systematized and people of the ruling and middle classes were required to learn the Confucian texts by heart. People were taught to accept the Confucian texts as the authority for socio-political principles as well as the daily practice of ethics and moral conduct. There was no critical evaluation of the texts, nor of their validity in the context of Korea, but they were regarded as given authority by the king and forefathers. People read them aloud or memorized them and recited them, and tried to follow their teaching literally. In the period when Protestant Christianity was introduced in Korea, Confucian philosophy was largely questioned by the educated people, due to the corruption of

31 *Report of National Bible Society of Scotland* (1930), p. 104.
32 William N. Blair and Bruce Hunt, *The Korean Pentecost and the Sufferings which Followed* (Edinburgh: The Banner of Truth Trust, 1977), p. 67.
33 *Report of British Foreign Bible Society* (1907), p. 70.

the government and division and infighting between different Confucian schools; nevertheless, the mode of learning it inculcated is dominant in the Korean education system even to the present day.

When the Bible was introduced to the Koreans, and once Korean Christians accepted it as the sacred text, it was reverenced as the authority above others. And they employed the Confucian method of learning as they studied the Christian scriptures. They tended to accept the literal meaning of the text and tried to put it into practice in their daily lives. In this conservative approach, any new understanding or interpretation of the text has to be scrutinized by the traditional understanding of the text. This approach has in turn shaped the Korean church where there is a strong commitment to the scriptures, which has contributed to its rapid growth. There has also been an eagerness to study the Bible and follow literally what the Bible teaches. The scriptures so well learnt have been a source of strength for Korean Christianity, especially in the time of persecution in the middle of the nineteenth century, during the Japanese occupation and the Korean War.

However, this rigid and radical affirmation of Christian scripture has also limited the development of Korean Christianity in various ways. Korean Christians tend to take the text literally and are reluctant to accept any new interpretations. The interpretation of the Bible by the missionaries, which came with the introduction of the scriptures, was 'accepted as the norm' or held 'authority'. Therefore any other interpretation has to be measured by this original interpretation. This is not to say that Koreans accepted the interpretation of the early missionaries simply because they brought a text, but rather Koreans accepted that particular version of Christianity and they wanted to maintain their initial commitment. 'Bible Christianity' could lead into biblicalism in which there could be no interpretation but only transmission of the text. This attitude may have contributed to a fundamentalist approach to the Christian faith and towards other scriptures, as well as to people of other faiths. This preoccupation with the study of the Bible as the only authoritative text of Christian living tends to lead Korean Christians to be less concerned about the actual application of the teaching. In other words, this lack of interpretation of the text hinders any experiment with creative approaches to the text, and as a result the text becomes law, which either demands the literal obedience of Christians or becomes irrelevant to contemporary Korean society.

In the cases of African, Indian and Korean Christianity, the attitudes of Christians towards the Bible were far from those of being mere recipients, but rather they actively participated in the translation, distribution and interpretation of the Bible even in the very early stages of the arrival of the Protestant missionaries. They took the Bible as their own and made it part and parcel of their culture and Christian practice so that scripture has been a key source in developing Christianity in these regions. As a part of this process, the Bible shaped the churches' response to the different socio-political and economic contexts.

Differing hermeneutics responding to changing contexts

The distinctive readings of the Bible in different regions, mentioned above, have in turn shaped the expressions and practices of Christianity in each case. In brief, African readings emphasize the inculturation of the Bible into the African tradition and culture; Indian readings are more concerned with creative interpretation of the text and interaction with the Hindu scriptures; Korean readings are in line with the Confucian method of learning, resulting in more rigid acceptance of conservative interpretations of the Bible.

However, the hermeneutical method is not uniform in each of these contexts. Especially in an age of globalization, Christian communities in different continents and regions are not isolated from one another. Ideas and methods from one context may be rapidly transmitted to another. So across different societies we can identify different methods of contextual theology. These fall into four main categories: liberation, feminist, cross-textual, and inculturation. These readings are not neat categories but they are helpful for us to examine here.

Liberation hermeneutics and postcolonial criticism

Liberation reading, without doubt, has been the most influential development of hermeneutical methodology in modern biblical and theological studies. Anthony Thiselton points out that in terms of hermeneutics, liberation theology, black and feminist theology have their roots in a hermeneutics of 'socio-critical theory', which is 'an approach to texts (or to traditions and institutions) which seeks to penetrate beneath their surface-function *to expose their role as instruments of power, domination or social manipulation*'.[34] Such a hermeneutics of suspicion has been influential around the world, especially since the 1960s.

According to Gustavo Gutiérrez, who is often regarded as the founder of liberation theology, liberation hermeneutics has four basic components. First, they construct a critique of the framework of the interpretation of the dominant traditions and this can be western, cap-

---

34 Anthony Thiselton, *New Horizons in Hermeneutics* (London: HarperCollins, 1992), p. 379.

italist, colonial, androcentric or patriarchal – ideologies of dominant traditions. They aim to offer an alternative interpretation from their own experience and seek to expose those uses of biblical texts that serve the social interests of dominant groups. Second, for the purpose of the first, 'socio-critical' tools are needed for hermeneutics and these can be used to 'conscientize'. Third, there is an intense identification of biblical texts, particularly the theme of Exodus. Fourth is the language of eschatology – bringing hope – and an emphasis on action (praxis).

There are many examples of liberation readings in Latin America and these have been immensely influential on the rest of the world, especially in Asia and Africa where the issue of economic and political injustice has been a dominant concern for Christians. Korea also developed its own version of liberation theology called minjung theology. The obvious starting point of minjung theology is the distinctive concept of minjung – common people. Ahn Byung-Mu, one of minjung theology's leading exponents, drew this concept from the Gospel of Mark. In his study of Mark, he identified the crowd who were surrounding Jesus – *ochlos* – and pointed out that this term was first used by Mark. He insisted that in comparison to the term *laos* in Luke, which means the 'people of God', *ochlos* is the common people, who belong to the 'marginalized and abandoned' group, and that *ochlos* is not consolidated into a concept but defined in a relational way.

> The *ochlos* are feared by the unjust and powerful, but they are not organized into a power group. Therefore, we cannot regard them as a political power bloc; rather, they should be regarded existentially as a crowd. They are minjung not because they have a common destiny, but simply because they are alienated, dispossessed, and powerless. They are never represented as a class which has a power base. They yearn for something.[35]

The identification of the people in the Bible with their own context is very common among liberation theologians. For example, Dalit theologians who represent outcaste communities of India (see Chapter 4) have been using Isaiah 3.12–15 to show that the Lord is defender of the poor, accuser and judge of the oppressors.[36] There is a strong identification with the people of Israel in Exodus stories by people in

---

35 Ahn Byung-Mu, 'Jesus and the Minjung in the Gospel of Mark', in Kim Yong Bock (ed.), *Minjung Theology: People as the Subjects of History* (Singapore: Commission on Theological Concerns and Christian Conference of Asia, 1981), p. 150.

36 George Koonthanam, 'Yahweh the Defender of the Dalits: A Reflection on Isaiah', in R. S. Sugirtharajah (ed.), *Voices from the Margin: Interpreting the Bible in the Third World* (London: SPCK, 1991), p. 107.

a marginalized situation,[37] and the Church adopts the liberating role of Christ within the society. Minjung theologians lived out their theology in the turbulent years of military government in South Korea and were instrumental in bringing about the transition to democracy and improvements in workers' rights and conditions. We shall look in more detail at the impact of this form of public theology in Korea in Chapter 5.

The main thrust of the liberation theological argument is based on the hermeneutics of suspicion, and this is shared with what is called postcolonial hermeneutics. But in his book, *The Bible and the Third World*, R. S. Sugirtharajah distinguishes the two and sharply criticizes liberation hermeneutics: for its conservative approach; its Christ-centred hermeneutics; its lack of critical self-reflectivity; pressure from conservative forces within the church hierarchy; over-eagerness to get the methods correct; and the seductive effects of dialoguing with western theologians.[38] Instead, he asserts that 'postcolonial criticism' aims to fulfil several tasks: scrutiny of biblical documents for their colonial entanglements; engagement in reconstructive reading of biblical texts considering the religious, cultural and political situations of the stories in the Bible; and interrogation of both colonial and metropolitan interpretations. He asserts that some distinctive characteristics of postcolonial critics are seeing the Bible as one among many liberating texts, and drawing resources from other religious traditions. He argues that this method employs the 'multi-disciplinary nature of the enterprise' and the 'empowerment of repressed voices through visual, oral and aural means'.[39]

Perhaps the most decisive difference in Sugirtharajah's mind is that liberation theologies maintain a metanarrative of liberation, whereas postcolonial approaches, in common with postmodern ones, do not. Liberation theologies situate themselves within the Christian story and Christian hope, whereas Sugirtharajah's postcolonial approach does not. But while Sugirtharajah helpfully highlights aspects of postcolonial method, in general it is difficult to draw a hard and fast line between the two. And we find aspects of postcolonial approaches being adopted by liberation theologians. One of the best examples of the postcolonial reading can be found in Samuel Rayan's article 'Caesar versus God'.[40] Rayan is used by Sugirtharajah to illustrate a classic postcolonial

---

37 Cyris Moon, 'A Korean Minjung Perspective: The Hebrews and the Exodus', in Sugirtharajah (ed.), *Voices from the Margin*, p. 236.

38 Sugirtharajah, *The Bible and the Third World*, pp. 242–3.

39 Sugirtharajah, *The Bible and the Third World*, pp. 262–5.

40 Samuel Rayan, 'Caesar versus God', in Sebastian Kappen (ed.), *Jesus Today* (Madras: AICUF, 1985), pp. 88–97.

approach (interrogation of both colonial and metropolitan interpretations), but at the same time he is a liberation theologian who has engaged in constructive dialogue with Gutiérrez and many others.[41]

Rayan's article examines the passage in Mark 12.13–17 (Matt. 22.15–22; Luke 20.20–26) in which, responding to some of the Pharisees and Herodians regarding the temple tax, Jesus answers, 'render to Caesar the things that are Caesar's, and to God the things that are God's'. Rayan has checked about 20 scholarly commentaries over 120 years (1857–1978) on this passage. Interestingly, he has observed that there are three tendencies in their interpretations. First, throughout the period, there is an interpretation that the payment of tax is both lawful and obligatory and that the Emperor, ruling over the country, has the right to demand just taxes; and that obedience to God included obedience and loyalty to the state. This is what Rayan sees as 'colonial theology's capacity to abstract from the history of oppression and to concentrate on the service of power'.[42] The second interpretation is that the question of tax is not central – in other words, Jesus goes beyond the political to the question of conscience. This trend of interpretation was found during the post-war era. The attention no longer centres on the question of tax but rather the question of the things of God. However, in this period, no unqualified blessing is bestowed on imperialism and these interpretations have a tendency to challenge people to religious discernment in political issues. There is also a tendency to secularize authority, expose it to criticism, and create room for rebellion.[43] The third trend was to ask whether God's people are free from making payment to Caesar – whether Caesar has any claim on God's people. This interpretation suggests that Jesus is not supporting any of Caesar's claims, nor endorsing any tribute to conquerors. He is rather grasping the situation in its totality – people are subject to God and to no one else. Rayan concludes that the early interpretation of Caesar as 'God's delegated authority is an ideologically conditioned position'.

As the example of Rayan shows, liberation theology and postcolonial theory may overlap to a considerable extent in postcolonial contexts. However, liberation theological approaches are not limited to postcolonial contexts. They have been applied in doing public theology in many different situations of injustice, as we shall see in this book.

---

41 See T. K. John (ed.), *Bread and Breath: Essays in Honor of Samuel Rayan* (Anand: Gujarat Sahitya Prakash, 1991).

42 Rayan, 'Caesar versus God', p. 91.

43 Rayan, 'Caesar versus God', p. 93.

African and Asian feminist readings

The Woman's Bible (1895) by Elizabeth Cady Stanton was a significant landmark for the reading of the Bible from a feminist perspective. According to Thiselton, the hermeneutics employed by feminist theology, black theology and liberation theology are all in the same category of 'socio-critical' hermeneutics, but I would like to put the feminist readings in a different category since they begin with women's experience and this becomes a critical principle for their reading of the Bible.[44] According to Fiorenza, the characteristics of the feminist hermeneutics lie in: first, not just analysing merely the biblical passages on women, nor accepting the construction of patriarchal texts at face value; second, an evaluation of biblical androcentric traditions and examining not only the Bible but all spectra of life and 'through women's struggle for liberation from all patriarchal oppression'; third, rejecting 'those elements within all biblical traditions and texts that perpetuate, in the name of God, violence, alienation, and patriarchal subordination, and eradicate women from historical–theological consciousness';[45] fourth, recovering the liberating visions of the people of God.

As Kirsteen Kim explains, there is general agreement that African and Asian feminist theologies can be distinguished from the feminist theology done by western women in North America and Europe. While there is a danger that this perceived division is simply a reflection of a northern view of the rest of the world that sees it as an undifferentiated bloc, it is a view that also finds support among feminist theologians who see themselves as part of the Third World or colonized world, and who do not regard northern feminist theology as addressing the issues affecting women's lives in their contexts, or as using appropriate method for their situation. In part the distinction is due to a conscious reaction of feminist writers from the Majority World to the feminist theology of the North and West, but it is also a reflection of the different contexts in which women are doing theology. The difference in context can be described in two ways: first, the difference of socio-economic status between the global North and the global South; and second, the difference in cultural and religious background, which is most marked in Asian theologies – a difference between West and East.[46] While some western feminist theologians are moving on from rereading the patriarchal text, or selecting 'women in the Bible' passages, towards going

---

44 Thiselton, *New Horizons of Hermeneutics*.

45 E. Schüssler Fiorenza, *In Memory of Her* (New York: Crossroad, 1983), pp. 32–3.

46 Kirsteen Kim, 'Gender Issues in Intercultural Theological Perspective', in Mark J. Cartledge and David Cheetham (eds), *Intercultural Theology: A Primer* (London: SCM Press, 2011).

beyond the text to become 'post-biblical feminists', Asian and African feminist approaches are by and large focused on 'women's experience' in their own contexts and reflect this in their reading of the Bible. I would like to discuss some examples of women's readings of the gospel from Asian and African contexts.

Japanese author Hisako Kinukawa examines the story of the Syrophoenician woman in Mark 7.24–30, who begged Jesus to cast out the demon from her daughter. Kinukawa objects to common aspects of the interpretation. For example: that the intelligent retort of her argument prevails over that of Jesus; that her bold faith wins Jesus' favour and he grants her request; that she shows wit and persistence; that her verbal riposte gives the twist to the story; that Jesus endorses the woman's indomitable spirit, etc. She insists that the woman is 'driven into an impossible situation and cannot find any other solution than to forget tradition, neglect social custom, and rush ahead recklessly to Jesus. She can no longer turn back. She risks everything on Jesus. And for Jesus, he 'is motivated to act, inviting the gentile, the socially outcast, the materially poor, the sick, the oppressed, the rejected into God's community'. Kinukawa expands this to include many Asian women who were the victims of Japanese aggression during the Second World War and found themselves in a similarly desperate situation; the story reassures them that they are accepted in God's community.[47]

Like Kinukawa, Asian and African feminists readings try to relate women's experience to the stories of the Bible, especially from the Gospels, and reread them from their contexts. They complain that the interpretation of the story is often focused on Jesus' words, thoughts and actions and not on the women – they are treated as background extras. But these authors wish to highlight the women's words, thoughts and actions so that the story can be fully appreciated.

Another example is the exposition of John 4, the woman of Samaria in her encounter with Jesus. Vandana from India, in her chapter on *Jeevan Dhara* ('Living Streams') in her book *Waters of Fire*, reads the story from the perspective of an Indian woman and against the background of Hindu traditions. She sees the metaphor of water as a symbol of life like the river Ganges and the scene in the Gospel as that of a Brahman man and outcast woman at a well, which could be pictured in India even today. Vandana understands Jesus' claim of 'I am He' as signifying that he is a guru. Water, in Hindu tradition, is a symbol of the Spirit and affirms the spirituality of India. Vandana skilfully integrates the story into an Indian village setting and brings the story alive by

---

47 Hisako Kinukawa, 'The Syrophoenician Woman: Mark 7.24–30', in Sugirtharajah (ed.), *Voices from the Margin*, pp. 138–55.

relating it to the reality of a lower-caste woman. She explains that the story can be appreciated more by relating it to Hindu spirituality.[48]

Mukti Barton, on the other hand, examines the same story from the standpoint of Bangladeshi women and from a liberation perspective. Barton, like Vandana, suggests the important relationship of water and life in the Bangladesh context and believes the scene at the well could be re-enacted in any village. She illustrates this by quoting a poem by Rabindranath Tagore based on a Buddhist story very similar to this biblical account and suggests that many women in Bangladesh, like the woman at the well, are humiliated not for what they have done but for who they are. She suggests a similarity between Samaritan and Bangladeshi women due to their lower status in society and their vulnerability in married life, especially on the issue of divorce. Barton sees that the traditional reading of the passage emphasizes Jesus as living water and his willing approach to the woman, but for her, the main issues here are the woman's situation as one that has been socially imposed upon her, her desire to go deeper into the conversation with Jesus, and her eventual finding of the source of the living water.[49]

> In the gospel account, the woman chooses to be truthful about her marital status and, instead of condemning her, Jesus compliments her for her truthfulness. The more Jesus honours her, the more the woman at the well starts to respect herself.[50]

Examining the text of Esther from the South African context, Itumeleng Mosala concludes that both the text itself and most of the interpretations of the text are heavily patriarchal. She objects to the text's choice of a female character to achieve what she sees as a 'patriarchal end' (Mordecai was honoured and well liked by ... He worked for the good of his people ...). She continues:

> The hero of the story is Mordecai who needless to say gives nothing of himself for what he gets. Esther struggles, but Mordecai reaps the fruit of the struggle. African women who work within liberation movements and other groups will be very familiar with this kind of dynamics.[51]

---

48 Vandana, *Waters of Fire* (Bangalore: ATC, 1989), pp. 76–92.

49 Mukti Barton, *Scripture as Empowerment for Liberation and Justice: The Experience of Christian and Muslim Women in Bangladesh* (Bristol: University of Bristol, 1999), pp. 107–18.

50 Barton, *Scripture as Empowerment*, p. 114.

51 Itumeleng Mosala, 'The Implications of the Text of Esther for African Women's Struggle for Liberation in South Africa', in Sugirtharajah (ed.), *Voices from the Margin*, p. 176.

Asian and African feminist readings are not as interested in the main characters of the texts as in the women in the texts, and trying to understand them or identify with them. As a result, these new readings bring new insights. In many cases, their readings challenge traditional readings and therefore the authority of the traditional interpreters of the scriptures. They are a reminder that the agents of public theology are not only elite academics and church leaders but that it is an activity of the whole Church and is enriched by the participation of all, especially those who experience the underside of history and oppression by traditional religious structures.

Inter-textual readings

The intertextual readings are well articulated in Chinese and Indian theological writings, largely due to these regions having rich traditions of the sacred texts. Indian theologian Stanley Samartha pointed out some of the basic presuppositions for these readings: first, acknowledgement of the plurality of scriptures ('a fact of history to be accepted, not a theological point to be discussed'); second, recognition of the fact that the traditions of other faith communities have developed their own hermeneutics suitable to their contexts; third, sensitivity and acceptance of the values and claims of other religious communities.[52] Addressing the context of Asia, he saw the Asians have a double heritage – the Bible and the other scriptures – and that Asian Christians could provide a 'bridge through which the insights of different scriptures might be shared in the larger community'.[53] He emphasized the importance of using other scriptures for our own spiritual enrichment:

> In every living religion, scriptures are not just sources of doctrine, but also of personal devotion, spiritual sustenance, and help in times of trouble, perplexity, and suffering. Therefore the *devotional* use of *other* scriptures by people of a particular tradition should not be rejected or looked upon with suspicion. In the lives of many people, reading from other scriptures is enlarging horizons and deepening inner life without in any way disturbing, diluting, or betraying one's own commitment.[54]

In this hermeneutical challenge, Kwok Pui Lan wishes go further, saying that 'biblical interpretation is never simply a religious matter, for the

---

52 Samartha, 'Scripture and Scriptures', in Sugirtharajah (ed.), *Voices from the Margin*, pp. 12–14, 19.
53 Samartha, 'Scripture and Scriptures', p. 21.
54 Samartha, 'Scripture and Scriptures', p. 31.

processes of formation, canonization and transmission of the Bible have been imbued with the issues of authority and power'. Concerning the question of the truth claims of the Christian scriptures, she suggests that we need to examine three areas: sacrality of the text, the issue of cannon, and the norm of interpretation. She asserts:

> Since I reject both the sacrality of the text and the canon as a guarantee of truth, I also do not think that the Bible provides the norm for interpretation in itself. For a long time, such 'mystified' doctrine has taken away the power from women, the poor and the powerless, for it helps to sustain the notion that the 'divine presence' is located somewhere else and not in ourselves. Today, we must claim back the power to look at the Bible with our own eyes and to stress that divine immanence is within us, not in something sealed off and handed down from almost two thousand years ago.[55]

Not all the biblical scholars who are trying to bridge the Bible and other religious texts fully agree with her, but they certainly challenge the notion of the norm of interpretation – that is, western tradition of historical–critical and other types of hermeneutics. Archie Lee is one of the Chinese scholars who has specialized in a cross-textual reading of the Bible. For example, he compares the Chinese creation myth of Nu Kua and the biblical narrative in Genesis. Here is a portion of the Chinese creation narrative:

> It is said that when the heaven and the earth were separated there was no human being. It was Nu Kua who first created human beings by moulding yellow earth. The work was so taxing that she was very exhausted. So she dipped a rope into the mud and then lifted it. The mud that dripped from the rope also became human beings. Those made by moulding yellow earth were rich and noble, while those made by dripped mud were poor and low.[56]

He compares the two texts and analyses the insights from each text and then tries to strengthen the interpretation of the other text. For example, he sees that the biblical texts have the divine dimension (for example, of God's breathing into the human being) whereas the Nu Kua text has a more anthropocentric emphasis and contains an explanation of the social hierarchy of the people. Furthermore, he sees that the Chinese

---

55 Kwok Pui Lan, 'Discovering the Bible in the Non-biblical World', in Sugirtharajah (ed.), *Voices from the Margin*, pp. 289–305.

56 Quoted in Archie Lee, 'The Chinese Creation Myth of Nu Kua and the Biblical Narrative in Genesis 1—2', in Sugirtharajah (ed.), *Voices from the Margin*, p. 368.

understanding of human beings becoming gods and the incarnation of gods in human form in history presents 'a theological challenge to the monotheistic faith of Christian faith'. He concludes:

> There are world views which cannot easily, if at all, be reconciled with the theology of creation which we derived from the biblical text and have developed in the doctrine of creation in the West. The issue of the universe being the body of the creator, as is conveyed in the creation myth of Pan Ku, and the idea of a close unity between the divine and the human (that human beings can somehow become 'gods' as well as that human beings can await the coming of the divine into our life) are significant topics for investigation in Asian theological endeavour.[57]

In India, these intertextual readings, which employ the concepts and philosophies of the Hindu religious traditions, are actively utilized in Christian theology. It is not too much to say that the predominant concern of Indian theology is this issue of relating the Christian text to the Hindu texts in their conceptual formulations and hermeneutics. This also includes the Christian expressions of art, music and literature. One of the early examples is Raymond Panikkar's well-known work, *The Unknown Christ of Hinduism* (1964).[58] Panikkar was convinced that there must be a 'meeting-place' between Christianity and Hinduism in the religious sphere.[59] He then argued that this meeting place should be Christ since Christ is the 'ontological meeting-point of any religion' and the 'only one mediator between God and the rest'; in fact, he further insisted that 'Christ is already there in Hinduism in so far as Hinduism is a true religion'. He then pointed out that *Ihsvara* in Hinduism was the 'link' between *Brahman* and the world, and that Christ is hidden in Hinduism, therefore Hindus, without realizing it, are acknowledging the 'hidden Christ' in Hinduism by having the concept of *Ihsvara*.[60] Panikkar believed that Hinduism can be and should be a vehicle for salvation because of the presence of the 'unknown Christ' within it. Panikkar's acceptance of Hinduism as a legitimate way of salvation laid the groundwork for Catholic theologians in India to move from 'Indian

---

57 Archie Lee, 'The Chinese Creation Myth', pp. 378–9. See also Archie Lee, 'Theological Reading of Chinese Creation Stories of P'an Ku and Nu Kua', in John England and Archie Lee (eds), *Doing Theology with Asian Resources* (Auckland: PTCA, 1993), pp. 230–7.

58 Raymond Panikkar, *The Unknown Christ of Hinduism* (London: Darton, Longman & Todd, 1964).

59 Panikkar, *The Unknown Christ*, pp. 11–18.

60 Panikkar, *The Unknown Christ*, p. 131.

Christianity' to 'Hindu Christianity'.[61] The use of Hindu concepts and terminologies in order to build bridges between Christianity and Hinduism can be found in most Indian theologians. Hindu–Christian dialogue is also an important agenda for Indian church leaders and theologians, and these intertextual readings play a vital role in this endeavour for dialogue.[62]

Reading one another's scriptures in dialogue with each other is an important part of doing theology in a multireligious society. It enables public theologians to relate their theology to the traditions of others in a way that resonates with them. One example of such public engagement with one another's religious texts is 'Scriptural Reasoning', an approach led by David Ford, Regius Professor of Divinity at the University of Cambridge, and a Jewish scholar, Peter Ochs, and also including Muslim colleagues. Scriptural Reasoning is defined as 'the communal practice of reading sacred scriptures, in small groups, together'. This practice originated in a university setting but it is now understood as a 'civic practice' in which people of different faiths 'engage with their holy scripture and with each other as neighbours and fellow citizens'. The participants have found this a challenging but ultimately transformative process leading to new conversations and relationships across religious boundaries in contemporary society.[63]

Inculturation readings of the scriptures

From the second half of the twentieth century, the term 'inculturation' was introduced. It soon became the dominant concept of Catholic theology, but the precise meaning of the term and its applications could range from interpreting the gospel to local culture to encouraging 'theology from below', or 'local theologies', as a way forward in Christian mission.[64] Aylward Shorter defines inculturation as a 'creative and dynamic relationship between the Christian message and a culture or cultures'. It is an ongoing process of dialogue between the gospel and culture and interaction between different cultures, since faith is

---

61 Aloysius Pieris, 'Inculturation in Non-Semitic Asia', *The Month* 19/3 (Mar. 1986), pp. 83–7.

62 See Harold Coward (ed.), *Hindu–Christian Dialogue: Perspectives and Encounters* (Maryknoll, NY: Orbis Books, 1989); Francis D'sa, 'How Is It that we Hear, Each of Us, in Our Own Native Language', in Wickeri, *Scripture, Community, and Mission*, pp. 127–51.

63 http://www.scripturalreasoning.org/ (accessed 6 Mar. 2011).

64 See Stephen B. Bevans, *Models of Contextual Theology* (Maryknoll, NY: Orbis Books, 1992); Robert J. Schreiter, *Constructing Local Theologies* (Maryknoll, NY: Orbis Books, 1985).

integrated in culture and it promotes the reinterpretation of culture 'enlivened by the Gospel from within'.[65]

Many African readings are in this category. David Adamo writes about the 'functional substitution' of the Bible with traditional ways of dealing with daily problems. In Africa, there are cultural ways of responding to problems, diseases, evil spirits and calamities, but Africans were told to abandon these practices by the missionaries. According to Adamo, this change created a kind of vacuum for African Christians since the mission churches could not provide alternative ways to deal with the problems. However, in the African Initiated Churches in Nigeria, they discovered rich resources in the book of Psalms that resembled the traditional resources. Adamo explains some distinctive usages of the psalms in new ways to protect from all kinds of enemy. The Church of the Lord classifies certain psalms as specially effective for certain purposes. For example, Psalms 5, 6, 28, 35, 37, 54, 55 and 83 (particularly Ps. 55) are considered to protect from evil ones.[66]

Yoruba society (in northern Nigeria) has a complex system of dealing with diseases and sickness through herbs and rituals. Some psalms are regarded as therapeutic, for example, Psalms 6, 20 and 40. They use the psalms along with traditional methods of healing. Another area is to help young people to be successful in the passing of exams, getting jobs, and so on. Psalms 4, 8.1–9, 9, 23, 24, 27, 46, 51, 119.9–16, and 134 are identified as ones for success. There are careful instructions by a village chief about how to use the psalms:

> Cut four candles into three each, light them round and be in the middle of the candles. Put some salts under each candle, read Psalm 4 eight times. Call the Holy Name *Alatula Ja Ajarahliah* 72 times. Pray for success. You will surely pass.[67]

Psalm 133 is the psalm identified as one that will aid villagers to secure the love of a woman or a man! Here are the instructions:

> Draw some water with your mouth into a bottle. Put some water that will fill the bottle into a bowl. Wash your face and armpit seven times in the water in the bowl. Add that water in the bowl to the one in the bottle to fill it up. Then call the name of the woman/man and the name Eve/Adam 21 times. Read Psalm 133, Ruth 1:16–17 and

---

65 Aylward Shorter, *Toward A Theology of Inculturation* (Maryknoll, NY: Orbis Books, 1988), pp. 10–12, 42.

66 David Adamo, 'The Use of Psalms in African Indigenous Churches in Nigeria', in West and Dube (eds), *The Bible in Africa*, p. 340.

67 Adamo, 'The Use of Psalms', p. 342.

Solomon 3:1–11 and John 1:1–4 into the water at midnight and if the person is known, give the water to her/him to drink.[68]

According to Adamo,[69] the villagers believe that these practices are effective, and he argues, rather controversially, that this is an example of Christians finding alternative resources to deal with the daily problems of healing, protection and success.

C. S. Song is perhaps the most articulate theologian in Asia when it comes to the utilizing of life story in his theologizing. He sees theology as intuition rather than reason, which 'breaks into the mystery of mysteries'. He sees the importance of using symbols in Asian theology and distinguishes his theology from systematized theology. One of the best examples of his reading of the Bible is his thesis on 'the seed of hope in the womb'. In this thesis, he starts by quoting a poem, 'First Tragedy', by a Vietnamese (Trieu Vu).

> The yellow telegram
> with its stark typewritten letters
> announces a death
>
> She knew it would be his death
> still she mumbles the words
> telling herself telling
> herself don't
> cry
> for this is common
> in war who is ever free of tragedy
>
> Just lie still lie still
> you are free now my darling
>
> Constantly thinking of the future
> with a withering faith
>
> she has painted her own portrait
> the high collar the still-life round eyes
> the bombs the grenades
> everything is black
> because nothing is left
> who has not suffered in a war

---

68 Adamo, 'The Use of Psalms', p. 345.
69 Adamo, 'The Use of Psalms', p. 347.

In confusion she looks down
at the seed coming to life in her
coming to the misery of life
try to grow up like your father my darling.[70]

He draws a powerful picture from the poem, seeing the agony of the people and yet a great hope for the future, as he argues:

> Throughout long centuries of suffering, Asians have learned to stake their hopes and their future in the seed hidden within the mysterious womb of humanity. A new life is in the making to succeed the life that has just passed out of the community of the living. The seed of life in the womb is the seed of hope for Asians. Their past, their present, and their future converge in the seed of hope carried in the mother's womb. The seed of life in the bereaved wife's womb is the power of hope that unites all the members of the family, including the deceased husband, in a communion of life and hope.[71]

Song then connects this story with the story of Sarah, Abraham's wife. Though she had already passed the age of having a child, the promise from God was delivered: 'the seed of life that was to be conceived and to grow there through divine intervention was to bear the meaning of salvation'. And 'Sarah's womb became an important point at which God's salvation took on a historical manifestation.'[72] Song then quickly mentions Isaiah's prophecy to King Ahaz (7.14) and points out that 'the seed of life in the womb is the fruition of the interaction between God's hope and humanity's hope'.

> Because God has chosen the human womb to manifest God's presence in the world and God's salvation for humankind, this is affirmation of the seed of life as the seed of hope. God has now created the seed of life in Mary's womb as the embodiment of the hope of God's salvation. It is a profound religious insight on the part of Luke to give his account of the birth of the Saviour in this way. The human womb thus becomes the embodiment of human hope. It is where God comes to meet us, to become united with us, to be one with us. In Mary's womb God is at work in the conception of her child. Mary's womb becomes a new universe, a new creation. God has intervened in the human womb for the creation of a new life, a life that will be

---

70 C. S. Song, *Third-Eye Theology: Theology in Formation in Asian Settings* (Guildford: Lutterworth Press, 1980), pp. 124–5.
71 Song, *Third-Eye Theology*, p. 146.
72 Song, *Third-Eye Theology*, p. 147.

responsible to both God and humanity, a life that binds God and humanity in a new bond of love and redemption.[73]

What Song does is to start with a life story in Asia, and relate it to the biblical passages. He then leads into a formulating theology, which Asians (particularly women) can identify with. He has done this in a very passionate and convincing way.

Consideration of inculturation readings is a reminder that public theology need not necessarily be expressed or conceived in the academic theological style used in this book. It starts with reflection on public life in specific cultural contexts, and if its conclusions are to be communicated and understood in the public square, then it may need to be expressed in the vernacular and in dynamic interaction with cultural forms.

Conclusion

It is exciting to see the development of various hermeneutical tools from world Christianity that enrich the reading of the Bible and its application to public life. By way of conclusion, I would like to consider some matters of concern as we examine these readings. First, the question of authority: where does the source of authority lie in biblical interpretation? Of course, ultimately individuals or a group all have a right to decide what the particular passage means in their own situation. But this decision is also by and large informed by various outside sources. When a group accepts a collective interpretation, often it has immense implications for our course of action. For example, the interpretation of the race issue in the Dutch Reformed Churches during the Apartheid era resulted in very negative consequences, whereas the Kairos Document (see Preface) made a significant contribution to the cause of a just society in South Africa. Uncritical and literal interpretations may lead to fundamentalist approaches to the Christian scriptures as we have seen in North America and elsewhere. A Marxist reading of the scriptures also has its limitations as it often uses the text with a pragmatic and manipulative attitude. David Lochhead, in his article 'The Liberation of the Bible', discusses this dilemma. He sees the praxis of hermeneutics as 'politics of understanding'. The process of seeing the text in our own context, as most contextual readings do, needs two conditions: the method must be available to ordinary people; and the people must be able to distinguish the perspective of the group from the

---

73 Song, *Third-Eye Theology*, p. 151.

perspective of the text. In the process, a group could call 'experts' but they do have their own ideological commitment. We could abandon the experts' help altogether, but this anti-intellectual approach often ends up giving prominence to 'more aggressive representatives of the unofficial ideology of the group: the most pious or the most militant'. Lochead suggests that 'what we need is not information about what the Bible *means*, but about the *context* within which the text has its basic meaning', and discovering the meaning of the text for a particular individual or group is a matter of 'creative insight'.[74]

Second, the issue of discernment is an important one. Readings have been influenced by various internal and external factors and these give a rich variety of insights to the understanding of scripture. It is inevitable that readings differ from one to another. But does this mean that the original intention of the text in that particular context does not matter? Does the Bible serve only as a 'proof text' for our intentions and action? I do not think the Bible is meant to be merely serving to support our course of action. The search for the original meaning of the text needs to continue in our reflection so that these meanings challenge us and contradict our ways of thinking and intention. The actual implications of the text in our contexts need to be constantly revised and updated, but the search for the intentions of the original texts should continue. Reflecting on the interpretations of other religious textual traditions are an interesting and a creative way of understanding the Christian text, but this also has its limitations of being naive and superficial in that it may not reflect in-depth understanding of either religious text, but may only remain as an academic exercise. Inculturation approaches have been immensely helpful for enlarging the meaning of the text and bringing a lively conversation with cultural contexts, but not all cultural interpretations are valid. Discernment is needed to bring out in cultural forms the public implications of a uniquely Christian theology.

Third, the issue of identity and ownership: often scholars from Asia and Africa describe themselves as 'we Asians', 'we Africans', as if they represent all Asians and Africans. However, often the reality on the ground of the faith and concerns of the people are different from what these theologians claim them to be. I am not saying that they are wrong, but they may not represent the Christians there and the people's reading of the Bible. This is particularly so when we look at the situation in Latin America. Though Latin American liberation theologians' reading was reflecting the situation of the poor and oppressed, many of them rather opted for Pentecostal Christianity, in which the reading of the

74 David Lochhead, 'The Liberation of the Bible', in Norman K. Gottwald (ed.), *The Bible and Liberation: Political and Social Hermeneutics* (Maryknoll, NY: Orbis Books, 1983), p. 133.

scriptures is significantly different from liberation readings. One academic describes this as liberation theology offering the 'option for the poor' but the 'option of the poor' has been for the Pentecostal faith or for the traditional Catholic Church. Minjung theology in contemporary Korea is also facing a similar dilemma. It is significant to listen to the alternative reading to the liberation theological readings as it expresses itself in Robert Warrior's article on the Native American (or First World Nations) reading of the Exodus story. From the perspective of Native American Indians, the God of the Exodus was the one who sided with the conqueror, and their land was given to the conquerors as the 'promised land'. Warrior warns of the dangers of selective readings of the biblical narratives without consideration of the history behind them.[75] While these theologians criticize the western hegemony of biblical interpretation as part of the imperial legacy, they may also be in danger of imposing their own ideological perspectives onto the Christian theological reflections in these regions. As a result, they may become either irrelevant to the very contexts in which they proudly claim to be rooted, or give a limited option to the readers in these regions by providing the ready-made 'meaning' of the text and not the 'tools' for them. As Lochhead rightly points out, 'a liberating reading of the Bible must be accompanied by a healthy exercise of suspicion'. These new readings need not be regarded as substitute readings for traditional hermeneutics but rather as 'alternative' readings so that our understanding can be enriched.

As theology is engaged in the public sphere, the question should be asked whether the Bible is able to provide resources for dealing with contemporary complex situations. Public theology starts with an affirmative answer to that question, but the challenge to public theologians, church leaders and congregations is constantly to discover and reinterpret the meaning of texts and apply them in different situations and to different issues.

---

75 Robert Warrior, 'A Native American Perspective: Canaanites, Cowboys, and Indians', in Sugirtharajah (ed.), *Voices from the Margin*, pp. 277–85.

3

Doing Public Theology:
The Example of Eco-Theology

The earth is the Lord's, for it is the Lord's self-manifestation. It is something God is saying and doing, an ongoing revelation, and unfolding word of God in which something of God's thought and heart are disclosed and much of God's attitude to us is conveyed: the way God holds us dear and precious, the way God relates to us in life-bearing gifts.[1]

The reality of climate change, and the challenges it presents to sustainable living, are perhaps the key issues facing humanity at present. The developing ecological crisis raises profound questions for theology, religious traditions, politics and economics. Governments, various NGOs and religious communities have been engaging with the issue and are actively involved in shaping responses in both theoretical and practical ways. In particular, the Christian churches have made conscious attempts to deal with the problem in recent years in three ways: by Christian leaders making the Church aware of its responsibility in the issue; by Christian groups and organizations providing practical tools for action; and by theologians reshaping our understanding of theology in relation to the ecological crisis.

In this chapter we will discuss the ways in which the churches have brought a variety of theological resources to bear on environmental issues. In particular, four different approaches to formulating eco-theology in the 1990s will serve as an illustration of the way in which public theology does not have a uniform theological method and is not done by only one section of the Church but is open to the participation of the whole Church from different confessions and geographical regions.

---

1 Samuel Rayan, 'The Earth is the Lord's', in David Hallman (ed.), *Ecotheology: Voices from South and North* (Geneva: World Council of Churches, 1994), pp. 130–54 at 132.

Churches' attempts to address the ecological crisis

In the first collective effort of Christian churches to address climate issues, the World Council of Churches initiated the programme 'Justice, Peace and the Integrity of Creation' (now 'Justice, Diakonia and Responsibility for Creation'). In particular, the Conference on World Mission and Evangelism (CWME) at San Antonio, meeting in 1989, reaffirmed the stewardship of human beings over God's creation and the importance of seeking justice in the sharing of land. Human beings have a ministry to be 'guardians of nature', as the San Antonio report affirms: 'Because the earth is the Lord's, the responsibility of the church towards the earth is a crucial part of the church's ministry.' The emphasis was on the mandate to human beings to 'till [the earth] and keep it' (Gen. 2.15) rather than 'to subdue it and have dominion over' it (Gen. 1.28). 'Justice, peace and the integrity of creation' has been a dominant theme for the ecumenical tradition for a number of years and has made a significant impact on the life of the churches. To bring justice, human beings need to recover the role in creation given to them by God. This means reaffirming God's creative activity in and through us human beings. This is characterized as 'stewardship' and needs to be reinforced in the theology and ministry of the Church.[2] In the lead-up to the United Nations Conference on Climate Change in Copenhagen (7–18 December 2009), the WCC mobilized the 'Countdown to Copenhagen'. It collected more than half a million signatures and conducted a bell-ringing and prayer campaign on 13 December. In a letter to the president of the conference, it stated that 'it will be a subject of justice and wisdom towards our planet and the entire good creation of God, to see the same promptness from the global community in responding to the climate change crisis, as the way in which it dealt with the financial and economic crisis', and concluded, 'Do not be afraid! Act now!'[3]

From the Roman Catholic Church, the Vatican's Council for Justice and Peace hosted the Pontifical Council on Climate Change and Development in April 2007, inviting prominent scientists, environment ministers and leaders of various religions from 20 different countries. The main issue discussed at the conference was the balance between

---

2 For a detailed report, see Frederick R. Wilson (ed.), *The San Antonio Report* (Geneva: World Council of Churches, 1990), pp. 52–68. See also 'The Church of England's Seven-Year Plan on Climate Change and Environment', at http://www.shrinkingthefootprint. cofe.anglican.org/misc_lib/14.pdf (accessed 15 Oct. 2010).

3 'A sign of hope for the future for people of good will', at http://www.oikoumene.org/ gr/resources/documents/wcc-programmes/justice-diakonia-and-responsibility-for-creation/ climate-change-water/statement-to-cop15-un-climate-conference-copenhagen.html (accessed 15 Oct. 2010).

environmental concern for nature and the developmental needs of people. The participants called for the Vatican to focus on the ethical and moral challenges posed by climate change.[4] In the recent Pontifical Encyclical of Pope Benedict XVI, *Caritas in Veritate* (Charity in Truth; 29 June 2009), the Catholic leadership has expressed its view on the issue of the environment. The encyclical emphasizes that the environment is God's gift to everyone, but that the Church has a particular responsibility to use it for the care of the poor. It also states that nature reflects the Creator and his love for humanity, but cautions against either seeing nature as something more important than human beings or treating it as the object of exploitation. It calls for *'renewed solidarity'* to share natural resources between the rich and the poor and *'responsible stewardship over nature'*. The Church in particular, it says, has this responsibility in the public sphere. The encyclical emphasizes the importance of human ecology, in which our attitudes towards other human beings and nature are interconnected, and that the *'decisive issue is the overall moral tenor of society'*.[5]

Meanwhile, among evangelicals, a significant step towards dealing with climate change was the statement made by some 280 American evangelical leaders in January 2006, entitled 'Climate Change: An Evangelical Call to Action'. The signatories recognized the impact of climate change on the poor and vulnerable, and on future generations, and made four claims: the reality of human-induced climate change; the devastating consequence of climate change on the poor; the responsibility of Christians on the basis of moral convictions; and the urgency of immediate action. On the basis of this, they called for Christians to 'make personal changes and rally action', and for policy-makers 'to make wise and moral choices' to protect God's world and its people.[6]

Second, it is also very encouraging to see various Christian NGOs specifically addressing the issue of climate change. A Rocha (a Portuguese word meaning 'a rock') is among the most active international Christian groups working for the environment. It is based on commitments that include: faith in God who entrusts the world to the care of human society; research and education for conservation and restoration of the natural world; and working with local communities and in partnership with wider communities and individuals. A Rocha

---

4 'Pontifical Council on Climate Change and Development', at http://www.religiouscon sultation.org/News_Tracker/pontifical_council_on_climate_change.htm (accessed 15 Oct. 2010).

5 *Caritas in Veritate*, at http://www.vatican.va/holy_father/benedict_xvi/encyclicals/ documents/hf_ben-xvi_enc_20090629_caritas-in-veritate_en.html (accessed 15 Oct. 2010).

6 'The Evangelical Climate Initiative', at http://christiansandclimate.org/ (accessed 15 Oct. 2010).

provides resources such as ideas for sermons, service outlines, material for children and young people, and group studies. Similarly, Operation Noah, Christian Ecology Link, Christian Aid, CAFOD, Tearfund, the European Christian Environment Network, and the Environment and Climate Change theme within the Churches Together in Britain and Ireland provide internet resources, printed materials, news updates and networking among those who are concerned. They also conduct regular conferences and workshops to encourage local congregations to get involved in promoting the cause. There is an increasing number of special projects within different church denominations and other faith organizations such as the Islamic Foundation for Ecology and Environmental Sciences, Ecological Buddhism and The Big Green Jewish Website.[7] The strength of these movements is their practical suggestions for local religious communities and individuals to do whatever they can in their own situation, and these local initiatives are increasingly gaining support from the general public as well.

Third, with the growing concern for ecological issues, there have been theological discussions on these issues, which provide resources and insights contributing to the development of what is commonly called 'eco-theology', led by such as Michael Northcott, Celia Deane-Drummond and David Hallman. Eco-theology is concerned with 'the environment and humanity's relationship with the natural world' and seeks to 'uncover the theological basis for a proper relationship between God, humanity and the cosmos'.[8] Michael Northcott insists that the environmental crisis requires a 'radical change to the predominant direction of human behaviour' rather than new technology and regulations. Although the latter are important, he is convinced that the issue is an ethical one, which demands 'recovery of a spiritual, moral and cosmological awareness of our place in the natural order', and ethical teaching from religious traditions could contribute in a significant way to dealing with the problem. He sees a purely material and scientific reading of the environment as missing the point that redemption requires moral and spiritual conversion as well.[9] Northcott emphasizes that the Hebrew Bible and the Christian doctrine of natural law offer significant insights into God's created order, an account of the interaction between human beings and the ecological order, and relations between these and God. A renewed examination of the Sabbath of the land and the shalom

7 See 'Environment and Climate Change Link', at http://www.ctbi.org.uk/BAA/67/#christian (accessed 15 Oct. 2010).

8 Celia E. Deane-Drummond, *Eco-Theology* (London: Darton, Longman & Todd, 2008), pp. x and xii.

9 Michael Northcott, *A Moral Climate: The Ethics of Global Warming* (London: Darton, Longman & Todd, 2007), pp. 13–16.

of the earth will show us our duty to preserve God's created order since we are part and parcel of the whole system rather than above it.[10] In her comprehensive study on eco-theology, Deane-Drummond discusses various theological attempts to relate ecology and theology and argues that ecology is the 'universal vocation' for Christians and should be at the heart of Christian faith and practice. She insists on the importance of the biblical wisdom traditions of the Sabbath, which she regards as the ethos for eco-theology: 'living from the Sabbath is a reminder to the human community to live according to covenant responsibility', and it also helps us to approach nature with respect and humility.[11]

There have been an increasing number of publications on the Church's response to the ecological crisis, and ecology has now become an important item on the agenda of theology. Eco-theology has challenged traditional theologies and given the Church and its ministry not only new and fresh insights but has also led to a re-examination of scripture and the understanding of human beings and nature. Eco-theology has emerged as theologians have wrestled with several challenges. These include, first, the criticism of traditional theologies, which are accused of being anthropocentric (human-centred) and androcentric (man- – not woman- – centred). As such they are accused of complicity in colonialism, environmental destruction and the oppression of women. This is seen as largely due to the understanding of the creation narrative (especially Gen. 1.28) as affirming human – particularly male – domination over other beings. Second is the failure of traditional theologies to respond to the problems of the ecosystem and their silence in the face of development and technology models that have been the main contributing factors to the present crisis. Third is the encounter with the people and philosophies of other religious traditions. Christian theologians have found deep insight among people of other faiths concerning the relationship between humankind and nature. This has brought to the fore the question of how and to what extent Christian theology can learn from these more integrated systems of some other religions and indigenous spiritualities.

From the writings of various theologians in the 1990s, four strands of eco-theology may be traced: social ecology, creation theology, eco-feminism and eco-spirituality. These are not distinct schools of thought because one author may exhibit two or three of them together, but

---

10 Michael Northcott, *Christianity and Environmental Ethics* (Cambridge: Cambridge University Press, 1996), pp. 164–98.

11 Deane-Drummond, *Eco-Theology*, pp. 95–6, 179, 181–2. See also Celia Deane-Drummond, *The Ethics of Nature* (Oxford: Blackwell, 2004); David Hallman (ed.), *Ecotheology: Voices from South and North* (Geneva: World Council of Churches, 1994).

each represents a thread or theme that may be distinguished from the others, while nevertheless forming part of the whole. The purpose of this chapter is to identify the essence of the public theologies of each of these four strands and to appraise these in the light of their contribution to contemporary debate.

Social ecology: public theology as a socio-political struggle for justice in the whole creation

'Our ecological crisis should be seen as a justice issue', writes K. C. Abraham,[12] who is one of the main advocates of ecological concerns in theology from the Two-Thirds World. Social ecology follows a liberation theology model for its methodology, seeking to see nature liberated from bondage. Social ecology tries to offer 'paradigms for the search to recognize society from a human and ecological perspectives'[13] by connecting social, ecological and theological elements together. The ecosystem is seen as intimately related to the social system but the problem of injustice is situated in the human systems. Therefore social ecology seeks social change to achieve justice towards the creation. 'A radical change in the socio-political structure' is to be brought about by the collective power of the people.[14] This 'liberative solidarity' is preferred to an 'ascetic or monastic' approach.[15]

Social ecology is based on a very positive view of creation as essentially good and innocent. But nature remains material, nature is not sacralized nor is God desacralized. God–humankind–nature forms a harmony yet each is distinct. Social ecology therefore rejects two extremes: 'Naturalism – nature as hypostatic subject, with sacred and unchangeable laws to which human beings must submit ... [and] anthropocentrism – human beings as the sovereigns of creation'.[16] Instead it stresses God's sovereignty over creation and human responsibility or stewardship to maintain it in a proper manner. The challenge of the ecological crisis must be met by human effort. This means bringing 'justice' to nature as we ought to do in society for the oppressed and the poor. Nature remains an object and mission is done on nature's behalf.

---

12 K. C. Abraham, 'A Theological Response to the Ecological Crisis', in Hallman (ed.), *Ecotheology*, p. 67.

13 Tony Brun, 'Social Ecology: A Timely Paradigm for Reflection and Praxis for Life in Latin America', in Hallman (ed.), *Ecotheology*, p. 82.

14 Lucius Nereparampil, 'An Eco-Theology Foreshadowed in the Gospel of John', *Bible Bhasyam* XIX/3 (1993), p. 191.

15 Abraham, 'A Theological Response', pp. 71–3.

16 Leonardo Boff, 'Social Theology: Poverty and Misery', in Hallman (ed.), *Ecotheology*, p. 243.

The integrity of creation should be affirmed since it belongs to God who created it and cares for it, therefore we are called to participate in 'God's love and concern for the entire cosmos and human's co-creative stewardship for promoting the unity and integrity of the whole cosmos for a human life in harmony with Nature'.[17] Stewardship is a traditional Christian doctrine but in social ecology it goes beyond simply using earth's resources wisely towards affirming 'the intrinsic value, goodness and worth of creation'.[18] Also mission is not limited to spiritual salvation only but has to do with the well-being of whole human environment, that is, society and the natural world. Therefore mission is holistic, that is, it emphasizes both the spiritual dimension and also the social and environmental. These insights should be welcomed and implemented in Christian theology. They also lay a common ground for Christians to work together with those of other faiths as we face ecological crisis.

However, in social ecology, there is a naive assumption that wrongs can be righted in this world simply by human beings pulling together. An overemphasis on human activism without an eschatological dimension can easily degenerate into idealism and ideology. The method of analysis is the method of liberation theology, therefore the problems of the environment are seen as structural problems of society caused by industrialization and technical development. All living creatures are thus victims of environmental injustice. In line with other liberation theologies, those who are oppressed and poor are 'empowered' as evil structures are overthrown. But how can nature be 'empowered' and to what extent can we treat nature as oppressed? Does nature have a 'right' over human need? Who decides that 'right'?

Social ecology encourages human beings to act on behalf of nature, but if human society has been 'corrupted' and become 'self-centred', how far can human beings help nature? What happens when 'justice' for the poor and 'justice' for nature conflict? For example, when a development project for the poor clashes with a project that may help the natural environment, what will be the choice? And who decides what is the better option? The very concept of humanization is in a dilemma. What is the responsibility of the individual human being for the ecological crisis? Is it only a problem of structure? Or has it also to do with personal sin? Will changing the structures alone solve the problem? In order to overcome the ecological crisis, and to do 'justice' to both human beings and the natural world, its nature and methodology need strengthening.

17 George Therukattil, 'Towards a Biblical Eco-Theology', *Jeevadhara*, XXI/126 (Nov. 1991), p. 467.

18 Therukattil, 'Towards a Biblical Eco-Theology', p. 474.

Creation theology: public theology as living with the earth to restore the interconnectedness of the whole creation

Creation theology starts with the phrase, 'God created the heavens and the earth ... it was very good.' Creation theologians view the original creation as the perfect model for God's relationship with humanity and the natural world. God–humankind–nature are seen as interconnected. And furthermore, creation theologians claim that the present ecological crisis is 'a logical Christian product'.[19] Creation theology sees that in the creation narrative the most important concept is the relationship of God–humankind–nature. This is not a hierarchical order, as traditional theology understands it, but an expression of the interconnectedness and integration of one with another. The theology of creation *ex nihilo* is rejected since it is the relationship that determines the existence of creation and even God cannot be acknowledged if there is no relationship. Therefore the very existence of God is also relational, not absolute. In creation, nothing is absolute but all is relative and interrelated – and God is no exception. 'The theological implications of such an organismic relationship between God and Creation is [*sic*] that we can no longer conceive of God apart from His/Her creation.'[20]

Creation theology adopts a 'creation-centred spirituality'[21] in opposition to traditional theology, and challenges Christians 'to take a cosmotheandric stand and move away from the traditional anthropocentrism'.[22] It issues a call to redefine the place and role of human beings in the context of creation not as rulers over nature but as a part of it, dependent on it, or even emanating from it. 'He [the human being] is not above but within and in creation.'[23] The relationship between humanity and nature is not seen as subject and object but rather as a responsibility to protect, serve and care for the creation – 'an ethical relationship'.[24] This will lead to a cosmic perspective on theology, 'ecology, economy and ecumenicity'.[25]

---

19 K. M. Matthew, 'In Search of a Theology of the Environment: The Message of the Earth Summit II', *Vidyajyoti* LVII/4 (Apr. 1993), p. 219.

20 Arvind P. Nirmal, 'Ecology, Ecumenics and Economics in Relation: A New Theological Paradigm', in Daniel D. Chetti (ed.), *Ecology and Development: Theological Perspectives* (Madras: Gurukul, 1991), p. 22.

21 K. M. Matthew, 'In Search of a Theology', p. 221.

22 Therukattil, 'Towards a Biblical Eco-Theology', p. 480.

23 Boff, 'Ecology and Theology', p. 113.

24 Boff, 'Ecology and Theology', p. 113.

25 Nirmal, 'Ecology, Ecumenics and Economics', p. 21.

A creation theological reading of scripture reveals that 'God's revelation to humans comes through nature'.[26] This means that our understanding of God and our relationship with him is through nature since nature provides this cosmic platform for human beings to conceptualize and formulate their ideas. Theology is no longer between God and human beings but nature in a mysterious way takes part in shaping it and transforming it. 'It is not just that nature seems to worship God; nature proclaims to man the beauty and the glory and wonder of God and invites man to worship him.'[27] For human beings, therefore, it is imperative to have interaction with nature in order to understand God's revelation in a deeper way. 'The Divine mystery is to be experienced in our deep communion with nature.'[28]

Creation theology has a theology of 'all in God' and 'God in all' — or panentheism.[29] This is also similar to 'naturalism', which sacralizes nature and has the concept of 'cosmic union of all beings'.[30] Since all life is interconnected and interdependent, the cosmos is conceptualized as an organism or body:

> ... trees and toads, water and rocks ... women and men. Each mirrors the Divine; each is unique in its expression and contribution to the whole. This is a creation-centred spirituality that elicits our wonder and awe, encourages new humility within the total earth community, and an urgent religious commitment to its preservation and enhancement.[31]

This broadens the concept of salvation. Salvation is no longer just for human beings but also for all creatures, as implied in Romans 8.19–22 and Colossians 1.20. And this salvation is not one way – humankind first then nature – but interconnected. Veeraraj explains the new paradigm of salvation in creation theology: 'Humans are not saved unless nature is saved in us ... Together with nature humans seek salvation in God. And in turn God seeks her realization in the redemption of both nature and humans.'[32] Furthermore, the concept of conversion is also no longer personal but collective:

---

26 Anand Veeraraj, 'Eco-Spirituality and the Religious Community', *NCCI Review*, CX/9 (Oct. 1990), p. 543.

27 R. H. Lesser, 'Ecology and Spirituality', *In Christo* 29/1 (Jan. 1991), p. 30.

28 Therukattil, 'Towards a Biblical Eco-Theology', p. 479.

29 Boff, 'Ecology and Theology', p. 117f.

30 Therukattil, 'Towards a Biblical Eco-Theology', p. 482.

31 Jane Blewett, 'The Greening of Catholic Social Thought?', *Pro Mundo Vita Studies* 13 (Feb. 1990), p. 29.

32 Veeraraj, 'Eco-Spirituality', p. 545.

Conversion would mean that we rediscover the finitude of nature as a balance of elements, which together harmonize to support life for all parts of the community of creation, so that no part can long flourish if the other parts are being injured or destroyed.[33]

Life in humans and in nature is God's gift in creation, therefore human beings cannot claim ownership of other elements of creation.[34] This means we move towards 'life-centrism', which will enable us to 'live with the earth, promoting harmony, sustainability and diversity'.[35] The emphasis in ministry is not on activism but on being who we were created to be and living in harmony with nature. Creation theology recognizes the culpability of Christians in ecological problems. It does not hesitate to point out that the plunder of the resources of the rest of the world and the dispossession of its peoples by first Catholic and then Protestant countries since the fifteenth century is the root of the present crisis. The richer countries of the world who continue to export ecological disasters to the poorer are still overwhelmingly Christian. Most writers consider this is due to a misinterpretation of the Christian gospel rather than a problem inherent in Christianity itself.[36]

Public theology emerging from the school of creation theology can be summarized as *living with the earth to restore the interconnectedness of the whole creation*. Creation is both the motive and goal of mission, its subject rather than its object. Human beings, who are integrated into creation and part of it, can be 'converted' and saved together with the whole creation. Public engagement of theology is not stewardship but rather participating in an organic relationship between God and nature.

Creation theology has made creation the starting point of theology whereas traditional theology (Protestant theology) tends to emphasize the incarnation or the cross. Consequently in our public theology, the spiritual and sociological needs of human beings have been the dominant concern. Creation-centred theology offers the Church fresh insight as to our starting point in mission and helps us to understand and explain the nature of God's missionary activity. The concept of *missio*

---

33 David C. Scott, 'Some Reflections on "A Theological Response to Ecological Crisis"', *Bangalore Theological Forum* XXV/1 (Mar. 1993), pp. 21–2.

34 Stan McKay, 'An Aboriginal Perspective on the Integrity of Creation', in Hallman (ed.), *Ecotheology*, p. 214.

35 Chung Hyun Kyung, 'Come, Holy Spirit – Renew the Whole Creation', in Michael Kinnamon, *Signs of the Spirit: The Official Report of the Seventh Assembly* (Geneva: World Council of Churches, 1991), p. 39.

36 See, for example, K. M. Matthew, who describes today's environmental disaster as 'a logical Christian product' but then dissociates this kind of 'Christian' from the Sermon on the Mount – Matthew, 'In Search of a Theology', pp. 218f.

Dei must begin with creation as the starting point of God's mission to the world. God's creative activity continues as God's mission continues. This also provides a theological platform for bringing a message from the scriptures to people who are not familiar with the Christian message (see Acts 17.23–31).

However, in creation theology, the distinction between Creator and creation is not clearly defined as it is in scripture, where it is clear that God is one who created humankind and nature, and creatures themselves do not have the creative power of life. Because God created the world, God owns it and also saves and maintains it. God is the object of our worship not nature itself. The God of the Bible does not need another vessel to contain him or an ideology by which to conceive of him. If God is part of creation then transcendent Christian hope is lost. Yahweh is a personal God and a self-existent personal being. God alone is the source of life, not one who draws life out from other sources, as creation theology seems to suggest. The relationship between God and creation should be one of dependency not one of interdependency. This means:

> To speak of the 'integrity of creation' is to reaffirm that everything which exists has God for the Author – signalling not only the dependence of all of creation on the Creator but also its inherent worth and dignity ... And 'integrity of creation' speaks of creation's 'wholeness' – an inclusive perspective.[37]

In other words, God's attributes flow in and through his creatures by his constant creative power. Mission starts from God himself in creation. God is the one who is responsible and who sends.

Although human beings are part of the organic system of the whole creation and follow the natural laws of every living being, human beings are created in the image and likeness of God in a unique way in which other beings are not. And therefore God has endowed human beings with responsibility and privileges towards creation. The issue is not whether nature is equal with human beings, but a right understanding of stewardship. (Putting human beings and nature in an equal position does not make human beings treat nature any better, as we have seen how human beings treat other human beings in our economically and socio-politically unjust world.) Creation-centred theology should be God (Creator)-centred theology otherwise it will become nature worship. If it is avoided then creation theology provides

---

37 Marlin Van Elderen, 'Integrity of Creation', *NCCI Review* CVIII/8 (Sept. 1988), p. 489.

a firm biblical basis for extending the scope of mission to encompass the whole created order. It also means Christian ministry should partake of God's creative nature and work with not against the interests of the natural environment.

Eco-feminism: public theology as overcoming dualisms to unite the whole cosmos

In recent years feminism has given new hermeneutical insight into male-dominated theology through rereading the scriptures from women's perspectives. It may also be said to have challenged the entire theological methodology through the call to embrace the feminine nature of God. Thus it enriches our experience of God by demanding perception and acceptance of the fundamental truth of the gospel: 'there is neither male nor female'. Eco-feminist theologians believe that they can offer a great deal to the search of eco-theology since feminism has much common ground with ecology:

> They share many basic premises – such as their world view, analysis, method, life-style and vision of the future. Both movements oppose 'power over' ... encourage 'power from within' and 'power with' ... They are searching for a spirituality which promotes the immanence of God, the sacredness of this world and wholeness of body, sensuality and sexuality.[38]

They note that, practically, women are the first victims of ecological crisis since their work depends directly on the availability of natural resources.[39] In many cultures women are associated with the earth and men are associated with the sky or heaven. Such dualism is used to subordinate the one to the other.

Eco-feminism thus identifies women with nature as victims of the dominating structure: for women this is experienced as sexism, discrimination, inequality, sexual harassment and so on; for nature this is experienced as exploitation, pollution, destruction of forests and such like. This similarity in patterns of exploitation and domination causes eco-feminists to see the 'the rape of women' as derived from the

---

38 Chung Hyun Kyung, 'Ecology, Feminism and African and Asian Spirituality: Towards a Spirituality of Eco-Feminism', in Hallman (ed.), *Ecotheology*, p. 179.

39 Aruna Gnanadason, 'Women, Economy and Ecology', in Hallman (ed.), *Ecotheology*, pp. 180f.

same root as the 'rape of earth' and vice versa[40] – that is, masculine or 'phallic' aggression. Eco-feminism further draws parallels between the oppression of women, colonialism or the oppression and exploitation of other peoples, and the exploitation of nature – tending to see all of these as the results of male-dominated western theology.[41]

Another obvious link between feminism and eco-theology is the feminist conception of God as Mother[42] and the ecological description of the earth as mother. The concept of Mother Earth originates with the primal religions and fertility cults – against which there is some polemic in the Old Testament. But the mother image of the earth is a challenge to see the earth not as something to possess or exploit for human ends but as something to respect and treat in a proper manner. It regards earth as subject not object. 'Mother Earth' reveals the motherness of the earth and at the same time the earthness of the mother.

The eco-feminist response to the ecological crisis is to affirm the feminine dimensions of both God and nature and to bring them together. This involves the rejection of all dualisms such as God versus creation, soul versus body, spirit versus matter, heaven versus earth, man versus woman.[43] The theological and philosophical models of West (and often East) in which man is associated with the higher principle and woman with the lower are seen as constructed by men and as the cause of both the oppression of nature and of women. In their place eco-feminists substitute a new pattern of relationship for all 'in the cosmos based on mutuality, interdependence and life-giving values'.[44] They affirm the interconnectedness and sacredness of all life:

> The eco-feminist vision emphasizes the life that is in everything, the value of all God's bounty ... affirms the sacredness of all God's gifts in creation ... It rejects anthropocentric worldviews, ... emphasizes the connectedness between women and nature, as between humanity and nature.[45]

---

40 Aruna Gnanadason, 'Towards a Feminist Eco-Theology for India', in Chetti (ed.), *Ecology and Development*, p. 33.

41 Mary Daly, *Beyond the Father: Toward a Philosophy of Women's Liberation* (London: The Women's Press, 1986), pp. 114–22.

42 This is a concept found in Scripture and Christian tradition; see Joseph Sebastian, *God As Feminine: Hindu and Christian Visions in Dialogue* (Tiruchirapalli: St Paul's Seminary, 1995), pp. 167–233, for a comprehensive treatment of this topic.

43 Rosemary Radford Ruether, 'Spirit and Matter, Public and Private: The Challenge of Feminism to Traditional Dualisms', in Paula M. Cooey, Sharon A. Farmer and Mary Ellen Ross (eds), *Embodied Love: Sensuality and Relationship as Feminist Values* (San Francisco: Harper & Row, 1987), pp. 65–76.

44 Chung, 'Ecology, Feminism and African and Asian Spirituality', p. 175.

45 Gnanadason, 'Women, Economy and Ecology', p. 184.

The contemplation of motherhood means that eco-feminism also sees the cosmic dimension of life not as linear and static but cyclical and dynamic. Life itself can create and recreate other life and this is a call to go deeper in understanding of life, to move towards a 'culture of life' in which women, together with nature, can participate. This replaces the 'culture of death' which men with their technology and machinery are accused of creating.[46] Thus eco-feminists promote a shift from a 'mega-machine' world-view to a 'Mother Earth' world-view[47] – from modernity to postmodernity. For eco-feminists God is not in isolation from the circle of life but very much part of it and very much integrated into it. Therefore the relationship of God and human beings with nature is not one of domination and rule or sovereignty but one of co-operation and mutual relationship and mutual support: 'We must transform relationships of domination and exploitation into relationships of mutual support. This transformation will not occur without a parallel change in our image of God, our image of the relationship between God and creation in all its dimensions.'[48] Eco-feminism thus tends towards a monism in which God–humankind–nature are in essence the same because any separation would lead to dualism.

Eco-feminist theologians draw their methodology from the feminist model of human society and apply it to the issue of ecology. They see the issue of ecology as the issue of women since the forces against women and nature are the same – male-dominated hierarchical social structure with anthropocentric ideology and technology. In the face of this they promote 'an alternative vision and hope' which is 'respect for life in nature and society'.[49] For this they find their inspiration in some of the traditional religions or spirituality from primal religions. They largely reject traditional Christian sources because of their perception that the Bible has a strong bias towards men, and they find it therefore limited in terms of models and methodology. The concept of feminine dynamic energy, *Shakti*, is one of the examples of this:

---

46 Chung, 'Come, Holy Spirit', pp. 43–6. In her controversial plenary paper at the Canberra Assembly of the World Council of Churches in 1991, she advocated three dimensions of change: from anthropocentrism to life-centrism; from dualism to interconnection; from the culture of death to the culture of life.

47 Rosemary Radford Ruether, 'Motherearth and the Megamachine: A Theology of Liberation in a Feminine, Somatic and Ecological Perspective', in Carol P. Christ and Judith Plaskow (eds), *Womanspirit Rising: A Feminist Reader in Religion* (San Francisco: HarperSanFrancisco, 1992), pp. 43–52.

48 Rosemary Radford Ruether, 'Eco-Feminism and Theology', in Hallman (ed.), *Eco-theology*, p. 204.

49 Gnanadason, 'Towards a Feminist Eco-Theology for India', p. 37.

God's creative power has been experienced by the people of India from ancient times as *Shakti* ... The powerless need to be empowered and we see the divine manifestation of empowerment through the expression of *Shakti* in the movement of dalit women and tribals.[50]

Dalits are the communities formerly known as outcastes in India and 'tribals' are the indigenous peoples of the land. Another model from Korea is *han*, which is an integrated term for explaining people's grief and resentment. *Han-pu-ri*, the activity of getting rid of *han*, which is mainly conducted by female shamans, then may mean becoming an instrument for helping people who are oppressed and exploited yet have nowhere to escape and express their anguish.[51] The attempt is made to identify women's grief with the grief of the earth and the grief of Jesus.

All these attempts are part of the feminist search for the new paradigm of 'eco-centred feminist spirituality'[52] to bring 'feminist theology into dialogue with a culturally-based critique of the ecological crisis'.[53] The public theology advocated by eco-feminism is a cosmic endeavour which brings God–women–men–nature together. Theology shifts from dualism to oneness. The material is affirmed. Concern for material things is no longer secondary to 'spiritual' work. Traditional aggressive missionary methods stemming from a sense of superiority are rejected. Mission is mutual and interpenetrating. Mission is reorientated from anthropocentrism to interconnectedness. The interdependence of all life is respected. Public theology means becoming part of the birthing process of new creation, being in travail with Mother Earth. It can be characterized as *overcoming dualisms to unite the whole cosmos*.

The public theology emerging from eco-feminism challenges us to see the whole creation as an integrated system rather than as dualistic. It is true that dichotomizing has done a great deal of damage in theology. Traditional mission has dualistic thinking behind it: evangelized–unevangelized; reached–unreached; christianized–heathen; civilized–uncivilized; developed–underdeveloped; rich–poor; etc. Therefore, missions have had a one-way approach (from ... to ...). Eco-feminism offers a new methodology – the possibility of mission being two-way, a mutual process of learning, where each side has something

---

50 See Joseph Mattam and Sebastian C. H. Kim, *Trends in Mission: Historical and Theological Perspectives* (Bombay: St Paul's, 1997).

51 For the concept of *han* and *han-pu-ri*, see Chung Hyun Kyung, '"Han-pu-ri": Doing Theology from Korean Women's Perspective', in R. S. Sugirtharajah (ed.), *Frontiers in Asian Christian Theology: Emerging Trends* (Maryknoll, NY: Orbis Books, 1994), pp. 52–62.

52 Gnanadason, 'Towards a Feminist Eco-Theology for India', p. 30.

53 Ruether, 'Eco-Feminism and Theology', p. 199.

to give. No longer are people described as the 'objects' or 'targets' of mission and defined in negative terms. But their full humanness and their way of life is respected.

But on the other hand, eco-feminism has broadened the scope of mission to the extent that God has no place in this process of uniting the whole cosmos. The transcendence of God, implied in the masculine language of Father, King and so on, is seen as an obstacle to overcoming dualism. Rather than seeing the hindrance to unification as on the human side – sin – there is a tendency to locate it on God's side. So for eco-feminists, God's holiness and absoluteness must be rejected as the Creator is merged with the creation, and heaven is brought down to earth. If the transcendence of God is lost, faith becomes materialistic and hope-less. The problem of the traditional dualisms is not in dualities themselves but in the philosophies constructed on them. The distinction of male and female needs to be affirmed as does the distinction of Creator and creation. But any parallel between the two must be very carefully drawn in view of the fact that male and female are both part of the creation.

The methods advocated by eco-feminists are generally conscientization together with social and political action. Salvation becomes self-awareness, an understanding closer to eastern mysticism than to Christian notions of redemption. The call to repentance is lacking, instead those who respond are seen as 'sinned against' rather than 'sinning'. Thus there is a certain naivity about both women and nature. They are idealized as if innocent and perfect, and evil tends to be located only in men. The eco-feminist gospel therefore has a certain exclusivity; men's role in theology is unclear. Feminists have not yet overcome that most fundamental dualism – male and female.

Eco-spirituality: public theology as being part of the work of the Spirit in creation

As the Church encounters the different religious traditions and their spirituality, Christian theology has to respond to the challenge of the eco-spirituality, which is deeply rooted, particularly in the primal religions. These can no longer be treated as merely superstitious or 'primitive' but are increasingly recognized as yielding deep eco-theological insights that Christian theology has failed to recognize until recently. The issues are twofold: first, accepting and learning spirituality from other faiths, especially from primal religions; second, redefining the nature and work of the Holy Spirit in and outside the Church. Eco-spirituality starts with the interconnectedness of humankind and nature. But it goes beyond to personify and sacralize nature. Human beings are to have 'a bio-centric world-view ... holistic and all-inclusive with nature'.[54] Humans and nature should work together towards 'cosmic order', which comes from the search for 'wholeness' and 'integrated' life.[55] It also challenges human beings to be in partnership with nature and 'facilitates communication that transcends species boundaries. This requires an enlarged understanding of the bio-spheric culture and community.'[56]

This approach opens up the spirituality of other religions and philosophies: 'We need to be more sensitive to ... the rich spiritual, philosophical heritage of our Asian religious traditions which are profoundly sensitive to the mystery of life in its unbroken totality and integrity.'[57] But in particular, it reaches to the grassroots, to 'popular religiosity', promoting a cosmic rather than a meta-cosmic religion, a folk religion rather than religion in its institutional form. Eco-spirituality affirms that the spirituality of indigenous people is the 'integrated web of life' and it 'exudes life-giving value'.[58] These insights from the indigenous people help us to see the 'essential interconnectedness of the divine, humanity, and the world of nature'.[59] Eco-spirituality has a strong pneumatological component. Proponents of eco-spirituality enlarge the scope of the work of the Holy Spirit to include not only human beings but also whole creation. What is more, the work of the Spirit in the natural world is also a work of redemption. As Veeraraj puts it, 'eco-spirituality enables the redemption of every entity in nature, every human being, and the divine as well'.[60]

But the new pneumatology is most radical in the theology of Chung Hyun Kyung, who called forth varied responses when she addressed a plenary session of the Canberra Assembly of the World Council of Churches in 1991. As she invoked the Holy Spirit, Chung also called the spirits of people in the past and even the spirits of nature: 'Come. The spirit of the Amazon rain forest now being murdered every day. Come. The spirit of earth, air and water, raped, tortured and exploited by human greed for money ...'[61] For Chung, the work of the Holy Spirit is carried out through the spirits: '[The spirits] are the icons of the Holy Spirit who became tangible and visible to us. Because of them we can

---

54 Veeraraj, 'Eco-Spirituality', p. 542.

55 McKay, 'An Aboriginal Perspective', p. 216.

56 Veeraraj, 'Eco-Spirituality', p. 542.

57 K. M. George, 'Integrity of Creation and the Church's Task', *NCCI Review* CVIII/8 (Sept. 1988), p. 481.

58 Chung, 'Ecology, Feminism and African and Asian Spirituality', p. 177.

59 Veeraraj, 'Eco-Spirituality', p. 541.

60 Veeraraj, 'Eco-Spirituality', p. 545.

61 Chung, 'Come, Holy Spirit', p. 39.

feel, touch and taste the concrete bodily historical presence of the Holy Spirit in our midst.'[62] Therefore the spirits are part of the manifestation of the Holy Spirit and, through the 'divine presence of the spirits in creation',[63] we experience the fullness of life in God. Chung's method is a combination of liberative political action and spiritual exorcism (after the manner of a Korean shamanist) to release the oppressed spirits and set the creation free. She called participants at Canberra to welcome the Spirit and dance with her, 'letting ourselves go in her wild rhythm of life'.[64]

The public theology of eco-spirituality emphasizes the activity of the Spirit. It recognizes the work of the Spirit beyond the boundaries of Christianity and therefore no longer rejects other spiritualities as 'primitive', 'heathen' or 'devilish'. Instead, it affirms them and seeks to learn from them. Mission becomes adopting the values of those societies that live close to nature to cultivate an ecologically sensitive spirituality. Public theology thus becomes *being part of the mission of the Spirit in creation.*

The study of the nature and work of the Holy Spirit is a recent concern that deserves more attention. The Holy Spirit plays a key role in creation (Gen. 1.2). The scope of the Spirit's work is wider than the Church or believing community in scripture. It could be said that the work of Holy Spirit in renewing the whole creation needs to be included in theology and reaffirmed. Since the unbounded activity of the Spirit cannot be limited to Christianity, learning from the spiritualities of other religious traditions should be encouraged. But the pneumatology of Chung Hyun Kyung as expressed at Canberra needs to be challenged. However much we may admire primal spiritualities, Christianity is not a primal religion. The boundaries between the spirits and the Holy Spirit must be defined. The Holy Spirit should be understood in the light of the Trinity. The Spirit is the Spirit of God who created the world and the Spirit of Jesus Christ, therefore the Spirit is the Spirit of salvation and forgiveness. The truth that the Holy Spirit moves unlimitedly throughout the whole creation does not mean necessarily that the Spirit has to use the form of other spirits. In particular, eco-spirituality is ambiguous about the evil spirits that we find so clearly referred to in scripture. The methodology for learning from other spiritualities needs to be explored and studied. Scripture has a great deal to say about spiritual warfare and discerning spirits, which is largely ignored.

---

62 Chung, 'Come, Holy Spirit', p. 39.
63 Canberra 1991, 'Report of Section I', in Kinnamon (ed.), *Signs of the Spirit*, p. 55.
64 Chung, 'Come, Holy Spirit', p. 46.

There is great potential here for the development of a biblical pneumatology of mission. The Spirit in scripture is the Spirit of creation and mission. Therefore there are strong grounds for saying that it is the Spirit that is responsible for the interconnectedness of the ecosystem. John Taylor, in particular, in describing the Spirit as the 'Go-Between God',[65] has opened up a whole new avenue for theological exploration.

Conclusion

Eco-theology is a new and exciting development that needs to be carefully examined biblically and theologically. For the purpose of this chapter, eco-theology has been looked at as a contribution to public theology. In our study of the strands in eco-theology, we have drawn out four distinct but closely related public theologies arising from different theological disciplines. Responding to the ecological challenge is a crucial task of public theology. We have a responsibility to face this overwhelming crisis. Eco-theology is especially important for public theology because it broadens the scope of public theology beyond human society to include the whole created order. As such it reflects the cosmic vision of the Bible, particularly in Genesis 1—3, the Psalms, Colossians, Ephesians and Revelation. As Donald Senior points out, commenting on Colossians and Ephesians, 'No longer can the church's horizons be narrow, its agenda timid. It serves a cosmic Lord: therefore its field of service is as wide as the world.'[66]

As Christians carry out their responsibility towards the creation, the Church must establish sound theological perspectives on the issue. Eco-theology has opened a new way of theologizing to meet the ecological crisis and has contributed a great deal to our understanding of the relationship of God, humankind and nature. The awareness of the interdependence of all life and the immanence of God in his creation is part of this contribution. The abuses of anthropocentric theology have been clearly brought out but the search for an alternative centre goes on. Life-centrism is a very attractive paradigm but we need to be clear that the life that is affirmed is not merely biological life but 'life in all its fullness', the life of the kingdom of God in Christ, the eternal life of the new age of the Spirit. It is important to welcome and learn from the insights offered by these approaches to the environment in

---

65 John V. Taylor, *The Go-Between God: The Holy Spirit and the Christian Mission* (London: SCM Press, 1972).

66 Donald Senior and Carroll Stuhlmueller, *The Biblical Foundations for Mission* (London: SCM Press, 1983), p. 208.

public theology today, but at the same time, we need to critique them positively so that we all grow into a deeper and more comprehensive understanding of the relevance of theology in the public sphere.

PART 2

Public Theology in Global Contexts

Habermas and the Public Sphere   HM24 Hab Reserve

After Habermas   new perspectives —
      the public sphere   HM 585 Aft.
                    Hab Short Loan

4

The Church as a Public Body: Exclusion and the Quest for Authentic Community in India

In this setting the Church must move away from being a communal entity to become an open fellowship, present *to* and possibly *in* all religious and secular communities to witness to Christ as the bearer of both true human life and salvation.[1]

The most contentious issue between Christian and Hindu communities in India has been the problem of conversion. The traditional understanding of conversion as manifested in joining the Christian community leads to serious difficulties in the life of the converts in South Asia, particularly in India, where change of religious community has major implications for relations with the wider Hindu community. Hindu leaders oppose Christian conversion as incompatible with Indian philosophies and social practices, and have countered it by legislation and by the re-conversion of Christian converts. In particular in the 1930s, M. K. Gandhi made his strong objection to Christian conversion activities a part of his political agenda in his struggle against the British Raj, because he feared mass conversions would increase communal disturbances. During and after Independence, the discussion about conversion was focused on the inclusion of the freedom to 'propagate' as one of the fundamental rights in the Indian Constitution Assembly (1947–49). Hindu objections to Christian missionary activities led to a public inquiry into missionary activities by the government of Madhya Pradesh in 1954. The resulting 'Niyogi Report', completed in 1956, was highly critical of converting activities, particularly the conversion of tribals and of the activities of foreign missionaries. Subsequently, Hindu objections to conversion were concretized in three main ways: by the introduction of Hindu 'personal laws', which were disadvantageous for caste Hindus who converted to another religion (1955–56), by the limitation of social benefits for converts from Scheduled Caste back-

---

1 M. M. Thomas, 'The Post-Colonial Crisis in Mission – A Comment', *Religion and Society* XVIII/1 (Mar. 1971), p. 70.

grounds (1950s), and by the passing of the 'freedom of religion acts' in various states (1960s and 1970s). The election of 2003 was won by the Congress Party, which promotes a secular approach to religious issues in the central government, and the tensions over the conversion issue seem to have been relaxed. As a result, there have been four distinctive models for dealing with the problem of conversion: the Ashram model, the secular model, the inculturation model and the liberation model. They also represent four theological strands respectively: the attempt to form an authentic Indian church, the Christ-centred secular fellowship, the Hindu–Catholic synthesis approach and the liberation model.

In this chapter, I will examine each of these models in turn as we wrestle with the wider question of the nature of the Church and its relationship to the public sphere. The challenges of the Indian context have led to a number of different experiments in public theology that are of much wider application. In every society churches face the question of the relationship between the Church or Christian community and the wider society and culture. Should there be a firm line between who is inside and who is outside of the Church? Is the Church a counter-cultural community that challenges the norms of society? Or should it be embedded within the culture and lead from within? Sometimes the answers to these questions may be largely determined by the context in which the Church finds itself. In other places we find a variety of approaches adopted by different churches.

The ashram model: authentic Indian church

In the context of mass conversion to the Christian Church and the reaction from Hindu leaders to Christian missionary approaches, there was strong disapproval of this church-centred mission. This was especially prominent when the 'Rethinking Group' of Madras produced a book, *Rethinking Christianity in India*.[2] The book was interpreted by many authors as a response to Kraemer's understanding of the theology of religions, but careful examination of the book informs us differently. It appears that the authors' concern was not the theology of religions, based on theological or philosophical arguments, but the practical problem of the Indian church in relation to the current debate on mass conversion – the problem of proselytism, the need for integration of the Hindu and Christian communities, the problem of Christian com-

---

2 D. M. Devasahyam and A. N. Sunarisanam, *Rethinking Christianity in India* (Madras: Hogarth Press, 1938).

munalism (as seen from a Hindu perspective),[3] and the search for an alternative model for Christian mission.[4]

In his article on 'the Church and the Indian Christian', Chenchiah questioned the choice of the Church as the central theme of the Conference. He asked openly 'by what right Christendom has all but jettisoned the kingdom of God which occupies so central a place in the message of Jesus and substituted in its place the Church of which the Master said so little and the disciples talked so much'.[5] In his article, 'Jesus and Non-Christian Faiths', he raised the question, 'Why should Hindu converts join the Church?' He criticized the missionaries' dogmatic view and insisted on the necessity of continuity in the life of Indian Christians in a Hindu context. But he soon moved to discuss the questions that Kraemer addressed concerning the Church, the message and the missionary mandate. First, he saw that the problem of the church in India was that it had become 'the centre of influence, the source of salvation, the object of loyalty' and it was 'identified with the core and acquired as it were the same value as the original nucleus'. Furthermore:

> The calamitous fact is that doctrines, institutions, sacraments, priests and pastors, all join together under the name of the Church and take the place of Jesus, whom they in doctrine exalt as God. The Christian does not go to Jesus direct, but clings to the Church as the author of his salvation.[6]

He rejected institutional Christianity by separating Christ from Christianity, and seeking what he called the 'Raw Fact of Christ'. His strongest criticism was that 'the Church with all its claims cannot lead us to the Christ'; 'the Church detracts our attention from the central fact'; 'the Church has never been the cradle of new life', but instead 'accommodator to the dominant forces of the old life';[7] 'we tremble before the Church'. In the Church's place, he insisted, Indian Christianity needs 'Christ, the Holy Spirit, the Kingdom of God'.[8]

---

3 Devasahyam and Sunarisanam (eds), *Rethinking Christianity in India*, p. 13.

4 When we read the whole book, the papers are heavily concentrated on the Church – out of 13 articles, more than 7 articles are dealing with the Church or the Christian community in India. In fact, the most quoted article by Chenchiah, which is a response to Kraemer, is in an appendix, though it is the longest article.

5 Devasahyam and Sunarisanam (eds), *Rethinking Christianity in India*, p. 82.

6 Devasahyam and Sunarisanam (eds), *Rethinking Christianity in India*, pp. 50–1. He further cynically commented that the Church insists to people of other faiths, 'Jesus does not save unless you interpret him as the Church does'.

7 Devasahyam and Sunarisanam (eds), *Rethinking Christianity in India*, pp. 53–62.

8 Devasahyam and Sunarisanam (eds), *Rethinking Christianity in India*, p. 99.

Second, on the Christian message to people of other faiths, Chenchiah, in his critique of Kraemer's book, said that the issue of interreligious relations is not merely theological or intellectual, but 'a matter of life and death', and furthermore, the Christian in India 'can never understand Jesus till he understands the drama of God's dealing with man in and through the other religions of the world'. For this, the 'Indian Christian naturally looks to Indian philosophy for guidance'. He criticized Kraemer's dogmatic approach – what he called 'juridical theology' – and instead emphasized the importance of faith and the Holy Spirit. However, agreeing with Kraemer, he rejected the fulfilment theory of religions since he believed that Hinduism is 'not only longing but also provides satisfaction to its adherents'. He focused on the distinctive nature of Christ over against Hinduism.

> Jesus stands in relation to man as a new creation stands towards the old. His is not perfect man, but a New Man. In Jesus we have the Creator's answer to creation's groaning for a new life … 'new given' that has entered the world. Hinduism makes the perfect man, Christianity the new Man … Jesus is the first fruit of a new creation. Hinduism the final fruits of the old creation.[9]

Third, regarding the missionary mandate, he argued that there are two obstacles to mission in India – communalism and the Church, and he hoped that eventually the 'social intolerance of the Hindu and excessive zeal of the missionary may disappear in India'. In order to achieve this, he argued that conversion should be separated from church membership. That is, he saw conversion as a change of life without insisting on affiliation to the Church, because he viewed mission as a 'movement in the Hindu social fold' rather than the creation of 'a solid society outside'. He strongly objected to either individual or mass conversion to the Christian Church, but supported a Christian mission in India that was 'prepared to see the gradual infusion of Hinduism by Christian ideals and above all Christian life' by creating 'a powerful Christian atmosphere within Hinduism'. He saw the heart of Christian mission as the creation of 'new life' as demonstrated in the life of Jesus, which he believed was able to fulfil the 'unrealized longing for a life here' of the Hindus.[10]

In similar vein, Vengal Chakkarai, another key figure in the Rethinking Group, asserted that the church in India had arisen out of the historical setting of western Christianity and that Indian Christians

9 Devasahyam and Sunarisanam (eds), *Rethinking Christianity in India*, pp. 10–44 at 43.

10 Devasahyam and Sunarisanam (eds), *Rethinking Christianity in India*, pp. 44–52.

are not obliged to follow its pattern. Whatever the positive elements of the Church might be, they cannot be included in the 'revelation of Christ Himself' since they are not eternal and not of 'divine essence'. He strongly rejected the western form of the Christian Church:

> In its witness to the Spirit of Christ, as the voice of one in the wilderness, calling ever unto men, hurrying on, to pause and reflect, to repent and to be reborn; protesting as an alien force against the world's life, its culture and civilisation, and its tower of Babel; it is a witness to the faith and as the faithful among the faithless ... that the church is the Body of the Lord.[11]

Therefore the Church should be inspiration not institution, and the institutionalized Church, for Chakkarai, is 'the tents put up by our Western friends; but they can never be our permanent habitation'. Instead, he emphasized that Indian Christians should seek the kingdom of God which the Lord 'announced and for which He gave His life'.[12]

G. V. Job advocated that the 'pure' and 'infant' Indian church should be born not through the 'transplanting' of the western Church in Indian soil, but by drawing its resources from Hindu tradition, just as the early Christians drew their resources from the Old Testament, and in this process the 'Lord alone matters'. He further insisted that what is needed is the idea of the 'new creation', which he regarded as lacking in traditional Christianity due to its preoccupation with personal salvation and the pursuit of the 'realities of Christ and His Kingdom', which is the 're-born humanity'.[13]

The rejection of the institutionalized Church and mass conversion to the Church was a common feature of the Rethinking Group, and this was supported by some missionaries. These were C. F. Andrews, E. Stanley Jones and A. G. Hogg, all of whom attended the Conference and tried to respond to the problem of mass conversion and its political implications in India. Although their approaches and theologies are quite different, the solution they came to was seeking the kingdom of God, in the sense of promoting Christian values in Indian society. As early as 1909, C. F. Andrews wrote:

> I am led more and more by missionary experience to regard the conversion of India, not as the aggregate of so many individual conversions, but far rather as a gradual process of growth and change in

11 Devasahyam and Sunarisanam (eds), *Rethinking Christianity in India*, pp. 119–21 at 120.

12 Devasahyam and Sunarisanam (eds), *Rethinking Christianity in India*, pp. 122–3.

13 Devasahyam and Sunarisanam (eds), *Rethinking Christianity in India*, pp. 20–7.

thought, idea, feeling, temperaments, conduct – a process which half creates and half reconstructs a truly Christian atmosphere, Indian at its best, and Christian at its best.[14]

Andrews considered that the major issue at the Conference was 'how the Christian duty of evangelism was to be truly conceived in relation to the non-Christian religious communities'.[15] Chaturvedi and Sykes recorded how Andrews was disturbed by the announcement of Ambedkar and controversy surrounding the conversion of the Scheduled Castes. He thought Ambedkar's move was a misuse of religious conversion, which he believed should be conducted with 'genuine religious experience and conviction'. However, he differed from Gandhi in that he did not exclude conversion involving change of religious affiliation and seeking baptism in the Christian Church. After a long discussion with Gandhi on this issue of conversion as change of religious affiliation, and just before Tambaram, he wrote to a friend:

> ... if conversion meant a denial of any living truth in one's own religion, then we must have nothing to do with it. But it is rather the discovery of a new and glorious truth for which one would sacrifice one's whole life. It does mean also, very often, passing from one fellowship to another, and this should never be done lightly. But if the new fellowship embodies the glorious new truth in such a way to make it more living and cogent than the old outworn truth, then I should say to the individual, 'Go forward'.[16]

During the Conference, the most vocal opponent to Kraemer was A. G. Hogg, who had just retired from principalship of Madras Christian College, and who challenged Kraemer's notions of discontinuity, Christian revelation, and the Christian attitude to people of other religions. Hogg distinguished faith, which he regarded as the religious life in other religions, from faiths, which are complexes of spiritual, ethical, intellectual and social elements of religions. He insisted that the religious life, faith, is 'hid in God' in people of other religions, therefore the missionary attitude towards non-Christian faiths should not be only 'respect or admiration' but a 'religious reverence', believing that this faith is the holy ground of communion between God and human beings. Furthermore, he asked:

---

14 Benarsidas Chaturvedi & Marjorie Sykes, *Charles Freer Andrews: A Narrative* (London: George Allen & Unwin Ltd, 1949), p. 39.

15 Chaturvedi and Sykes, *Charles Freer Andrews*, p. 309.

16 Chaturvedi and Sykes, *Charles Freer Andrews*, p. 310.

In non-Christian faith may we meet with something that is not merely a seeking but in real measure a finding, and a finding by contact with which a Christian may be helped to make fresh discoveries in his own findings of God *in Christ*?[17]

Just as Kraemer separated the revelation of Christ from empirical Christianity, Hogg opposed the idea of identifying faith (the divine initiative of self-disclosure) with its empirical forms, since he was convinced that there must be a Divine response to human seeking. Therefore, with this understanding, he insisted:

> It is radically wrong for the missionary to approach men of other faiths under a conviction ... that he and his fellow-believers are witnesses to a Divine revelation, while other religions are exclusively the product of a human 'religious consciousness'.[18]

The greatest difference between Kraemer and Hogg was that Hogg believed 'God reveals *Himself*', not ready-made truths about himself, in both Christian and non-Christian faiths. He asserted that Christianity is unique not because of a unique *occurrence* of revelation but because of the unique *content* (Christ) of revelation. In other words, it is Christ that matters, and whether he was revealed in Christianity or non-Christian religions is secondary. Moreover, since there is continuity of nature, between Christian faith and non-Christian faiths, the life of the people of other faiths must be 'hid in God'.[19]

Hogg was not happy with Kraemer's treatment of Hinduism as a 'religious consciousness', his ill-defined term 'biblical realism', and the exclusiveness of revelation in the Christian gospel in Kraemer's theology. Responding to Kraemer, Hogg used the philosophical analysis of separating faith and faiths, just as Kraemer separated Christ from Christianity. They both tried to present Christ in the non-Christian context but in different ways. The question is not whether one is arrogant and the other is not – they both struggled to find appropriate means to present the gospel with respect to people of other faiths. Kraemer saw that by acknowledging the differences and discontinuity, Christians could respect the separate integrity of other religions, and that the only way to present Christ was through proclaiming the gospel and incorporating converts into the body of Christ, the Church. Hogg,

---

17 A. G. Hogg, 'The Christian Attitude to Non-Christian Faith', in International Missionary Council (IMC), *The Authority of the Faith* (Oxford: Oxford University Press, 1939), p. 103.

18 Hogg, 'The Christian Attitude', p. 106.

19 Hogg, 'The Christian Attitude', p. 108.

however, understood that there was clear continuity in terms of faith (singular) and in that Christ was somehow present himself in the Hindu context, without the aid of the Church or missionaries, so he held that Hinduism was capable of bearing God's revelation directly, the content of which is Christ. Both Hogg and Kraemer were missionaries and their concern was to understand other faiths and how to approach them. Therefore O. V. Jathanna's observation that Kraemer and Hogg were basically in agreement was not an unjustified perception.[20]

Hogg's missionary concern is clear in his article in *Evangelism for the World Today*, in which he emphasized the legitimacy of Christians seeking converts, but distinguished evangelization as a manifestation of 'religious instinct' from proselytism as 'herd instinct'. That is, evangelism is leading people to Christ and proselytism is calling people to join our own party, the Church. He also distinguished manifesting Christ, that is seeking the kingdom of God, from seeking converts to the Church, which he regarded as the root cause of the problem of communalism in India.[21] On the question of a relevant presentation of the Gospel in India, he wrote:

So, when Jesus received at His baptism, the commission to win for man a perfect world – the 'Kingdom of God', He realized that the only way He could fulfil this commission was by bringing into being the kind of community that could be trusted with such a perfect world.[22]

He insisted that this community should be 'divinely created', not by 'human contriving' but by personal commitment to Jesus himself, and implied that the Church might not be 'fit' to be trusted to be the one.

As a result of two and a half weeks of intensive discussions and reflections, the participants of each section drew up their findings. The findings of sections III and IV affirmed the Conference's strong position that the Church and mission are inseparable, the Church 'must so present Christ Jesus to the world ... that men shall come to put their trust in God through Him their Saviour and serve Him as their Lord in the fellowship of His Church'. Furthermore it stated:

We stress the fact that nothing in the present world situation in any way invalidates the Gospel. It is still the power of God unto salva-

---

20 Origen Vasantha Jathanna, *The Decisiveness of the Christ-Event and the Universality of Christianity in a World of Religious Plurality* (Berne: Peter Lang, 1981), p. 298.

21 A. G. Hogg, in John R. Mott (eds), *Evangelism for the World Today as Interpreted by Christian Leaders throughout the World* (New York and London: IMC, 1938), pp. 20–5.

22 Hogg, in Mott, *Evangelism for the World Today*, pp. 118–22.

tion. Our fundamental purpose in evangelism is still the same and we agree that every missionary activity should be judged by its effectiveness in conveying the message of the Gospel.[23]

Moreover, even in the findings of sections I and V, we find strong support for the Church and mission. It was stated that although the Church should 'only be obedient to the will of the Good Shepherd' and 'proclaim the Kingdom of God', it should also 'call men of all faiths by word and deed into the one life of the Beloved Community', that is, the Church. Regarding the goal of missionary work, it rejected the 'permeation' of the gospel as the goal of Christian mission but found that the 'end and aim of our evangelistic work is not achieved until all men everywhere are brought to a knowledge of God in Jesus Christ and to a saving faith in Him'. Furthermore, although they affirmed that other religions do contain values resulting from deep religious experience and great moral achievement, the findings stated, 'yet we are bold enough to call men out from them to the feet of Christ. We do so because we believe that in Him alone is the full salvation which man needs.'[24] The findings concluded:

> Whatever new emphasis may mark our presentation of Christianity in face of the changes in the non-Christian faiths, the heart of the Gospel remains eternally unchanged, and the obligation of the Church to carry its witness to all mankind stands central to its obedience to the will of its Lord.[25]

E. Stanley Jones was especially unhappy with the discussions and findings of the Conference. In his highly critical article, he asserted 'centrally and fundamentally the Conference missed its way'. The problem he saw was that the Conference set 'the Religious Community, the Church' as the main theme. He regarded the Church as a 'pseudo-absolute' and insisted instead that the kingdom of God is 'God's absolute order', just as Christ is the 'absolute Person'.[26] He further argued that the kingdom of God as the goal of mission means advocating 'secular movements which have a social passion and a demand for social justice' instead of trying to get church members and building up the church organization, which he saw as the main emphasis of the Conference.[27]

---

23 IMC, *The World Mission of the Church* (London: IMC, 1939), pp. 33–40 at 39.
24 IMC, *The World Mission of the Church*, p. 51.
25 IMC, *The World Mission of the Church*, p. 55.
26 *Guardian*, 23 February 1939.
27 *Guardian*, 9 March 1939.

The theological question of the kingdom of God and the Church is important when it comes to the integrity of Christians, because it relates to the practical life of the converts in their relationship with their past religious experiences and the wider community. The Rethinking Group represented Christians of a higher caste background who regarded the Hindu tradition as part of their heritage and did not wish to be excluded from the wider Hindu society. They also saw themselves as sharing a common identity with Hindus in their search for the welfare of India and its people in a time of national struggle against colonial rule. These approaches are recurring themes of Indian theologians, and they arise out of their sincere attempt to solve the problems of communalism and proselytism, for which they saw the Church in its western pattern and theology as responsible. The debate at Tambaram was the result of a painstaking search to answer the question of what it means to be Christian in their seeking to follow Christ who preached the kingdom of God and also shared his life with the community of believers. What is the place of the Church and the kingdom of God in Christianity? The Christian Church, in spite of its weaknesses, or rather because of its weaknesses, can bear witness to Christ and continue to be a place for worship and sharing. The Church as a visible community, rather than a hindrance, can make an impact on the wider community, and more importantly, the Christian community need not be understood merely in a functional way, but as the body of Christ and therefore of the essence of the gospel. On the other hand, the Church constantly needs to be shaped and challenged by the kingdom perspective that there is a hope in Christ beyond the boundaries of the exclusive visible community of believers. The kingdom of God is not limited by historical and cultural traditions of religious affiliation, but open to the possibilities in Christ who has called believers to be part of his ongoing 'new creation'.

The secular model: 'Christ-centred secular fellowship'

Towards and after Independence, the concern of Indian Protestant theologians was more to do with the relationship between the Christian community and the Hindu community, particularly the question of whether converts should leave the Hindu community in order to join the Christian community and what joining the Church entailed. During the 1940s, Manilal Parekh, who had been baptized but later declined to identify himself with any church, became a prime opponent of the Church on the conversion issue. He strongly condemned Christians for forming a community that he saw as a distinctly social and political body, anti-national and not spiritual in character. He believed this was the direct result of the 'proselytizing' activities of the missionaries.[28] His radical approach was to advocate a 'Hindu Church of Christ' as 'the only possible Church of Christ in Hindustan'. His attempt to bring 'harmony and synthesis' between Hinduism and Christianity brought controversy and led to a debate with Bishop Azariah who rejected Parekh's pure spiritualization of baptism and Christian life.[29] Robin Boyd argued that his bitter opposition to the Church and his syncretistic approach did not lead 'to a positive stage of Indian theological construction', but on the other hand, it had considerable influence on the thoughts of M. M. Thomas and Kaj Baago in their approach to conversion,[30] and these then played major roles in advocating new approaches.

In 1966 an article by Kaj Baago, Professor of Church History at United Theological College, Bangalore, triggered controversy among Christian theologians in India. Baago argued that, in the light of the contemporary postcolonial situation, Christian mission must rethink its objectives and goals, and that the most important issue should be the Christian attitude to other religions, especially the 'problem of conversion'. Baago strongly questioned the legitimacy of conversion: 'Shall they [people of another religion] be converted at all?' and 'Do they have to be incorporated into church organizations which are utterly alien to their religious traditions?' He alleged that Christian mission was carried on with ideas of 'expansion', 'victory', 'progress' or 'religious conquest' in a way contrary to the practice of Jesus and the early Church.[31] He not only called for the abandonment of the conversion activities of Christian mission, but also declared:

> The missionary task of today cannot, therefore, be to draw men out of their religions into another religion, but rather to leave Christianity (the organized religion) and go inside Hinduism and Buddhism, accepting these religions as one's own, in so far as they do not conflict with Christ, and regarding them as the presupposition, the background and the framework of the Christian gospel in Asia. Such a mission ... might lead to the creation of Hindu Christianity.[32]

---

28 Manilal Parekh, 'The Spiritual Significance and Value of Baptism', *National Council of Churches Review* (NCCR) XLIV/9 (Sept. 1924), pp. 324–9.

29 Manilal Parekh, 'Keshub Chunder Sen: His Relation to Christianity', *International Review of Mission* (IRM) XVII/65 (Jan. 1928), pp. 145–54. V. S. Azariah responded to Parekh's article in the same issue – 'India and Christ', pp. 154–9.

30 Robin Boyd, *An Introduction to Indian Christian Theology*, rev. edn (Delhi: ISPCK, 1975), pp. 267–71.

31 Kaj Baago, 'The Post-Colonial Crisis of Missions', *IRM* LV/219 (July 1966), pp. 322–32.

32 Baago, 'The Post-Colonial Crisis', pp. 331–2.

Although the idea of 'Hindu Christianity' was not a new one among Indian theologians and some missionaries, Baago's suggestion of Christians 'converting' into Hinduism was contentious. Baago saw Christianity as tainted by the institutionalized Church, a colonial legacy, which he wished to separate from Christ, the 'norm and rule' of Christian faith. Since Christ transcends all things, including culture and religion, he thought Christ must be free from Christianity and particularly from the Church, which is neither compatible with their culture nor acceptable to modern Hindus because of its historical past in India. He believed Christianity, as it was manifested in western church forms, did not make any impact in India. He identified the solution to be not an attempt to find a meeting-point between Christianity and Hinduism, but a rejection of Christianity as a legitimate vessel to hold the gospel. Instead the gospel should be allowed to grow within Hinduism since, as he tried to show in his historical analysis of the mission history of the Church, Christ and his gospel are not bound by Christianity.

Baago's radical approach to conversion was echoed by M. M. Thomas, who also questioned the role of the Church in the contemporary situation. In the Nasrapur Consultation in 1966, Thomas developed his thoughts on conversion and raised the question of the 'form' of the Christian community within the human community.[33] He argued that the most urgent task for contemporary Christian mission is to participate in the people's struggle for the 'realization of humanity' rather than following the traditional missionary task of conversion. He further insisted that the secular fellowship was the 'point of contact' and could be in 'partnership in the struggle' and called on the Church to break the communal structure and build up a new partnership of Christians and non-Christians – the 'human *koinonia*'.

Thomas, reflecting on the Uppsala Assembly (1968), published a booklet, *Salvation and Humanisation* (1971), which was the outcome of his search for the 'point of contact', and perhaps represents his most mature thinking on the issue,[34] but it brought about a direct confrontation with Lesslie Newbigin.[35] Thomas insisted that the mission of

---

33 M. M. Thomas, 'The Struggle for Human Dignity as a Preparation for the Gospel', *NCCR* LXXXVI/9 (Sept. 1966), pp. 356–9.

34 M. M. Thomas, *Salvation and Humanisation: Some Critical Issues of the Theology of Mission in Contemporary India* (Madras: Christian Literature Society (CLS), 1971).

35 The discussion first started when Newbigin made his critique on Thomas' comments during his 1965 debate with Berkhof – see Lesslie Newbigin, 'The Call to Mission – A Call to Unity?', in *The Church Crossing Frontiers* (Uppsala: Gleerup, 1969), pp. 254–65. In *Salvation and Humanisation*, Thomas was responding to Newbigin's comments. After its publication, Newbigin wrote a review of Thomas' booklet – Lesslie Newbigin, 'Salvation and Humanisation – Book Review', *Religion and Society* XVIII/1 (Mar. 1971), pp. 71–80. The ensuing correspondence between Thomas and Newbigin from October to December

the Church must take into account the 'religious and secular movements which express men's search for the spiritual foundations for a
fuller and richer human life' in the present 'revolutionary' period. In his
critique of dichotomic approaches that separated salvation and humanization – concepts he saw as 'integrally related' – he alleged the main
problems of Indian Christianity were 'pietistic individualism', which
emphasized dogmatic belief and the inner experience of conversion,
and the communal tendency of the Christian community, which isolated and closed off Christians from others. He then introduced the
concept of the 'Christ-centred secular fellowship outside the Church', a
koinonia which was the 'manifestation of the new reality of the Kingdom at work in the world of men in world history'. He perceived that
the Indian understanding of Jesus Christ was as the 'Divine Head of
Humanity' through whom the Holy Spirit brings all men into sonship
of the Father, ultimately uniting all their struggles for humanization.
Therefore, 'Salvation itself could be defined as humanization in a total
and eschatological sense.'[36]

In order to cultivate the fellowship or *koinonia*, overcoming the
'form' of the Church was of vital importance for Thomas. Therefore
he stressed that the Church must 'move away from being a communal
entity to become an open fellowship able to witness, in all religious and
secular communities, to Christ as the bearer of both true human life
and salvation'. As a result, he envisaged a 'new pattern of combining
Christian self-identity and secular solidarity with all men',[37] in that

> conversion to Christ does not necessarily imply conversion to the
> Christian community isolated from the communities in which they
> live but rather ... it implies the building up of a Christ-centred fel-
> lowship of faith within the society, culture and religion in which they
> live, transforming their structures and values from within.[38]

Therefore, he insisted that 'the Church must be bearer of Christ in all
Indian communities' as it 'extends' into both religious and secular soci-
ety, and saw this as the 'only way in which the form of church life in
India could be renewed'.[39]

As Baago had done, Thomas rejected a Christian mission of calling people to convert to Christianity and also saw the limitations of

---

1971 was published as 'Baptism, the Church and *Koinonia*', *Religion and Society* XIX/1
(Mar. 1972), pp. 69–90.

36 Thomas, *Salvation and Humanisation*, pp. 1–19.
37 Thomas, *Salvation and Humanisation*, pp. 40–60.
38 Thomas, in 'Baptism, the Church and *Koinonia*', pp. 72–3.
39 Thomas, in 'Baptism, the Church and *Koinonia*', p. 74.

attempting a synthesis by finding a meeting-point between and within Christianity and Hinduism. However, he differed from Baago in that he tried to find the common ground in the emerging *secular* Hindu society. He believed that, by secularizing itself, Christianity could meet the needs of the people in India, which were caused by the rapid secularization of Hinduism. The main concern for Thomas was not the conversion of individual Hindus to Christianity nor creating a 'Hindu Christianity', but rather a perceived need for a conversion of both Christian and Hindu faiths into the common ground, which he saw as a 'human *koinonia*' or, as he later called it, 'the Christ-centred secular fellowship'.

It is important to notice that for Thomas, 'secular fellowship' does not mean making the gospel secular. What he intended was not for Christians to lose the religious or spiritual aspect of the gospel, nor for Christianity to be absorbed into Hindu religion, but for the secularization of the Christian *community* in order to bridge the gap with the wider Hindu community and identify with Hindus. Secular for him meant the Christian community becoming 'truly "religious" without being "communal"'.[40] Thomas wanted to overcome the problem of the Christian community becoming more and more isolated from the main community in India, especially because of the insistence on a radical discontinuity between the gospel and Hindu religion through the means of conversion. This led to the exclusion of Christians by the Hindu majority as 'outcastes', which resulted in the fact that the Christian community was no longer able to make an impact on Hindu society – as was plain especially in the case of the Hindu personal laws. He was confident that secularism would override religious differences and shatter the values that Christianity and Hinduism held as religions, but that the 'human *koinonia*' would remain as the meeting-point and that since Christ is in all, he is to be found there too.

The Protestant thinking on conversion in the 1960s and the early 1970s was part of the wider Christian discussion in the face of the political and social revolutions taking place in many parts of the world and urgent calls for the Church to take part in the struggle for humanization. There was a conscious shift of emphasis in mission from evangelism (leading to conversion) towards social involvement. In India, Christian theologians faced increasing challenges from the Hindu nationalist movement, especially as it started to gain support from certain states and pressured the central government for the rights of Hindus over against other minority communities. In search of a solution, some Indian Protestant theologians suggested that the Christian

---

40 Thomas, in 'Baptism, the Church and *Koinonia*', p. 88.

community in India should be part of the wider Hindu community in an apparently rapidly secularizing India, for they believed that not only was secularization an inevitable process of modernity but also that it would gradually overcome communal tensions. They insisted that a 'point of contact' between the Christian community and the Hindu community must be established so that Hindus would not need to convert to the Christian community. This point of contact must be located inside the wider Hindu community since the Christian community was either a stumbling block in this process (Baago), or an entity that naturally transcended religious divides to produce a secular fellowship (Thomas).

One of the key points at issue in the debate among the Protestant theologians was the question of whether the Church is a legitimate 'point of contact' for Christians and Hindus. Thomas (and Baago) rejected the Church and found the 'point of contact' outside the Church. In contrast to Catholic theologians (see next sections), many Protestants were ready to discard the Church as an essential part of the gospel. This was also evident in conciliar debates of the 1960s, swayed by J. C. Hoekendijk, in which the Church tended to be understood as merely functional.[41] The problem of the association of the Church with the colonial authority and, even after Independence, the continued dependency of Indian churches on western churches, particularly in the area of leadership and finance, made it difficult for Thomas and others to treat the Church as an essential part of the gospel.

However, the attempts of Thomas and others at creating a 'secular fellowship' within the Hindu community may have led to an identity crisis for caste Hindu converts who found themselves fully belonging to neither the Hindu community nor the Christian one. The dilemma was even more acute for Christians from a dalit or outcaste background, who made up the vast majority of the Indian churches. They had not regarded themselves as Hindus before conversion nor had Hindus treated them as such. For them, conversion to Christianity was part of a struggle for religious and social identity that they had previously lacked, and now they were being expected to deny this identity. The problem of Thomas's approach was that Indian Christians would become individuals who follow Christ but have no ground for their social and religious interaction with their fellow believers. In the midst of commu-

---

41 See David J. Bosch, *Transforming Mission: Paradigm Shifts in Theology of Mission* (Maryknoll, NY: Orbis Books, 1992), pp. 382–5; Timothy Yates, *Christian Mission in the Twentieth Century* (Cambridge: Cambridge University Press, 1994), pp. 196–7. Hoekendijk put it bluntly: 'The *nature* of the Church can be sufficiently defined by its *function*, i.e. its participation in Christ's apostolic ministry.' J. C. Hoekendijk, 'The Church in Missionary Thinking', *IRM* XLI/163 (July 1952), pp. 334–5.

nal tension and rising Hindu nationalist movements, Christian converts would find themselves rootless individuals fearing that any support of the Christian community would be understood as communal and therefore unethical. There was a tendency to think that anything particular to Christianity and against the interests of the larger Hindu community was incompatible with the search for a 'common humanity' and must therefore be rejected, not on the grounds of whether it was right or wrong but on the grounds that it contributed to communal tension. Religious conversion was certainly viewed as being in this category; among all the Christian teachings and practices it was regarded as most destructive for communalism in India in general and for communal tension between Hindus and Christians in particular. In spite of their honest search for an answer to the communal problems supposedly caused by conversion, Indian Protestant theologians appear, by limiting the implications of conversion to the individual and spiritual realms of life, to have caused a weakening of the self-identity of the Christian community.

The inculturation model: 'Hindu–Catholic' synthesis

While Protestant attempts to solve the problem of conversion involved finding a 'meeting-point' within Hindu society, such as that expressed by M. M. Thomas in his 'Christ-centred secular fellowship', Catholics in India initially found it hard to share this theological premise because of the traditional Roman Catholic emphasis on the doctrine of *extra ecclesiam nulla salus* (no salvation outside the Church). In the 1970s and 1980s, the development of Indian Catholic thinking on conversion was greatly influenced by two competing approaches to contextualizing the gospel, the inculturation model and the liberation model,[42] representing the 'double confrontation' of contemporary Christianity 'with the great world religions on the one hand and with the non-Christian "secular" humanisms on the other'.[43] In Asia these were responses to the dominant realities of the context: religiousness and poverty.[44] The tension between these two loose movements in the 1980s was due to

---

42 See David Bosch's analysis of models of contextualization, *Transforming Mission*, pp. 420–1.

43 Hans Küng, *On Being a Christian*, trans. Edward Quinn (London: Collins, 1977), p. 25.

44 Aloysius Pieris, *An Asian Theology of Liberation* (Maryknoll, NY: Orbis Books, 1988), pp. 45–50. George Gispert-Sauch also identifies these two movements in India – 'Asian Theology', in David F. Ford (ed.), *The Modern Theologians: An Introduction to Christian Theology in the Twentieth Century*, 2nd edn (Oxford: Blackwell, 1997), pp. 460–1.

a number of factors, chief among which was the fact that inculturationists tended to relate to the upper castes and Brahmanical religion,
whereas liberationists were concerned for the interests of the outcastes,
whom they believed were victims of caste Hinduism. Liberationists thus
accused inculturationists of indifference to matters of social justice and
even of complicity with high-caste oppression, whereas inculturationists saw liberationists as insensitive to Hindu religion and as a threat
to communal harmony.[45] Applied to the issue of conversion, the inculturation movement attempted to synthesize Christian faith with Hindu
religion and culture to make conversion as a change of religion and
community avoidable, and the liberation movement tended to see conversion as a social 'protest' of dalits and their 'liberation' as a legitimate
aim of conversion.

In the open climate fostered by the Second Vatican Council, an
attempt to deal with the problem of the relationship between Christianity and Hinduism was presented in the shape of Raymond Panikkar's
well-known work, *The Unknown Christ of Hinduism* (1964). Panikkar
was convinced that there must be a 'meeting place' between Christianity and Hinduism in the religious sphere. He then argued that this
meeting place must be Christ, because Christ is the 'ontological meeting-point of any religion' and the 'only one mediator between God and
the rest'.[46] He concluded that 'Christ is already there in Hinduism in so
far as Hinduism is a true religion' and that the Christian mission was to
unveil the 'unknown Christ' in Hinduism. Hence conversion

> does not mean ... a changing 'over' to another culture, another tradi-
> tion or even 'another' religion, but a changing 'in', a changing into a
> new life, a new existence, a new creation, which is precisely the old
> one – and not another – but transformed, lifted up, risen again.[47]

Although the work of Panikkar was in many ways in line with the
new thinking of the Second Vatican Council and with Karl Rahner's
theology, there was a significant difference in that Panikkar affirmed
Hinduism itself as a way of salvation, which neither the Vatican documents nor Rahner did. Both Rahner and Panikkar attempted to bring

---

45 These issues are illustrated in, for example, the criticism of the ashram movement
by George Soares-Prabhu, 'From Alienation to Inculturation: Some Reflections on Doing
Theology in India Today', in T. K. John (ed.), *Bread and Breath: Essays in Honour of
Samuel Rayan, S.J.* (Anand: Gujarat Sahitya Prakash, 1991), pp. 55–99, and the letter from
Soares-Prabhu and response from the leaders of the ashram movement in Vandana Mataji
(ed.), *Christian Ashrams: A Movement with a Future?* (Delhi: ISPCK, 1993), pp. 153–60.

46 Raymond Panikkar, *The Unknown Christ of Hinduism* (London: Darton, Longman
& Todd, 1964), pp. 11–28 and 119–31.

47 Panikkar, *The Unknown Christ*, p. 18.

Christianity and Hinduism (and other religions for Rahner) together in a normative salvation, though in different ways. For Rahner, salvation was through God's grace offered to 'anonymous Christians', and for Panikkar, it was by acknowledging the 'unknown Christ' within Hinduism. In Rahner's theology of religions, the non-Christian religions were not really the focus of discussion, which was on individuals of other faiths; this led to Hans Küng's criticism that he was reaffirming the doctrine of *extra ecclesiam nulla salus* through the 'back door'.[48] Panikkar, on the other hand, believed that Hinduism can be and should be a vehicle for salvation because of the presence of the 'unknown Christ' within it, and this rendered conversion unnecessary. Christianity and the Church were not his concern since it is Christ who mediates and brings salvation. However, although he may have appeared to solve the problem of conversion of Hindus, his approach was still based on the concept of Christ and relied on the acceptance by Hindus of the need for one mediator. Although Panikkar's combination of Thomistic and Vedantic terminology very much impressed Boyd and others,[49] many critics saw him as still holding the superiority of Christianity over Hinduism,[50] which pleased neither those theologians who wanted to acknowledge the legitimacy of Hinduism on a par with Christianity, nor Hindus, who felt insulted. For some he was a follower of the 'fulfilment' theory set down by J. N. Farquhar a half-century before;[51] for others, his approach lacked genuine 'respect' for Hinduism as though he was only trying to 'interpret' it according to his own perspective.[52] Nevertheless, Panikkar's acceptance of Hinduism as a legitimate way of salvation laid the groundwork for Catholic theologians in India to move from 'Indian Christianity' to 'Hindu Christianity'.[53]

It was Hans Staffner, an Austrian Jesuit, and Bede Griffiths, an English Benedictine, who made the inculturation approach applicable to solving the problem of conversion in India by attempting a synthesis of the two religions. Staffner, following Upadhyay's Hindu–Catholic approach, looked for complementarities in the two faiths that do not

---

48 Küng, *On Being a Christian*, p. 98.

49 Boyd, *An Introduction to Indian Christian Theology*, pp. 222–5.

50 Panikkar described Christianity as 'a risen Hinduism' – *The Unknown Christ*, p. 17 – and Hinduism as 'a vestibule of Christianity', with Christianity providing the 'essential contents' to Hinduism – p. 19. Notice his revised edition (1981) in which he omitted these sentences – Raimundo Panikkar, *The Unknown Christ of Hinduism: Towards an Ecumenical Christophany*, rev. edn (Maryknoll, NY: Orbis Books, 1981).

51 See Eric J. Sharpe, *Faith Meets Faith: Some Christian Attitudes to Hinduism in the Nineteenth and Twentieth Centuries*, London: SCM Press, 1977, p. 118–31.

52 See Küng, *On Being a Christian*, p. 98.

53 Aloysius Pieris, 'Inculturation in Non-Semitic Asia', *The Month* 19/3 (Mar. 1986), pp. 83–7.

conflict with the vital belief and practice of either. Staffner's theological synthesis clearly originated in the struggle of Indian Christians over conversion. It was his conviction that conversion was a 'purely spiritual event' and that therefore changing one's community should not be any part of it.[54] He argued that, since Hinduism is the religion of the Hindus and is defined by race or geography (like Greek or Roman religions), membership of the Hindu community was not based on definite creeds or beliefs. Reiterating Upadhyay, he regarded religions as having two dimensions: *samaj dharma* (social customs, ritual purity, diet, etc.) and *sadhana dharma* (the way of salvation). Hinduism, he believed, falls primarily into the former category but, since the essence of Catholic Christianity is doctrine and faith in God and it is quite accommodating of social customs and culture, Christianity is primarily *sadhana dharma*. Therefore, Christianity and Hinduism can be synthesized and the two religious traditions complement each other. Conversion is then no longer necessary, since adherents of each can 'embrace' rather than 'renounce' the essence of the other's religious tradition while remaining in their own community.[55] Hindu–Catholic theology was very influential among Indian Catholic theologians in the 1970s and stimulated the Catholic ashram movement.[56]

Although there had been some Protestant ashrams,[57] the leading proponents of ashrams after the Second Vatican Council were Catholics, led by Fr Jules Monchanin and Swami Abhishiktananda, who were both French Benedictines.[58] In the 1970s, Griffiths became a leading figure in the Catholic ashram movement and became engaged in debate with Hindus.[59] The theological understanding of Griffiths is clearly expressed in his book *Christ in India* (1966), a collection of his

54 Hans Staffner, 'Conversion to Christianity, Seen from the Hindu Point of View', in Joseph Pathvapankal (ed.), *Service and Salvation: Nagpur Theological Conference on Evangelization* (Bangalore: Theological Publications in India, 1973), pp. 235–48.

55 See also Staffner's later publications, *The Significance of Jesus Christ in Asia* (Anand: Gujarat Sahitya Prakash, 1985) and *Jesus Christ and the Hindu Community: Is a Synthesis of Hinduism and Christianity Possible?* (Anand: Gujarat Sahitya Prakash, 1988), where he continued to argue for a synthesis of Christian faith and Hindu culture, envisaging them in a seed-and-soil relationship.

56 See Vandana Mataji, *Gurus, Ashrams and Christians* (Delhi: ISPCK, 1978); *Christian Ashrams: A Movement with a Future?* (Delhi: ISPCK 1993).

57 See Richard W. Taylor, 'Christian Ashrams as a Style of Mission in India', *IRM* LXVIII/271 (July 1979), pp. 281–93.

58 Monchanin, also known as Swami Param Arubi Anndam, started Saccidananda Ashram at Tiruchirapalli in South Tamil Nadu in 1950. Abhishiktananda, formerly Dom Henri Le Saux, worked with him there and later lived the life of a *sannyasin*. For a summary of their theologies, see Boyd, *An Introduction to Indian Christian Theology*, pp. 218–22, 287–97.

59 Griffiths founded Kurisumala Ashram in Kerala and later became the leader of Saccidananda Ashram.

papers.[60] Like Panikkar, he believed that the meeting place between Christianity and Hinduism must be in Christ, insisting that Christ is 'reality', whereas Christianity and Hinduism are religions, that is, manifestations of the reality and not reality itself. He sought to present Christ by adapting the *sarvodaya* or 'service of all' movement popularized by Gandhi's disciple Vinoba Bhave. It is based on the Hindu philosophy of self-realization, that is, Christ is found by entering into a deeper realm of spiritual reality, and conversion to Christianity is not required.[61] Though, in his interpretation of Hinduism, he exhibited a great sense of respect and appreciation of Hindu culture, in his theological thinking, like Staffner, he held a 'fulfilment' approach to Hinduism, separating Hindu religion from Hindu culture. He regarded the Hindu deities as 'symbols of the divine mystery', having no 'reality in themselves' but only as 'shadows of the mystery of Christ', the true reality. He concluded that the Church's mission is to identify the 'true place of Christ in India' for the purpose of 'saving' anything good and true in Hinduism and 'purifying' anything erroneous or corrupt so that Hindus could learn to 'discover Christ as the true fulfilment'.[62]

The inculturation theologians' synthesis of Christian faith and Hindu culture had a theological basis in the concept of fulfilment but it was also supported by Catholic anthropologists in the 1980s, led principally by Louis Luzbetak, who distinguished gospel and culture as meaning and form respectively, and argued that the former transcends the latter.[63] However, this Catholic approach was questioned on anthropological grounds by David Mosse in his study of Catholic–Hindu synthesis in a village in Tamil Nadu. Mosse observed that the local Jesuit attempt – dating back to de Nobili – to accommodate Hindu culture on the basis of the superiority and universality of the Christian religion, had led in practice to a large measure of retention of Hindu religious beliefs which were embodied in and not separate from cultural forms.[64] This was particularly so in the case of the caste system. The net result, Mosse suggests, was that both the Catholic missionaries and the caste leaders 'accommodated' each other in order to sustain their own polit-

---

60 Bede Griffiths, *Christ in India: Essays Towards a Hindu–Christian Dialogue* (New York: Charles Scribner's Sons, 1966). For a critical appraisal, see K. P. Aleaz, *Christian Thought through Advaita Vedānta* (Delhi: ISPCK, 1996), pp. 148–55.

61 Griffiths, *Christ in India*, pp. 9–37.

62 Griffiths, *Christ in India*, pp. 77–111.

63 Louis Luzbetak, *The Church and Cultures: New Perspectives in Missiological Anthropology*, 2nd edn (Maryknoll, NY: Orbis Books, 1988), pp. 75–83.

64 David Mosse, 'The Politics of Religious Synthesis: Roman Catholicism and Hindu Village Society in Tamil Nadu, India', in Charles Stewart and Rosalind Shaw (eds), *Syncretism/Anti-Syncretism: The Politics of Religious Synthesis* (London: Routledge, 1994), pp. 87–92.

ical influence in the village, and therefore, from the *dalit* perspective, the Hindu–Catholic synthesis appeared 'as simply a Christian form of high-caste Hindu hegemony'.[65] Mosse's work illustrates the dilemma of the Catholic Church in India: in their attempt to 'inculturate' the gospel in Hindu society, they had tolerated the caste system, but the resulting Christian community had a membership that was overwhelmingly low caste or tribal, who strongly objected to caste discrimination, and moreover resented the approach of inculturation because it drew on high-caste or Brahmanical traditions. Moves to eliminate caste from Catholic ritual alienated caste-Hindus and raised communal boundaries; at the same time, interfaith dialogue initiatives were viewed with suspicion by dalit groups.

The Hindu response to the Christian ashram movement was initially either to ignore it or to tolerate it, but in the mid-1980s Hindus started to raise objections and this led to vigorous debates between Griffiths and three Hindus: Swami Devananda, Ram Swarup and Sita Ram Goel.[66] For example, Sita Ram Goel, a Hindu writer and publisher, in his analysis of the above debate and his examination of Christian inculturation, alleged that Catholic ashrams were yet another 'assault' on Hinduism, and that the attempt to exclude any religious dimension from Hindu culture was a 'deliberate and calculated design' to implant the Christian meaning of Christ into Hindu culture. He pointed out that in the planting process, what happens to the Hindu religion is not the missionary's concern.[67] He insisted that Hindu culture grew out of Hindu religion and thus any attempt at separating religion and culture is damaging to both. He also questioned whether any Hindu practices, so deeply rooted in Hindu theological concepts, could be adopted by Christianity without hypocrisy. He claimed that Christian use of Sanskrit terminology 'implies a close relationship of Hindu theology to Catholic theology, a relationship which does not really exist'. Further he found '[s]uch missionaries speak authoritatively on Hindu scriptures and argue that their [Christian] teachings are consonant with everything Hindu, but add a finishing touch, a "fullness", to the traditional faith ...'. In short, he alleged that Catholic aspirations to share spiritual experience and bring about unity among the religions through Christian ashrams were only 'unethical conversion strategies'.[68]

The above criticism makes it clear that the Hindu–Catholic approach, as an effort to solve the problem of conversion, faced serious objections

---

65 Mosse, 'The Politics of Religious Synthesis, pp. 92–5, 100–1.

66 See Sita Ram Goel, *Catholic Ashrams: Sannyasins or Swindlers?*, 2nd edn (New Delhi: Voice of India, 1994).

67 Goel, *Catholic Ashrams*, pp. 3–13.

68 Goel, *Catholic Ashrams*, pp. 87–90.

from Hindus. The main objection made by Hindus in the debate was to the Christian insistence that Hinduism is primarily a cultural and social concept and not a 'religion'. The radical separation between spiritual and socio-cultural elements and the attempt to create a religious synthesis was unrealistic in the context of the caste system, Hindu worship of many deities, and Hindu monism, as Staffner himself admitted. These aspects of Hinduism clearly contradict Christian principles, and moreover, they are not only socio-cultural phenomena but are embodied in Hindu beliefs.[69]

Though Staffner, Griffiths and others were motivated by their genuine appreciation of Hinduism, they necessarily selected the common 'meeting-points' between the two different religious systems and, in the process, they split the religious system of Hinduism into the concepts of *sadhana dharma* and *samaj dharma*. As we have seen, this Hindu–Catholic synthesis has been criticized at various points: on the one hand, by dalit Christians, who saw its exclusive association with Brahmanic Hinduism as rendering it unable to demonstrate the liberative nature of the Christian gospel; and on the other hand, by Hindu nationalists who reacted strongly, claiming that synthetic approaches are a subtle way to convert Hindus and undermine Hindu religions by appropriating their sacred symbols and religious practices. Furthermore, they refused to accept 'outside' interpretations of their religions and insisted that Hinduism, without the help of Christianity, does provide salvation for the people of India. Neither radical discontinuity in conversion from one religion to another nor radical continuity between religions was satisfying. The imposed discontinuity of Christian campaigns of conversion and the imposed continuity of *Hindutva* are attempts to obliterate a tension that must necessarily exist between the two. The Hindu–Catholic approach can be developed beyond creating a meeting-point. The extent of 'enreligionization' of different individuals, communities and religions varies, and both continuity and discontinuity co-exist in the experience of another religion. At the meeting-point of faiths, conversion may be experienced both as a change of religion and as a transformation within a religious tradition.

The liberation model: conversion as a search for liberation from caste oppression

Despite the efforts to reach the elite, in the late nineteenth and early twentieth centuries, all the churches in India grew rapidly by 'mass

---

69 See Staffner, *Jesus Christ*, pp. 230–3.

conversions' of communities of outcaste and tribal groups, and these make up the overwhelming majority of Indian Christians today (70–80 per cent of Indian Christians). Many of these poor Christians, formally known as 'untouchables' but who now choose to designate themselves 'dalit' (which means broken, crushed or torn), used conversion as a protest against Hindu caste practices, and also as a means of improving their socio-economic status. In keeping with the socialist model of national development, Protestant lay theologian M. M. Thomas, Jesuit activist and theologian Samuel Rayan and others developed theologies of revolution and humanization. Rayan was one of the first to welcome the Latin American liberation theology and the Christian option for the poor and oppressed. While acknowledging a debt to Marxist analysis, Indian liberation theologians soon recognized its limitations in dealing with the caste system. They also challenged the historical and rational framework of Latin American liberation theology and led the way among Third World theologians in developing a spirituality of liberation which draws on indigenous cultural traditions and experience.[70] There are now a number of paths of liberation theology in India. Not only does each provide different resources, it also offers a different method, enabling Indian theology to break out of the rigidity of the western academic method and embrace new creative forms.[71]

Although caste distinctions are being broken down by urbanization, a market-oriented society and positive discrimination by government, especially in rural areas dalit communities still face harassment, exclusion from water supplies and exploitation by the higher castes.[72] But caste practices are by no means eradicated in the churches. Despite the reputation of Jesus Christ for eating with outcastes and sinners, in all the churches – Orthodox, Catholic and Protestant – there are many instances of outcastes not being invited to share the same loaf or communion cup.[73] Christian dalits suffer doubly, being discriminated

70 Samuel Rayan, 'Theological priorities in India today', in Virginia Fabella and Sergio Torres (eds), *Irruption of the Third World – Challenge to Theology. Papers from the Fifth International Conference of the Ecumenical Association of Third World Theologians* (Maryknoll, NY: Orbis Books, 1983), pp. 30–41; Michael Amaladoss, 'Ashrams and Social Justice', in D. S. Amalorpavadass (ed.), *The Indian Church in the Struggle for a New Society* (Bangalore: NBCLC, 1981), pp. 370–8.

71 Felix Wilfred, 'Towards a Better Understanding of Asian Theology: Some Basic Issues', *Vidyajyoti* 62/12 (1998), pp. 890–915; Israel Selvanayagam (ed.), *Moving Forms of Theology: Faith Talk's Changing Contexts* (Delhi: ISPCK, 2002).

72 For examples, see J. Aruldoss, 'Dalits and Salvation', in Andrew Wingate, Kevin Ward, Carrie Pemberton and Wilson Sitshebo (eds), *Anglicanism: A Global Communion* (London: Mowbray, 1998), pp. 294–300.

73 Rowena Robinson, *Christians of India* (New Delhi: Sage, 2003), pp. 70–92; Duncan B. Forrester, *Caste and Christianity: Attitudes and Policies on Caste of Anglo-Saxon Protestant Missions in India* (London: Curzon, 1980).

against in the Church and also socially, in that they do not qualify for government benefits intended to counter discrimination on the grounds that Christianity does not (officially) acknowledge caste.[74] Thus the dalit Christian struggle is both with Hindu society and with the Christian community.

The liberation model of theology in India emerged from a critical analysis of development projects, in which many Catholics workers were involved, and a consciousness of the oppression of dalits and tribals. It was influenced by other contemporary liberation theologies, particularly from the Americas, and majored on issues of human dignity and identity as well as economic concerns.[75] The emergence of liberation theology in Latin America had led to a major reinterpretation of conversion in the Catholic Church. The document produced by the Latin American Bishops' meeting at Medellín, Colombia in 1968, regarded as foundational to liberation theology, stated that the Church should follow the example of Christ who demonstrated the 'preference to the poor' and called for a 'sincere conversion in people's outlook, from individualistic self-concern to a concern for the common welfare' of others. Furthermore, the bishops affirmed 'the value and legitimate autonomy of temporal tasks', which means what was regarded as outside the scope of 'spiritual salvation' was no longer treated as secondary or inferior.[76] Thus the focus of conversion to God became 'conversion to the neighbour' as a vital part of any 'spirituality of liberation'.[77] For liberation theologians, redemption relates to liberation in the context of present historical reality but the exact relationship between the two is unclear,[78] and in practice liberation theology tends to treat social liberation as a visible manifestation of redemption.

The liberation understanding of conversion appeared to be an answer for the problem of the mass conversion of the depressed classes in India in that the motivation for their conversion was put down to their search for social justice or a social protest against caste-dominated

---

74 John Parratt, 'Recent Writing on Dalit Theology: A Bibliographical Essay', *IRM*, 83/329 (1994), pp. 329–37.

75 See Sathianathan Clarke, *Dalits and Christianity: Subaltern Religion and Liberation Theology in India* (New Delhi: Oxford University Press, 1999); S. M. Michael (ed.), *Dalits in Modern India: Vision and Values* (New Delhi: Vistaar Publications, 1999); Samuel Jayakumar, *Dalit Consciousness and Christian Conversion: Historical Resources for a Contemporary Debate* (Delhi: ISPCK, 1999); Gispert-Sauch, 'Asian Theology', pp. 460–1.

76 'Medellín Document on Poverty' (9, 17, 18), in Maryknoll Documentation, *Between Honesty and Hope* (Maryknoll, NY: Maryknoll Documentation Series, 1970), pp. 211–16.

77 Gustavo Gutiérrez, *A Theology of Liberation: History, Politics and Salvation*, rev. edn (London: SCM Press, 1973), pp. 116–20.

78 Rebecca Chopp, 'Latin American Liberation Theology', in Ford (ed.), *The Modern Theologians*, pp. 409–25.

Hindu society. In this view, the conversion of dalits was due neither to the proselytizing activities of 'outsiders', nor to the depressed classes being swayed by 'ulterior motives', but rather to their own search for a liberation that involved social equality. Because their conversion was a move towards liberation from caste-bondage, the Church, which proclaims liberation, must not only accept this movement, but the Church itself must also 'convert' towards these people who are in need of solidarity. This idea of accepting the motives of converts as the legitimate ones in Christian conversion was not new, but the liberation view on conversion tended to see conversion as entirely due to social problems of Indian society and set aside any religious convictions of converts.

In 1981, the conversions that took place in several villages in South Tamil Nadu brought about unprecedented public controversy.[79] The first mass conversion took place in Meenakshipuram on 19 February when about 200 families of the Pallan community converted to Islam.[80] This developed into a nationwide religious and political scandal as the further conversion of 27 families took place in the same village on 23 May and the movement spread to other villages in Tamil Nadu. This led to Christian reflection on what were the reasons for the Hindu conversion to Islam (instead of Christianity) and, even more seriously, why there were considerable numbers of Christian converts to Islam in the same movement. Like the Muslim writers,[81] Christians saw the reason as the social injustice of the Hindu caste system. The conversions were not only 'an act of revolt against society' but also 'against religious practices legitimized by religion'.[82] They saw a 'protest movement aimed at disowning the existing inequality structures in society', and, believing that conversion was an option for the repudiation of caste, found that in this case it had caused a 'repudiation of religion'.[83] Andrew Wingate, in his studies of the Christian conversions to Islam, found 'no evidence of anyone who claims to have had any experience we can liken to a so-called "conversion experience" as in Christianity'; but he

---

79 The news of dalit conversion in Meenakshipuram was broken as early as 21 March 1981 on the front page of the *Times of India*.

80 Also called Pallar.

81 See Mumtaz Ali Khan, 'A Brief Summary of the Study on "Mass Conversions of Meenakshipuram: A Sociological Enquiry"', *Religion and Society* XXVIII/4 (4 Dec. 1981), pp. 37–50. See also Mohammed A. Kalam, 'Why the Harijan Convert to Islam Views Reservations with Reservation', *South Asia Research* 4/2 (Nov. 1984), pp. 153–67; Imtiaz Ahmad, 'The Tamilnadu Conversions, Conversion Threats and the Anti-Reservation Campaign: Some Hypotheses', in Asghar Engineer (ed.), *Communal Riots in Post-Independence India* (Hyderabad: Sangam Books, 1984), pp. 118–29.

82 P. A. Augustine, 'Conversion as Social Protest', *Religion and Society* XXVIII/4 (Dec. 1981), p. 51.

83 S. Albones Raj, 'Mass Religious Conversion as Protest Movement: A Framework', *Religion and Society* XXVIII/4 (Dec. 1981), pp. 59 and 64.

maintained that Islam's emphasis on the oneness of God appealed to the people, though faith was not the guiding factor but only followed thereafter.[84] George Mathew, in his comprehensive analysis of the issue, described the motives for conversion as: the economic independence of the group; critical awareness through education; the inadequacy of the political process of Sanskritization; and the presence of an 'alternative' that offers 'brotherhood and sense of equality'.[85] The question of why the dalits preferred Islam to Christianity was answered by many by pointing to the caste discrimination within the Christian community. S. Albones Raj, for instance, observed that '[t]he Harijan Christian, so to speak, is disillusioned not only because Christianity has failed to make him socially mobile but also because the injustice perpetrated on him by his Hindu brethren is being repeated by his fellow Christians.'[86]

The *Indian Missiological Review* (*IMR*), a Catholic journal, treated the issue of conversion in 1983 and in 1984, when the most significant articles were those by Felix Wilfred and Walter Fernandes. Wilfred, a leading liberation theologian, insisted that the Church should reinterpret the meaning of conversion in the context of the socio-economic situation of India. For him, conversion is not 'a turning of our minds to some salvific events of the past and subscribing to some ideological system connected with it', nor 'a question of the Church trying to win more members to her fold from other religious groups to assure them a place in heaven', but a 'response of commitment to the voice of God speaking through the yearnings and aspirations of the millions of our countrymen, through their misery and want'.[87] He concluded that the Church in India should

> convert herself to the poor rather than aiming to convert the poor to her fold. Conversion of the Church to the poor is the concrete sign today of her fidelity to the Gospel ... To the degree of her conversion to God's poor, she proportionately becomes an *environment* for conversion to God's Kingdom which is different from being just an institution or agent.[88]

---

84 Andrew Wingate, 'A Study of Conversion from Christianity to Islam in Two Tamil Villages', *Religion and Society* XXVIII/4 (Dec. 1981), pp. 32–4. See also his book, *The Church and Conversion: A Study of Recent Conversions to and from Christianity in the Tamil Area of South India* (New Delhi: ISPCK, 1997), pp. 164–5, 175–9.

85 George Mathew, 'Politicisation of Religion: Conversions to Islam in Tamil Nadu', *Economic and Political Weekly* (19 and 26 June 1982), pp. 1032–3, 1068–9.

86 Raj, 'Mass Religious Conversion', p. 65.

87 Felix Wilfred, 'Understanding Conversion in India Today', *IMR* 5/1 (Jan. 1983), pp. 61–73.

88 Wilfred, 'Understanding Conversion', p. 69.

In the same vein, Fernandes, a Catholic sociologist, argued that conversion in India has to be understood as a caste struggle of the dalits against their inhuman treatment and that, although conversion involves both spiritual experience and social change, the latter has primary importance for their motive.[89] Therefore he discarded some Christians' insistence on its being spiritual and the Hindu accusation of its being material, insisting that conversion in India was a 'social movement' in the process of 'awakening [dalits] to the reality of their oppression' in the social context of 'caste mobility'.[90] He criticized the Catholic missionary view for giving positive value to the caste system in order to bring about conversion and, in so doing, allowing the unjust system of caste in the Church. Since salvation had to be 'real' to dalits in their sub-human condition, in his view, conversion was a by-product of the movement among dalits for their uplift that took a 'religious form'. He saw it as the Church's duty to be part of a movement to liberate people who are oppressed and believed this was the true meaning of conversion in India.

For both Wilfred and Fernandes, conversion was regarded as a means to achieve the social end of socio-economic justice for the dalits and the poor in Indian society. The realization by Christians that the injustices of the caste system were also practised by Christians encouraged both Wilfred and Fernandes to call for the Church to 'convert' to the world, to their neighbours, to the dalits themselves, to identify with them and bear their burdens. They criticized the Church's preoccupation with salvation as redemption through a spiritual experience of conversion that was confirmed by baptism, and saw liberation through breaking any form of oppression as the vital part of God's salvation.

The shift in the definition of conversion in the Indian context to mean a protest against social injustice or the Church's turning to the world to be part of the people's struggle was evident in the writings of these and other Catholic theologians. Perhaps George Mathew best summed up the new Catholic understanding of conversion as the 'politicisation of religion', understood in the sense of 'using religion as an instrument for changing the power balance', describing conversion in India as 'part of the proliferation of an ideology that questions the *status quo*' and as a 'structural question'.[91]

---

89 Walter Fernandes, 'Conversion, the Caste Factor and Dominant Reaction', *IMR* 6/4 (Oct. 1984), pp. 289–306.

90 In his earlier writing, he argued that caste mobility had already begun before the Christian missionaries started work among dalits – 'Caste and Conversion Movements in India', *Social Action* 31 (July–Sept. 1981), pp. 261–90.

91 Mathew, 'Politicisation of Religion', pp. 1071–2.

However, this reduction of conversion to a 'structural question' fails to reflect the complex nature of Indian society and the fact that dalits, like other human beings, have mixed motives that may have to do with more than just the socio-economic problems of their present life. In emphasizing the liberation motive so strongly, conversion almost loses any spiritual meaning to people under oppression. In other words, any religion or ideology, which is willing to be part of the dalit struggle, regardless of its 'spiritual dimension', could be chosen. As we have seen, it is striking that neither Muslim nor Christian commentators found that the conversions in South Tamil Nadu had any religious motives behind them, only sociological ones. It is entirely possible that this interpretation may not reflect the full picture of what was going on in the hearts and minds of the dalits, and that this may have been due to the particular methodological framework used by scholars to deal with social issues, or to the desire to play down religious differences for political reasons. Deryck Schreuder and Geoffrey Oddie have shown that studies of conversion in India during the 1970s and 1980s tended to focus on socio-economic factors rather than 'religious ideas and conviction'. This was because the methodological difficulties of discussing motives meant that scholars could do little more than 'leave room for some spiritual factors and religious beliefs in the conversion process'.[92] Socio-economic theories of conversion, by definition, can give only limited recognition to the religious awareness of the converts and the religious appeal of the missionary message. Moreover, in a political context of increasing opposition from Hindus, conversion appeared as disrespectful of Hindu religion so Christians were under pressure to find a different justification for it. The argument that it was the common struggle against the social injustices of Indian society avoided the religious issue since caste could be argued to be a social not a religious problem.

Dhirendra Vajpeyi's study of Muslim fundamentalism in India shows how social and religious motives went hand in hand in the conversion movement. Towards the end of the 1970s, increasing numbers of Muslim Indians found employment in Arab countries. Vajpeyi observes that the experience brought them closer and '[w]hen they returned to India they not only brought money ... they also came back with a new awareness and assertive spirit, the spirit of *din e-ilahi* [the religion of light]'.[93]

92 Deryck Schreuder and Geoffrey Oddie, 'What is "Conversion"? History, Christianity and Religious Change in Colonial Africa and South Asia', *The Journal of Religious History* 15/4 (Dec. 1989), pp. 512–13.

93 Dhirendra Vajpeyi, 'Muslim Fundamentalism in India: A Crisis of Identity in a Secular State', in Dhirendra Vajpeyi and Yogendra K. Malik (eds), *Religious and Ethnic Minority Politics in South Asia* (New Delhi: Manohar, 1989), pp. 66–7.

This new consciousness of their religious heritage and confidence in the Islamic faith undoubtedly led to a new zeal to spread their religion. Imtiaz Ahmad pointed to the influence of this new enthusiasm on the rise of the Islamic missionary movement in the 1970s in South Tamil Nadu.[94] It would be an oversimplification to say that these Islamic missionary groups were presenting only the egalitarian principles of the Muslim community and not Islam as a religion, and it is evident that the converts to Islam had at least been exposed to – and plausibly also embraced – *both* Islam as social organization *and* Islam as a faith.

The sociological interpretation of the conversion of dalits is problematic for Christians in two respects. First, it provides room for Hindu accusations that conversion of dalits is political rather than religious. Hindus can argue that conversion, especially mass conversion, lacks spiritual motives; it is merely a means to escape injustice or a social protest. Hindu resentment is not that dalits and *adivasis* are protesting against socio-economic injustice, nor do they deny the existence of social problems within the Hindu community, but they object to the fact that the converts choose to abandon Hinduism. Moreover, Christianity (or Islam) has been shown not to be free of caste and class inequality either, so this confirms their view that conversion is being used as a tool to increase Christian political power. That this is the case is confirmed when they find that 'spiritual' motives are lacking in Christian interpretations of conversion and that a this-worldly approach is supported by Christian theology. Second, and more seriously still, the result is that in their sociological interpretations, Christians and Muslims, just like caste Hindus, give the impression that dalits are motivated only by desire for their own material betterment or social uplift. The obvious inference is that dalits lack their own spirituality. Hence conversion itself is seen negatively as opportunism and not as the outcome of an active and considered search by a community for an answer to a spiritual quest. When theologians themselves argue that dalit conversion must be understood sociologically, dalits are in danger of being deprived again, this time of a fully rounded conversion, which has both sociological and spiritual, both temporal and eschatological dimensions.

Conclusion

The four theological models of the Indian attempt to solve the problem of conversion have made significant contributions towards the answer to the question in India. Although the terms and concepts of theologic-

---

94 See Ahmad, 'The Tamilnadu Conversions', pp. 121–2.

al interpretation may be specific to India, they could also be applied to other contexts as well. The issue of conversion is not unique to India, nor are the theological premises of the authentic, secular, inculturation and liberation models. But in order that these theologies may engage wider contexts, they need to be examined and sharpened in their own context first so there can be a hermeneutical circle of reflection and evaluation of these models and openness to the possibilities of new models of church that are applicable to our own situations.

The key issue here is the place of a religious minority community in the wider society, which is a question that is not just limited to the Indian situation. The ashram and inculturation models concern the shared identity of Christians with Hindus and the search for common meeting places and ways in which the different communities can share their common heritage together while maintaining their own identities. Although both parties are asked to make room for others, these two models give precedence to the cultural and religious outlook of the wider community. The 'secular fellowship' model seeks to create a different platform where various communities share together in a secular fellowship, which is intended to be truly religious but not locked into communal interests. This model seems to share the idea of 'public philosophy' presented by John Courtney Murray (in Chapter 1). The liberation model is of radical separation from the tradition, which regards conversion as a part of dealing with the structural question of an oppressive system and a way to solve the caste struggle. The Indian models are especially relevant in considering the nature of the Church as an inclusive or exclusive community in different societies today, or indeed the way any minority community (religious, ethnic or socio-economic) relates to other communities, as well as to the wider society and the state. This involves dealing with different and even sometimes conflicting values, traditions and world-views in order to establish a fair, open and inclusive public sphere.

5

Socio-Political Reconciliation: Struggles against Injustice and Division in Korea

Instead, we should take *han* as our theme, which is indeed the language of the *minjung* and signifies the reality of their experience. If one does not hear the signs of the *han* of the *minjung*, one cannot hear the voice of Christ knocking on our doors.[1]

Nobody expected that the South Korean team, which was ranked fortieth by FIFA, would get to the semi-final of the World Cup in 2002. It was estimated that 6.5 million South Koreans were on the street supporting the team all over the country. Since the fans were dressed in red, the *Observer* described the plaza in front of Seoul City Hall as the 'New Red Square' and said, after the defeat by Germany, 'the Korean dream ends but the party goes on'.[2] It was indeed a great festival for South Koreans, not only because they were World Cup co-hosts but also because their team did exceptionally well and reached the semi-finals. In quite a remarkable coincidence, the day the South Korean team played against Germany was 25 June, which all Koreans remember as 'yuk-i-oh', or six-two-five. This was the date of the first North Korean attack on South Korea in 1950, which led to the terrible war between the two that lasted for three years. The war claimed 4 million deaths, the majority of them were civilians, and both countries were virtually wiped out. Most of the older generation in Korea remember those days of despair and poverty, and many older people in other countries identify Korea with pictures of terrible cold weather and women and children crying over so many dead bodies. Perhaps the excitement of competing with the world superpowers of the football game was a kind of 'Han-pu-ri' – the shamanistic ceremony to get rid of deep despair, anger and sadness – for Koreans to exorcize those memories of war and suffering. As one

---

1 Suh Nam-Dong, 'Toward a Theology of Han', in Kim Yong Bock (ed.), *Minjung Theology: People as the Subjects of History* (Maryknoll, NY: Orbis Books, 1983), pp. 51–65.

2 *Observer*, 26 June 2002.

commentator said, it was almost a fairy tale – but for many Koreans it was a reality for which they had longed over many years.

After the Korean War in 1953, South Korea went through political turmoil with corruption and dictatorship. Eventually the military took over the government and through a series of coups d'états a military-backed government continued in power until 1988. High on successive government agendas was overcoming poverty. This legitimized their rule and their oppression of the opposition party and disregard for the civil liberties of the people. The catchphrase in those days was 'let's become wealthy (*jal-sal-a-bo-se*)!' But in the process of the remarkable economic growth, there was political injustice and exploitation of the workers and the farmers. The churches in South Korea grew, along with the modernization of the Korean society and rapid growth of the economy. The revival movement of seeking eschatological hope and church growth dominated the Korean church in the second half of the last century and, as a result, the Church rapidly grew numerically, forming a largely conservative evangelical constituency. However, the churches in post-war South Korea were facing the same problem of poverty and later economic and political injustice. The Korean church in this situation took two different directions, the *Kibock Sinang*, or 'faith of seeking blessings', on the one hand, and Minjung theology, on the other hand. I see both of these as contextual attempts to bring reconciliation in a situation of tremendous alienation by poverty and inequality in society. Reconciliation was also a key theme for Korean theology in view of the continuing division of the two Koreas. In this chapter we will examine the distinctive approaches of Korean theologians who developed theologies of blessing, minjung and unification.

The problem of poverty and *kibock sinang*

Kibock sinang, or 'faith of seeking blessings', in modern Korean Christianity has roots in Shamanism, the traditional religiosity of the Korean people, and is also closely related to revival movements that started in 1907 in the present-day North Korea. Revival has been described as a characteristic of Korean churches, and a Korean scholar even says, 'If anyone wants to understand the Korean church he has to understand its revivals.'[3] This series of revivals has led to several dynamics in the practices of the Korean church in which Korean Christians experience an outpouring of the Holy Spirit, genuine repentance and forgiveness,

---

3 The most prominent revival took place in 1907 in Pyeungyang, now the capital of North Korea. The great revival, known as the Korean Pentecost, broke out during the Annual Ten-day Bible Study Conference.

and this gives them tremendous confidence to preach the gospel and keep the faith in times of difficulty. The earlier revival meetings were to do with seeking blessings, particularly 'spiritual' blessings such as forgiveness of sins and eternal salvation. Studies suggested that during the time of the Japanese threat to the Korean peninsula, many of the western missionaries tried to direct the Korean Christians' attention to these 'spiritual matters' rather than to a political struggle that they foresaw would inevitably end in Japan's favour.[4] The message of the preachers and expectations of congregations were more towards something beyond this world, towards future expectation.

However, in the context of post-war Korea, as Min Kyeung Bae describes, people were desperately looking for a way to meet their material needs that was both eschatological and experiential; they were seeking the eternal kingdom in the reality of the present situation.[5] There was a rapid increase in revival meetings and the messages preached were to meet people's need of material blessing and healing. *Kibock sinang* became the dominant aspect of Korean Christianity as these meetings became popular and various religious groups took root soon after the war. There were also a growing number of 'prayer mountains', where people stayed for prayer and fasting and where there were often reports of miracles and healing. People wandered from mountain to mountain following well-known miracle-workers or revival preachers. It was indeed a time of great turmoil and testing for Korean Christianity. People were confused, and yet they wanted to see God's blessings here and now rather than rely on a future hope. It was not that they were not interested in matters of belief, ethics and ultimate destiny, but as they had recently faced the challenge of life and death in a real sense, their faith had to be met by the immediate result of healing and miracles and above all by liberation from desperate poverty.

Kibock sinang, or seeking blessings, is not new to the Korean church, nor is it unique to Korean religiosity as it is a common phenomenon of people who profess any form of religion known as *do ut des*: I will do this in the expectation of receiving something from the deity. What is interesting in the particular context of the post-war Korean church was that there was a shift in thinking from the early revival phenomenon of emphasizing 'spiritual blessings' in the eschatological dimensions to include the material manifestation of those blessings. This was in line with the government campaigns for economic growth at all costs and the rise of the *jaebul*, Korean family-run mega-companies. In the midst

---

4 See Min Kyeung Bae, *Korean Christianity and Reunification Movement* (Seoul: Korean Institute of Church History, 2001), pp. 59–114.

5 Min Kyeung Bae, *History of Christian Church in Korea* (Seoul: Christian Literature Society of Korea, 1982), pp. 470–1.

of it all, the Korean church experienced rapid growth in numbers and produced mega-churches. So in the 1960s and 1970s, Korea experienced tremendous growth in both business and church congregations, and the poor felt the changes taking place. They also witnessed changes in their own lives or those of other Christians, who testified to God's blessing that had brought them out of poverty. In other words, Christians had not only set the material manifestation of spiritual blessings as an achievable goal of Christian life, but also actually experienced it in their lives and the life of the whole nation as the economy rapidly grew.

The man who epitomizes this approach is Paul (David) Yonggi Cho of the Full Gospel Church in Seoul. The story of the church is one of remarkable transformation of a church that started as a tent church in 1958. The official history of the Full Gospel Church explains the situation:

> In the 1950s however, especially toward the close of the decade, Korea's situation, both economically and politically, was not rosy by any means. It was not long after the Korean War and there were many suffering poverty and chaos from the war's aftermath. Pastor Cho Yonggi was no exception. It was not uncommon for Pastor Cho Yonggi to satisfy his hunger with nothing other than three meals of porridge given him by an American evangelist. He also battled poverty along with the members of his congregation. In such desperate times, Pastor Cho Yonggi called out to God for messages appropriate for such harsh reality.[6]

It was this harsh reality that brought Pastor Cho to seek the meaning of the gospel and come up with his famous threefold blessing.[7] The

---

6 The official website of the Yoido Full Gospel Church is http://english.fgtv.com.

7 The threefold blessing, the blessing of the Spirit, the soul and the body, has been the dominant theme for the message of Pastor Cho, particularly in his emphasis on 'our general well-being'. He uses 'positive thinking' terminology such as 'change your thought patterns'. He utilizes the law of blessing (the law of tithes; the law of sowing and reaping; the law of reverberation) and regards fulfilling these laws as a prerequisite for receiving blessing from God. This threefold blessing is based on the idea that God is a good God who is ever ready to bless those who are coming to him with expectation. See the section on 'Full Gospel Theology', at http://english.fgtv.com. See also Yonggi Cho, *Threefold Blessing* (Seoul: Yongsan Publications, 1977); *The Fourth Dimension* (Seoul: Seoul Word Publications, 1996). For more detailed studies on the theology of Cho and of the Yoido Full Gospel Church, see Wonsuk Ma, William W. Menzies and Hyeon-sung Bae (eds), *David Yonggi Cho: A Close Look at his Theology and Ministry* (Goonpo, Korea: Hansei University Press, 2004); Hong Young-gi, Myung Sung-Hoon (eds), *Charis and Charisma: David Yonggi Cho and the Growth of Yoido Full Gospel Church* (Bletchley: Regnum Books, 2003). See also the papers presented at the 2002 Young San International Theological Symposium (26–27 Sept. 2002).

testimonies of the people who have experienced these blessings are numerous. The following is from a BBC television interview:

> [Che Su Hwan] was taken ill. He knew his sickness was not only of the body; he was on the edge of total collapse. When he was over the worst of the physical malady, he was taken by a friend to hear Dr Paul Yonggi Cho, of the Full Gospel Church in Seoul ... At one of Dr Cho's services, he had an intense emotional experience, accompanied by uncontrollable tears and a sense of being caught between modes of living.
>
> ... Dr Cho's promise of blessings had been delivered. 'Astonishing, astonishing,' murmurs Su Hwan, 'We are blessed in the Spirit and everything else is added unto us.'[8]

Though the threefold blessing is what Pastor Cho preached, the idea of holistic blessing is not limited to the Full Gospel Church, indeed it is across whole sections of the Korean churches. As revival is character- istic of the Korean church regardless of denomination, so the message of the expected blessings for those who seek is common to most of the mainline Korean churches. Good news to the poor in the Korean context in the 1950s and 1960s was seen as this gospel of threefold blessing, and it seemed the message prevailed. Is it a genuine incultura- tion of the gospel to deal with the problem of the poor in the Korean context? Pastor Cho and others certainly have succeeded in exploring the Korean traditional religiosity of seeking blessings and expanded the meaning of blessing in the context of poverty. But the approach is not without problems.

There has been considerable opposition to this *kibock sinang* approach from both moderate and conservative sections of the Korean church. In fact, most of the articles written on *kibock sinang* in Christian aca- demic or popular journals condemn this approach.[9] They have various reasons. First, they see it as unbiblical and influenced by shamanism,

---

8 Charles Elliott, *Sword and Spirit: Christianity in a Divided World* (London: BBC Books), pp. 20–1.

9 See Kim Byeung-Seo, 'Well Established Kibock Sinang', *Sinang Saekae* (Apr. 1989), pp. 34–9; Kim Eun-Hong, 'Overcoming Family Based Kibock Sinang', *Kidockyo Sasang* (Mar. 2000), pp. 138–42; Kang Chun-Mo, 'Korean Church under Kibock Sinang', *Pulbit Mockhea* (Sept. 1996), pp. 15–31; Kang Seung-Jae, 'Critique on Kibock Sinang', *Pulbit Mockhea* (Mar. 1990), pp. 82–98; Lee Moon-Jang, 'What about Kibock Sinang of the Koreans?', *Mockhea ywa Sinhack* (Dec. 1999), pp. 52–9; Kim Jin-Hong, 'The Shadow of Kibock Sinang in the Church', ibid., pp. 60–6; Min Jong-Ki, 'Let Us Remove Kibock Sinang from the Church', ibid., pp. 67–73; Kim Young Jae, 'The Relationship between Kibock Sinang of the Korean Church and the Church Growth', ibid., pp. 74–8; Song Jae- Keun, 'The Danger of Kibock Sinang from the Perspective of Covenant Theology', ibid., pp. 79–91; Jung Hoon-Taek, 'The "Blessed" in the New Testament', ibid., pp. 92–104.

which they regard as this-worldly, unethical, anti-historical and temporal. Second, they object to *kibock sinang*'s belief that poverty is a curse and the result of wrong actions and attitudes towards God. Third, they interpret *kibock sinang* worship, offerings to God and good deeds as performed in expectation of receiving from God something in return. Fourth, they blame it for contributing to the lack of social participation of the Korean church and sharing its resources with others. It was described as a 'corrupted faith' and 'making Christianity a lower religion'. In addition, some claimed that biblical blessings are not meant to be material and that the gospel of Jesus is a gospel of suffering not blessing. Believing in Jesus, they claim, is for eternal salvation, and the gospel is the gospel of the kingdom of heaven, of righteousness and forgiveness.

The critics focus on the negative outcome of excessive seeking of blessings, particularly what we see in the revival meetings and services. They criticize the revival preachers for their unethical approaches towards material blessings and healing.[10] It is not uncommon to see revival meetings dominated by stories and testimonies of those who received blessing of wealth, healing and success. There is an excessive drive to increase church membership and construct new church buildings or church prayer halls in the mountains, often by borrowing money from the bank in 'faith' that God will fulfil his promise. The critics are right in that the extravagant demonstration of material blessings in church buildings and membership has become a disease in the Korean church. This preoccupation with self-interest and allegations of corruption have tarnished *kibock sinang*'s attraction to the growing middle classes.

However, these critics have their own biased perspectives. First, the critics focus on the fact that *kibock sinang* is somehow related to Korean religiosity, Shamanism, and they uncritically condemn Shamanism as unethical, selfish, materialistic, this-worldly, temporal and non-historical. The fact that Korean Christianity has been influenced by a shamanistic understanding of traditional Korean religiosity is not

---

10 The typical biblical verses are: Deuteronomy 28.1–2, 'if you obey faithfully the voice of the LORD your God, being careful to do all his commandments that I command you today, the LORD your God will set you high above all the nations of the earth. And all these blessings shall come upon you and overtake you …'; Malachi 3.10–12, 'Bring the full tithes into the storehouse, that there may be food in my house. And thereby put me to the test, says the LORD of hosts, if I will not open the windows of heaven for you and pour down for you a blessing'; Luke 6.38, 'give, and it will be given to you. Good measure, pressed down, shaken together, running over, will be put into your lap. For with the measure you use it will be measured back to you until there is no more need'; 3 John 1.2, 'Dear friend, I pray that you may enjoy good health and that all may go well with you, even as your soul is getting along well' (ESV/NIV)

necessarily a negative point. The religious tradition of Korean people, including Shamanism, cannot just be dismissed as unworthy. This interpretation is rather the result of a traditional Christian understanding of the religiosity of the people as something inferior, unacceptable or even evil, and anything to do with it is labelled as syncretism. According to Yoo Dong-Sik, Korean tradition combines *han* (oneness), *sam* (life) and *myuet* (beauty), and Korean theology has developed in these three directions: conservative fundamentalist theology, progressive social involvement theology and culturally liberal theology respectively.[11] However, I would like to add one more dimension to this: *kum* (dream or hope) is vital to Korean religiosity in that somehow, in the midst of despair and poverty, people look for hope either in this world or the next. While conservative theology may meet the need for spiritual fulfilment and eschatological hope, *kibock sinang* has harnessed the people's desire for *kum* in the present context. In Korean religiosity, the desire for something better, both spiritual and material, is expressed as seeking blessings. It is the humble desire of those who have not experienced fullness of life and who are constantly facing despair and poverty.

Second, it seems the critics are emphasizing the other-worldly aspect of the Christian gospel and also following the example of the suffering of Christ and the cross. It may be relevant to those who have already received material blessing to preach on suffering, the cross, inner spirituality and future hope, but the poor have already experienced suffering, they have already carried the cross. What they need is the message of deliverance and liberation from poverty and the promise of God's blessing, in the here and now. Besides, both in the Old Testament and in Jesus' teaching, blessing is not limited to the other-worldly nor is 'spiritual' blessing superior to 'material' blessing – they are part and parcel of the whole blessing from God, often expressed as 'shalom', the peace and well-being of God's people. This tendency to make blessing in the next world more desirable than in this world has been consistent in Christian tradition and also in the Confucian understanding of life, but *kibock sinang* challenges this. It cannot be said that the poor are cursed because they are not in a right relationship with God, but neither can it be said that seeking material blessings from God is improper or less 'spiritual' than seeking this-worldly blessings. The poor are blessed when they are fed and provided for, as in the example of Jesus' ministry. In the context of post-war Korea, many of the Korean church leaders responded to the problem of the poor by tapping into the traditional religiosity and also interpreting the gospel as seeking holistic blessing.

---

11 Yoo Dong-Sik, *The Mineral Vein of Korean Theology* (Seoul: Jun Mang Sa, 1984), pp. 14–20.

Though the problem of *kibock sinang* still remains and often threatens the gospel principle of the cross and suffering by employing the method of 'the end justifies the means', *kibock sinang* represents one way the Korean church has responded to the problem of poverty, and it has indeed been good news to the poor. It has provided the people of Korea with hope here and now through Christian faith, and resilience to endure the hardship and to persevere through the turmoil of post-war Korea. This hope, I believe, was not only limited to Christians only but spread to the nation as whole.[12]

The problem of injustice and minjung theology

Between the 1950s and 1970s, South Korea witnessed the rapid rise of the *jaebul*, with the help of government policy, which started to dominate the Korean economy. As a consequence, there was serious exploitation of the factory workers in their working conditions as well as their wages. The majority of pastors saw this problem as simply a matter of the 'process' of development and concentrated their emphasis on church growth. In this period, *jaebuls* and mega-churches rose in parallel and the church leadership believed that the growth of the Christian population and the growth of the national economy went hand in hand. There were large evangelistic meetings, for example the Billy Graham Crusade in 1973 and EXPLO '74 organized by Campus Crusade for Christ (CCC), both of which drew more than one million people. This speech by the head of CCC in Korea on the 'total evangelization of Korea' is typical:

> They [total evangelization] cover pre-evangelism, evangelization, discipleship, socialization, and the total Christianization of this nation. When they are realized, the amazing blessing promised in Deuteronomy 28.1–4 will apply to us. In Christ all things will be made new.[13]

However, Charles Elliott rightly points out the lack of social ethics regarding achieving material blessings and church growth:

---

12 Since the term *kibock sinang* carries such negative connotations in the Korean churches, there have been some attempts to find alternative terms. *Chukbock sinang*, meaning 'faith of invoking blessings', has been introduced by some Korean churches, and perhaps it may be appropriate to use this rather than reinterpret *kibock sinang*. See http://yfgc.fgtv.com/Y_5/WY_514_1.htm (in Korean).

13 Kim Joon-Gon, 'Korea's Total Evangelization Movement', in Ro Bong-Rin and Marlin L. Nelson (eds), *Korean Church Growth Explosion* (Seoul: Word of Life Press, 1983), p. 23.

Those offers – attractive as they are to people deeply troubled by the processes of transition in which they find themselves caught – are, however, predicated on the assumption that nothing can be done to modify the processes. It is at that point that Cho and the great majority of church leaders who think like him are at their weakest.[14]

In the context of 1970s Korea, there was a need for a new theological paradigm to meet the needs of the urban poor who were victims of a highly competitive capitalist market. The philosophies of *kibock sinang* and evangelistic campaigns did not seem to have a mechanism to deal with this problem of 'process' in modern Korean society. The problem of poverty is not just an individual matter, or to do with a congregation, but has to do with the structure of the Korean economy and society. It is at this point, some Christian intellectuals realized, that the poor are not just poor in the sense of lacking material things: they are also exploited and unjustly treated in socio-political reality, and the gap between the poor and the rich and between employee and employer is widening. The minjung movement was sparked when Jun Tae-Ill set himself on fire in November 1970 as his protest against the exploitation of fellow factory workers. The incident shook the country, and soon Christian leaders took this as a major issue and stood for and with the poor and exploited. This meant challenging the status quo of the government and the capitalist market economy of the *jaebul*. In 1973, they declared 'The Korean Christian Manifesto', which says:

> We believe in God who, by his righteousness, will surely protect people who are oppressed, weak and the poor and judge the power of evil in history. We believe that Jesus, the Messiah proclaimed that the evil power will be destroyed and the kingdom of Messiah will come, and this kingdom of Messiah will be the haven of rest for the poor, oppressed and despised.[15]

Following this, Suh Nam-Dong, among the most well known of minjung theologians, presented his thesis in 1975 that Jesus identified with the poor, sick and oppressed and that the gospel of Jesus is the gospel of salvation and liberation. For him, it is manifested in the struggle with those evil powers; liberation is not individual or spiritual but rather communal and political. Suh systematized his minjung theology in the following years, seeing the minjung as subjects of history and the dealing with *han* as the key theme for theology in a Korean context.

---

14 Elliott, *Sword and Spirit*, p. 38.
15 In Yoo Dong-Sik, *The Mineral Vein of Korean Theology*, pp. 258–9.

Let us hold in abeyance discussions on doctrines and theories about sin which are heavily charged with the bias of the ruling class and are often nothing more than the labels the ruling class have for the deprived. Instead, we should take *han* as our theme, which is indeed the language of the *minjung* and signifies the reality of their experience. If one does not hear the signs of the *han* of the *minjung*, one cannot hear the voice of Christ knocking on our doors.[16]

Ahn Byung-Mu, another well-known minjung theologian, asserted that Jesus identified in such a way that Jesus *is minjung* and *minjung is* Jesus as he shared his life with minjung, and the event of the cross is the climax of the suffering of minjung.[17] Therefore the presence of Christ is not when the word is preached nor when the sacrament is celebrated, but when we participate with or in the suffering of minjung. Jesus is God becoming flesh and body, which means material being and reality in everyday life not an ideology or philosophy.[18] Therefore, he argued, the minjung is the owner of the Jesus community, which is fundamentally a 'food community' – a community sharing food – and the concept of a worshipping community comes later.[19]

Ahn and Suh and other minjung theologians were deeply influenced by Kim Chi Ha, a prominent activist and poet who expressed in poetry this concept of sharing food in Christian life and theology:

Rice is heaven
As you cannot possess heaven by yourself
Rice is to be shared

Rice is heaven
As you see the stars in heaven together
Rice is to be shared by everybody

When rice goes into a mouth
Heaven is worshipped in the mind

Rice is heaven
Ah, ah, rice is
To be shared by everybody.[20]

---

16 Suh Nam-Dong, 'Toward a Theology of Han', in Kim Yong Bock (ed.), *Minjung Theology: People as the Subjects of History* (Maryknoll, NY: Orbis Books, 1983), pp. 51–65.

17 Ahn Byung-Moo, *The Story of Minjung Theology* (Seoul: Korea Institute of Theology, 1990), pp. 31–7.

18 Ahn, *The Story of Minjung Theology*, pp. 87–128.

19 Ahn, *The Story of Minjung Theology*, pp. 156–85.

20 Kim Chi Ha, *The Gold-Crowned Jesus and Other Writings* (Maryknoll, NY: Orbis Books, 1978), p. 30.

Minjung theologians captured people's imagination and brought the issue of poverty and exploitation into the Church. Here we see minjung theology as a 'protest' theology on behalf of the minjung against injustice and exploitation. Their interpretation of the poor is not in isolation from others but it is 'relational'. The poor are poor not necessarily because they are sinners or do not have a 'right' relationship with God, but because of the greediness of some others and the unjust system of modern capitalism. Therefore their main concern was not dealing with individual poor people but rather had to do with social process and the system that prevents the minjung from coming out of their misery. In this respect, minjung theologians' main concern is with anything anti-minjung rather than with the minjung themselves as they try to deal with economic and political injustice.[21] Minjung theology has made a great contribution to the Korean church and society through its understanding of liberation and justice, and by showing the poor and oppressed that they are not, or should not be, the objects of exploitation, that their protest is a legitimate one. It has been good news to the poor and, like *kibock sinang*, it was intended to uplift the poor. However, in its identification of the problem and the way to deal with it, it is vastly different from the latter.

There has been criticism of minjung theology in three areas.[22] First, is minjung theology by minjung or of the minjung, or is it a theology by elites for minjung? Second, who are the minjung in contemporary Korea and how do they see themselves? Are they only a conceptual group that is created by theologians for the purpose of their argument? Third, in the context of the changing situation in Korea, is there a place for minjung theology? Are there enough issues to deal with?

On the question of the identity of Minjung theologians, and therefore of Minjung theology itself, Minjung theologians *did* identify themselves with minjung by participating in sufferings with them. Many theologians went to prison and went through hardship. Because they identified with Jesus and the minjung in their theology, they suffered with the minjung and so the minjung theologians, at least in the first generation in the 1970s, *became* minjung. Though they may not have come from a minjung background – in fact, most of them were intellectuals – they qualified as minjung theologians in that they shared the experience of the poor. The leaders of the minjung church deliberately put themselves in a vulnerable situation and participated in the poverty

---

21 Moon Dong-Hwan, '21st Century and *Minjung* Theology', *Shinhack Sasang* (Summer 2000), pp. 5–29.

22 See Moon Dong-Hwan, '21st Century and *Minjung* Theology', pp. 30–54; Na Young-Hwan, 'Minjung Theology from the Evangelical Perspective', *Mockhea ywa Sinhack* (Aug. 1992), pp. 40–50.

and suffering of minjung, and their theology was the outcome of their struggle against what they saw as an evil system. Therefore minjung theology has a legitimate place in the life of Korean people as *of* the minjung and thus gives self-identity to the minjung.[23]

However, when we come to the second generation in the 1980s, this claim is not so firmly founded. The issue for the former was mainly the socio-economic problem of poor workers and farmers; for the latter, it was political and ideological tensions in relation to democracy. At least the first generation had the 'mass' of workers and farmers – the lower or middle-class people – over against the employers and land owners, who are relatively small. But the second generation minjung theologians had only minority support because they rather uncritically adopted Marxist-Leninist ideology in theologizing. Moreover, they perceived minjung theology as a protest ideology and so they rejected the present system and thereby also, wittingly or unwittingly, excluded those who supported the system. Particularly after the Kwangju massacre in 1980 by a military-backed government, minjung theologians shifted their attention to ideological issues, taking a socialist-communist line, favouring North Korea, and confronting the government of the South, which they perceived as illegitimate and associated with American 'imperialism'. This created a large gap between minjung who were not prepared to be on the side of the North and those who tried to integrate minjung theology into their ideological combat.[24] They seemed to have misread the mind of the minjung and perhaps undermined the minjung by having a rather arrogant and dogmatic approach to complex ideological issues and by being naive about the reality of the North.[25]

The second question of the identity of the minjung is a more difficult one. The term minjung, which is a Chinese word for ordinary people or citizens, is quite a new and unfamiliar one for contemporary South Koreans. This term was also often exploited by the South Korean government since the term has a similar nuance to the word used by North Koreans to describe the people – *Inmin*. In addition, people find it difficult to identify themselves with this heavily loaded term without definite or immediate benefits to be associated with. In a rapidly changing society like contemporary Korea, people are not prepared to commit themselves to such a static concept as minjung, and for the

---

23 Baek Nak-Chung, 'Who are Minjung?', in *Essays on Minjung* (Seoul: Korea Theological Study Institute, 1984), pp. 13–28.

24 Kim Sun-Jae, 'Yesterday, Today and Tomorrow of *Minjung* Theology', *Shinhack Sasang* (Spring 1998), pp. 8–9.

25 See Kim Jin-Ho and Lee Sook-jin, 'A Retrospect and Prospect on the Korean Modernity and Minjung Theology', *The Journal of Theologies and Cultures in Asia* (Feb. 2002), pp. 157–75.

cause of the minjung; in contrast, they rather wish to rise out of the minjung. Ham Seok-Hun, who is not regarded as a minjung theologian, but has contributed significantly in this discussion, introduced the different term, *Ssi-al*, a made-up Korean word to mean people, taken from the Korean word for 'seed'. Though this term has had rather limited usage, it represents an attempt to extend the meaning of minjung.[26] The fact that many articles were devoted to defining the minjung indicates that there have been difficulties of identifying this term with a concrete and tangible group, unlike black theology, feminist theology and dalit theology.

Nevertheless, in spite of these problems, minjung theology has made a vital contribution to the identity of the minjung and challenged them to stand up and speak. Though Latin American liberation theology made the point that the poor and oppressed are the ones who need to be liberated, minjung theology further asserts that the minjung are the subjects of this liberation as well as the subjects of the history and culture of their particular contexts. This was expressed in the relationship between Jesus and the minjung:

> Jesus proclaims the coming of God's Kingdom. He stands with the minjung, and promises them the future of God ... God's will is to side with the minjung completely and unconditionally. This notion was not comprehensive within the framework of established ethics, cult, and laws. God's will is revealed in the event of Jesus being with them in which he loves the minjung.[27]

This led to the idea of Jesus as the minjung and the minjung as Jesus, as developed for example by Ahn Byung Mu (see Chapter 2). The former formulation is acceptable to most theologians but the latter is a problem for many. This is because the question of the identity of the minjung depends on ontological questions of who the minjung are in relation to 'the other' and the ideological division of 'us and them'. But minjung theologians, particularly the third-generation theologians, asserted that the minjung has to be understood as an experiential entity identified with the event of Jesus in his life and words, especially of the cross. The minjung as Jesus does not mean for them an ontological identification,

---

26 Ham Seok-Heon, 'The True Meaning of Ssi-al', in NCC (ed.), *Minjung and Korean Theology* (Seoul: Korea Theological Study Institute, 1982), pp. 9–13; Park Sung-Jun, 'Reflection on Minjung Theology in the Context of 21st Century', *Shinhack Sasang* (Summer 2000), pp. 70–89.

27 Ahn Byung-Mu, 'Jesus and Minjung', in Kim Yong Bock (ed.), *Minjung Theology: People as the Subjects of History* (Maryknoll, NY: Orbis Books, 1983), pp. 138–51. He further explained the meaning of minjung as *ochlos* in Mark's Gospel (see p. 41 above).

but that by participating in the life and death of Jesus, the minjung are part of the Jesus event, and in that sense the minjung are Jesus. This has further consequences in that being minjung requires being in Christ for others – it is being a part of God's transformation for others.[28]

The focus of the minjung movement has been twofold: to safeguard the rights of the poor, weak and oppressed, and to change the society to a better system to protect them. It is for the minjung only. But being part of the Jesus event requires the minjung to serve others, and this could be the way forward for minjung theology in the future. There are already discussions of minjung theologies (plural) in the context of the globalization and ecological crisis. In particular, there is deep concern for foreign factory workers in Korea who are exploited and mistreated by employers as well as the Korean minjung themselves. Perhaps identifying the minjung is the most difficult and important question for the future of minjung theology and this should be an ongoing search. On the whole, minjung theology, has been a major instrument of the minjung or civil movement that challenged both the Church and society to deal with the problems of socio-economic and political injustice, brought democracy in Korea in the late 1980s, and certainly played a 'prophetic' role in Korean history.

Kibock sinang and minjung theology can be described as two major contextual theologies intended to address the problems of poverty and injustice. In order to do this, the former integrates traditional religiosity and Christian teaching on blessing, and the latter employs socio-political tools developed in the West and articulated in Latin America. *Kibock sinang* focuses on the individual poor and helped people in the context of post-war Korea to hope for material blessings by committing themselves to God, who is understood as being ready to bless his people. Minjung theology was formulated in the 1970s as a protest theology against both conservative evangelical theologies and *kibock sinang*, on the one hand, and against the unjust system of modern and divided Korea, on the other. These two approaches are products of the search for an answer to a particular problem in a particular time and place, therefore they have their limits. But with all their weaknesses, these two approaches are the outcome of a sincere quest to solve what is perhaps the most difficult problem for the Christian Church: the problem of poverty and injustice.

Though both minjung theology and *kibock sinang* affirm the poor and meet their needs, and are therefore both truly contextual, they cannot afford to remain as they are. First, if they are to be dynamic

---

28 See Choi Hyeung-Mook, 'Some Issues of Minjung Theology in 1990s', *Sidae ywa Minjung Theology* (1998), pp. 345-69.

and not static, they must keep in contact with the people. By associating with one particular ideology, minjung theology has distanced itself from the majority of the people. *Kibock sinang* has led to excessive accumulation of wealth and power at the cost of ethics and social concern, and therefore lost credibility in the public eye. Second, as we face the twenty-first century, there is a need for a new paradigm for Korean theology to deal with issues such as poverty in North Korea, reunification of North and South Korea, the rights of foreign workers in Korea, ecological issues and globalization. In other words, both minjung theology and *kibock sinang* need to discuss the question of 'the other'. Both approaches largely focus on the self, either collectively or individually, and have tended to neglect discussion of how to deal with others and how God's blessings can be shared with others. *Kibock sinang* needs to extend its seeking of blessings to asking for blessings on others beyond self, family and Church. Minjung theology needs to extend the meaning of minjung beyond a Korean group confined to a particular context and time. The development of methodologies is a positive step in this direction. Third, as part of this opening up, they need to lay themselves open to critique and to contribute to world Christianity, if they are not to remain sectarian and on the margins of theological discourse. Now that South Korea has also become part of the harmful effects of globalization, minjung theologians cannot always reject western theologies as contrary to Korean perspectives. According to the criteria of *kibock sinang*, the 'poor' have received the blessing they asked for and now have a responsibility to ask for blessings on others, which may entail a sacrifice of self. Above all *kibock sinang* and minjung theology need to be brought into interaction with each other to both change society and meet the individual needs of the poor.

Reconciling theology: reunification of the divided Korea

The conflict between the two Koreas is certainly the dominant concern for its people and has affected their lives ever since the division of Korea, which began in 1945 after the end of the Japanese occupation. Though the desire for reunification has been the most important agenda item for political leaders, the ways to achieve the goal have differed widely, because the two Koreas have been at the forefront of the ideological conflict of the Cold War. In this context, the churches in South Korea have gone through various stages in attempting to deal with the issue of division, and theological thinking has often made a significant impact on the wider society through Christian-initiated peace and reconciliation movements. I would like to look at some of the main political encounters between North and South Korea, discuss the churches' efforts for reconciliation and, lastly, make some suggestions towards a theology of reconciliation.

As in the case of politics, the South Korean churches are deeply divided into conservative and liberal positions, and this has been a constant struggle for Christians as they grapple with the political situation. Christian attitudes on the issue could be classified in three ways: unification as part of an anti-communist campaign and mission agenda (conservative Christians), promoting dialogue between two nations (liberal Christians), and involvement in a supportive and sharing humanitarian campaign (both conservative and liberal Christians).

Even before the Korean War, Korean Christians, like Christians in Europe, held a negative attitude towards communist ideology because of its anti-religious stance. This was confirmed by the persecution of churches by the government in the North and even greater suffering during the war. About 400 ministers were killed, and more than 2,000 churches were burnt or damaged by the communists in 1950–53.[29] As a result, during and after the war, Christians were at the forefront of anti-communist movements; they were against the ceasefire and regarded communists as evil. The immediate post-war reflections by Christians were more sombre. Some saw the war as a punishment by God towards Korean Christians for their unfaithfulness, including the way the Church had succumbed to Japanese pressure to practise Shinto worship, and the many divisions among Christians. Others understood the war as part of a sacrifice for the greater good of the nation in line with the sacrifice of Christ for human beings, which gave a salvific dimension to the tragedy.[30] But the dominant interpretation by Christians in the South was that the war was the result of the communist aggression, and this needed to be responded to with decisive force and vigour, on the one hand, and with prayer and mission towards the people of North Korea, on the other. This response was particularly common since many of the senior leadership of the churches in the South were those who had escaped from persecution by the communist regime in the North during the war, and also because, on this issue, the conservative sections of the Christian Church and the military-backed government shared the same attitude towards the communist government in the North. They believed regime change was the ultimate solution for peace and stability, and co-existence with the communist

---

29 Yi Mahn-Yol, *Korean Christianity and the National Unification Movement* (Seoul: Institute for Korean Church History, 2001), pp. 371–74.

30 Chung Sung-Han, *A History of Unification Movements in Korean Churches* (Seoul: Grisim, 2003), pp. 150–73.

North was not an option. So, in this understanding, the evangelization of North Korea was understood as prior to unification.[31]

This rigid and hostile attitude towards the North was soon countered by a more sympathetic acceptance of the people of the North as blood relations. This coincided with the rise of the democratic movement among the students and 'progressive' thinkers, increasing awareness of Christians' role in peace and reconciliation, and the sustaining support of the World Council of Churches for peace and reconciliation. An initiative was taken by a group of overseas Korean Christians, who met North Korean Christian delegates in the early 1980s, and this created fresh new beginnings.[32] However, the declarations after the meetings were heavily critical of the South Korean and US governments and supportive of the North. They were therefore rejected by the South Korean media and the general public, and did not really make any impact. Meanwhile, in this period, the World Council of Churches took an initiative to bring dialogue between the two parties. The most significant direct dialogue was a meeting between representatives from the North and South Korean churches at a seminar on the 'Christian perspectives on biblical and theological foundations for peace' in Glion, Switzerland, in September 1986.[33] The meeting reached an emotional climax during the worship, when all the participants were encouraged to greet one another. The representatives of South and North first shook hands but soon embraced each other. By participating in the Eucharist together – the heart of Christ's gospel of peace and reconciliation – they demonstrated the desire and hope of the people of divided Korea.

Meanwhile, in the midst of a series meetings sponsored by the World Council of Churches, in February 1988 the Korean National Council of Churches (KNCC) issued the 'Declaration of the Korean National Council of Churches towards the unification and peace of the Korean people', which made a significant impact both within the Church and on the whole nation.[34] The KNCC declaration was welcomed by many Christians but also generated a heated discussion among Christians. It brought the issue of peace and reconciliation within the churches, which motivated conservative Christians to participate in the debate. The declaration starts with the affirmation that Christ came to the earth as the servant of peace and proclaimed the kingdom of God, which represents peace, reconciliation and liberation. It claims that, accord-

---

31 See detailed discussion on this: Chung, *A History of Unification Movements in Korean Churches*, pp. 203–17, 240–60; Yi, *Korean Christianity and the National Unification Movement*, pp. 371–4.

32 In Austria (Nov. 1981), Helsinki (Dec. 1982) and Vienna (Dec. 1984).

33 See Yi, *Korean Christianity and the National Unification Movement*, pp. 382–8.

34 See Yi, *Korean Christianity and the National Unification Movement*, pp. 389–414.

ingly, the Korean church is trying to be with people who are suffering. In its main thesis, the declaration acknowledges and confesses the sins of mutual hatred, justifying the division of Korea, and accepting each ideology as absolute, which is contrary to God's absolute authority.

> We confess that throughout the history of our national division the churches of Korea have not only remained silent and continuously ignored the ongoing stream of movements for autonomous reunification of our people, but have further sinned by trying to justify the division. The Christians of both North and South have made absolute idols of the ideologies enforced by their respective systems. This is a betrayal of the ultimate sovereignty of God (Exodus 20:3–5), and is a sin, for the church must follow the will of God rather than the will of any political regime (Acts 4:19).[35]

The declaration, while affirming the three principles expressed in the Joint Declaration (1972; self-determination, peace, and grassroots unification of the Koreas), added the priority of humanitarian practice and the participation of the minjung, who are the victims of the divided Korea, in the unification discussions. The document made practical suggestions to both governments, including the change from 'ceasefire' to 'peace' and, after a peace treaty is signed and the peace and security of the peninsula guaranteed by the international community, the withdrawal of the US army and the dismantling of the UN head office. The Declaration then proclaimed the year 1995 as a jubilee year for peace and unification when Koreans could celebrate the fiftieth anniversary of the liberation from Japan. Reflecting on the biblical pattern of restoration of a just community (Lev. 25), it set down practical steps towards the jubilee year, including church renewal – the Church becoming a faith community for peace and reconciliation and working together with all the churches, employing all the necessary means towards peace and reconciliation.

> The Korean churches proclaim 1995, the fiftieth year after Liberation, as a Jubilee Year, to express our belief in the historical presence of God, who has ruled over those fifty years of history – indeed, over all of human history; to proclaim the restoration of the covenant community of peace; and to declare our resolution to achieve this restoration in the history of the Korean peninsula today. As we march forward with high aspirations toward the Year of Jubilee, we

---

35 KNCC, 'Declaration of the Churches of Korea on National Reunification and Peace' (1988).

should experience a revitalized faith in the sovereignty of God, who works within our people's history, and renewed commitment to the calling of God's mission.[36]

The declaration was welcomed by many South Korean churches and also by the Council of Chosun Christian Church in the North, but provoked severe criticism from conservative sections of the churches. They expressed deep concern over what they saw as naive views towards the North with regard to the peace treaty, to the suggestion of the withdrawal of US troops from South Korea and to the acknowledgement of the official Christian Church in the North, which the conservatives saw as a part of the Communist Party. They viewed the Declaration as a theologically one-sided approach towards the issues, and politically in line with the North Korean position.[37] However, the Declaration brought the issue of reunification onto the main agenda of Korean Christians and challenged many conservative sections of the Church to rethink their traditional approaches towards the North, moving from evangelism or relief to partnership for the common goal of peace and reconciliation. Furthermore, the Declaration expressed the vital concerns not only of Christians but also of the whole nation on the issue, and set the future direction of the Korean church on the unification issue. In spite of its limitations and shortcomings, the Declaration was the most significant landmark in the Korean Christian attempt to bring peace and reconciliation.

It seems the gap between the conservative and liberal approaches towards reunification has been as deep as that between North and South Korea. The situation was aggravated especially when Moon Ik-Hwan, a Protestant minister and activist for the reunification movement, made his controversial visit to Pyongyang to meet the leader of North Korea in March 1989 and when the Christian Council of Korea (CCK), consisting of some 20 South Korean Protestant denominations, was founded in the following month.[38] Since then the KNCC and CCK have often expressed sharply differing views, especially on the issue of reunification, and these have been reinforced by their theological positions, liberal and conservative respectively. However, more recently, this theological and ideological distance has been bridged by various

---

36 KNCC, 'Declaration of the Churches of Korea'.

37 See Chung, *A History of Unification Movements in Korean Churches*, pp. 276–80.

38 For details of the formation of CCK, see Chung, *A History of Unification Movements in Korean Churches*, pp. 276–99. Its main activities on North Korea include reconstructing the churches in North Korea, co-operating in mission to North Korea, supporting North Korean refugees and campaigning for human rights in North Korea. See http://cck.or.kr/ (accessed 12 Dec. 2010).

ecumenical projects. 'The South–North Sharing Campaign', founded in 1993, is perhaps the best example of a common project participated in by both camps, and it has gained increasing support from the Korean church as a whole. In its founding declaration, the participants express a wish to accept both 'prophetic mission' and 'priestly sacrifice', and for this purpose they seek to own commonly and share spiritual and material resources for the task of 'national reconciliation and peaceful reunification based upon a firm commitment to the Christian foundation of piety and temperance'.[39] The changing policy of the South Korean government since the early 1990s, and also the increasing voices from younger generations, mean that the church leadership is no longer saddled with the old pattern of a dichotomy of conservatives and liberals but has to work together regardless of denomination and theological differences.

Peace and reconciliation are vital theological concepts: God reconciles himself with us through Christ, and likewise we are called to become reconciled with one another. But how can this theological understanding be applicable to peace and reconciliation between the two Koreas? As we have seen, there is a sharp division among Korean Christians on the issue of reunification, and this is clearly demonstrated in the recent survey on socio-political opinions of Korean Protestant Christians conducted by the Institute of Theological Research at Hanshin University in Seoul.[40] However, it is important to notice that despite the differences, they are in agreement in three areas: the overwhelming majority of respondents desire the reunification of the two Koreas (97.9 per cent),[41] believe humanitarian support to North Korea should continue (91.4 per cent),[42] and see the mode of reunification as gradual and with mutual consultation between the two nations rather than by means of the South absorbing the North or through violent means (80.6 per cent). This survey reflects the desire and aspirations of Korean Christians for peace and reconciliation, the seeking of partnership and

---

39 www.sharing.net (accessed 12 Dec. 2010). In addition to this, many of the large churches – Young Nak Church, So Mang Church, Myeung Sung Church and Chung Shin Church – for example, are involved in humanitarian support of various projects in North Korea as well as in supporting North Korean defectors, recently renamed by the South Korean government, *Saetemin*, which means people who start home in a new context.

40 The Institute of Theological Studies, *Research on Socio-Political Consciousness of Korean Protestant Christians* (Seoul, 2004), pp. 40–52.

41 Reasons for the support of reunification are: because it enables the sharing of the Christian message to the people in the North (34.5 per cent), the opportunity to recover a common identity as Koreans (24.9 per cent), and to save the North Koreans from oppression (19.9 per cent). Reasons given against reunification included: fear of social chaos (42.9 per cent) and the economic burden (19.0 per cent).

42 The support should continue regardless of the political situation (57 per cent) and support should be given, but strategically (37.4 per cent).

sharing of a common identity as the same people, which are important aspects of the Christian message. If Christian theology is to address this issue, it is necessary to explore further the meaning of jubilee, *han* and shared identity.

The jubilee principle and the call for a restored sharing community

The jubilee is most clearly presented in Leviticus 25.8–55 (see also Lev. 27.16–25; Num. 36.4), which has a close textual relationship to the declaration of the sabbatical year in Exodus 21 and 23. Although there is no evidence whether the jubilee principle was practised in the history of Israel, the idea has been a challenge to the people of Israel and to Christians. This idea of jubilee and sabbatical year was picked up by Jesus' proclamation of the 'year of the Lord' (Isaiah 61.1–2) in Luke 4.21. The jubilee principle has several dimensions: sabbatical year, restoration of land to the original owners and liberation of slaves. When the KNCC declared 1995 as the Year of Jubilee, it focused on the third aspect of liberation, and also more on the proclamation than the actualization of unification in any particular year. Though many sincerely expected and wished that it could be achieved, the important point was that the jubilee was proclaimed. It is the proclamation of the liberation of the Korean people from the bondage of ideological hegemony and from political systems that hinder the formation of a common community.[43] This theme is also related to the remembering of God's grace in spite of the present situation, so that Christians are called to hold faith in confidence.

Kim Chang-Rak, in his support of the employment of jubilee law in the unification of the Korean peninsula, argues that the difference between the jubilee year and the 'year of the Lord' is that the *Sitz im Leben* of the jubilee principle relies on and affirms the present system, whereas the year of the Lord requires God's immediate intervention in a situation where there is no hope. The belief in God's immediate intervention was why the author of the Gospel of Luke recorded that Jesus read the passage and declared that the passage was fulfilled today (Luke 4.21).[44] Though there are problems in applying the jubilee law directly to the situation of the Korean peninsula and also in setting the year

---

43 See Park Jong Hwa, 'Theological and Political Task for Jubilee in the Church and People in Korea', in Korean Association for Christian Studies (ed.), *50th Anniversary of Liberation and Jubilee* (Seoul, 1995), pp. 25–44.

44 Kim Chang Rak, 'Jubilee in the Bible and Jubilee in the Korean Peninsula', in Institute of Theological Studies, *People's Unification and Peace* (Seoul: Institute of Theological Studies, 1995), pp. 157–215.

1995 as a jubilee year, the declaration exhibits the Korean Christians' insistence on the agenda of the reunification of two Koreas as they trust God's sovereign power over the problem of division, the slavery of hatred and the bondage of ideological conflict. Indeed, it was argued that the jubilee movement should be carried out in the form of creating a 'people community' of justice, restoring a common identity of Koreans sharing common struggle and pain.[45] The purpose of jubilee is bringing God's justice into the Korean context.[46] This is not only a religious notion but is manifested in socio-political reality, which requires participating in the justice and peace of God's kingdom in Korea and together celebrating God's works of liberation.[47]

The jubilee principle is also useful for Koreans in encouraging the search for a restored sharing community, employing the concepts of *koinonia* (community, sharing) and *oikoumene* (household of God). The separation of the people in the North and South over 60 years into two very different socio-economic and political systems means that there are very few shared identities. What could be the contribution of theology in this context? Perhaps, as Ahn Byeung-Mu insists, the early Church in Acts was primarily a food community, which shared the basic needs of humanity with others, rather than a worshipping community.[48] The restoration of this concept of *koinonia* between the South and the North is most urgent, especially as this is a time of severe economic hardship and even starvation in the North. Sharing of resources is a theological imperative that the Church should be actively engaged in. It is a central affirmation of Christian faith that the people of God is catholic, or universal. It is in this sense that *oikoumene* has been taken up by the ecumenical movement to express its mission of unity of the Church and humanity. Since God is one, the household of God must be one. This is not limited just to Christians but includes all – not least the people of North and South Korea.

David Kwang-sun Suh, in his 'theology of reunification', sees restoration of community as creating a sharing community. He writes metaphorically of the cross of division and the resurrection of hope. He expresses his resentment that, in spite of Korea being the victim of imperial aggression, Korea had to be divided again by the imperialistic

---

45 Min Yong-Jin, *Peace, Unification and Jubilee* (Seoul: The Christian Literature Society of Korea, 1995), pp. 295–305.

46 Kang Sa-Moon, 'The Problem of Application of Jubilee Law to 50th Anniversary of Liberation', in Korean Association for Christian Studies (ed.), *50th Anniversary of Liberation and Jubilee*, pp. 47–82.

47 Kim Yong-Bock, 'Preface', in Korean Association for Christian Studies (ed.), *50th Anniversary of Liberation and Jubilee*, pp. 5–14. See also Park Soon-Kyeung, *The Future of Unification Theology* (Seoul: Sakaejul, 1997), pp. 106–17.

48 Ahn, *The Story of Minjung Theology*, pp. 156–85.

policy of the superpowers, and in that sense Koreans are bearing the cross of division. He then argues that under this cross, Christians in the North and the South yearn for the resurrection that was demonstrated through Christ and promised to his disciples, and that this will be manifested through sharing at table together.

> Resurrection is the hope of the community of the table; it is the search for people coming together at the Lord's Table as a community. Resurrection is eating and drinking together at the same table with the Lord in a community ... we believe in the resurrection of the divided people from the cross of division, in Korea ... as the reclaiming of the community. In the resurrected body of Christ, we struggle for the community, the unity and commonwealth of peace and justice.[49]

The keys to seeking restored shared identity are understanding, accepting and sharing of life together, and this includes radical changes in past perceptions of each other. *Welcome to Dongmakgol* is a fine example of a film reflecting this dilemma of animosity and yet deep-rooted shared identity even between soldiers from the North and the South. The film is a comedy set in a remote mountain village during the Korean War. The villagers are happily unaware of the war until one day two separate groups of soldiers – one from the South and one from the North – stumble upon the village and confront one another in the square. As the bemused villagers look on and try to continue their normal lives, there is a stand-off between the soldiers, which lasts through pouring rain and all through the night. We discover that each group is bluffing – neither is as fearsome as they look, and neither really knows what is going on in the larger theatre of the war. Eventually one of the exhausted soldiers tosses away what he thinks is a dud grenade and accidentally blows up the store of food for the whole village for the winter. The distraught villagers round on the soldiers, forcing them to help to bring in more harvest. Eventually, they encourage them to take off their different uniforms and put on common village clothes. Working together for the good of the village, the soldiers gradually let down their guard and, living together, they become friends. When, eventually, the war catches up with them, they work together to save the village from being bombed. The film is very funny and seems far from present reality – but it is also very poignant. It touches the hearts

---

49 David Kwang-sun Suh, *The Korean Minjung in Christ* (Hong Kong: Christian Conference of Asia, 1991), p. 183.

of Koreans, who have been separated as enemies for over 60 years, and yet long to be reunited in one community.

Overcoming han *and building up trust and hope*

Koreans have experienced *han* through the constant cycle of hope and despair during the last half-century, and still there is no immediate sign of improvement in the relationship between the two nations. Koreans understand and identify in a national way with the story of Israel in Old Testament times, and with the meaning of the cross. The separation is understood as the cross that Koreans have to bear, and it is through these experiences of bitter conflicts and division that Koreans understand the reality of human nature and yet seek hope in the midst of despair. This concept of *han* was well articulated by minjung theologians, who struggled to find meaningful theological engagement in the context of the unjust society of the 1970s.

As we have seen in the previous section, the minjung theologians have further asserted that the minjung are the Koreans, both rich and poor, both North and South, who are struggling to be reunited, and that *han* is felt by every Korean in the yearning for reunification. David Kwang-sun Suh argues that the cross of division is the cross of *han*, and expresses his frustration with it:

> With a clear Christian conscience, we hear the agonizing cry on the cross of division, *Eli Eli lama sabachthani?* This cry of *han* is a cry to God from the forsaken people on the cross of division. Has God forsaken the Korean people on the cross of division? When we hear the cries of the cross of division, we feel numb and powerless. We are lost, we do not know how to respond to these cries.[50]

However, though the identification of the cross of division as the *han* of Koreans is vital in understanding the agony and despair, the hope of resurrection must be found and this seems to require a further development of the socio-political efforts for unification. In other words, the emphasis on political reunification without a concrete process of reconciliation between the two peoples may lead to further alienation of the one from the other. On the issue of the process of reunification, there has been ample discussion from political, economic, social and anthropological perspectives, but one of the deep problems of the relationship between the two Koreas lies in the profound sense of suspicion and distrust of the other – resulting from decades of conflict

---

50 Suh, *The Korean Minjung in Christ*, p. 181.

and the breakdown of dialogue. How can two parties establish mutual trust after having experienced so many incidences of hurt and hatred? Not only this, but how can the deeply divided opinions among the people in South Korea on the issue of unification be reconciled? Moon Ik-Hwan, the Protestant minister who made a controversial visit to North Korea in 1989 and was imprisoned by the South Korean government several times, has expressed his dream and hope for the future in his poem:

> Living in history means ...
> Changing night into day and day into night,
> Changing sky into earth and earth into sky,
> Scattering rocks with bare feet
> and being buried under them,
> Surviving as soul only,
> waving the flag of freedom high.
>
> Living in history in this land means ...
> Walking through a wall as a door,
> Refusing the separation with whole body,
> Shouting that there is no border line,
> Insisting on a railway ticket for Pyongyang
> from the stations in Seoul, Pusan or Kwangju.
>
> This person is crazy!
>
> Yes, I am crazy, truly crazy.
> You can't live in the history without being crazy.
> You with a clear mind,
> If you can't sell a ticket for Pyongyang,
> let it be.
>
> I shall walk.
> I shall swim Imjin River[51]
> If I am shot, let it be,
> I shall go with my soul like cloud and wind.[52]

---

51 This tributary of the Han River flows from North into South Korea.

52 Moon Ik-Hwan, *I Shall Go Even on Foot* (Seoul: Silchon Munwhasa, 1990), pp. 18–19.

Bringing about the process of reconciliation by forming shared identity

Reflecting on the South African situation, John de Gruchy, in his discussion on the 'art of reconciliation', makes the point that 'creating space is critical, irrespective of the nature of the reconciliation we seek' and that 'reconciliation cannot be pursued without the alienated parties facing each other'.[53] This idea of creating space is also affirmed by Gerhard Sauter. Reflecting on the German experience of reunification, Sauter insists that 'common identity demands mutual respect and a sharp sense of reality, especially if this identity is having to be built upon very different historical presuppositions'. He regretted that German reunification was largely based on common German pre-war history and did not create a 'common cultural memory' of the most recent German history. So he urges his Korean counterparts:

> The Korean Christians in the North and South will contribute decisively to achieving their common identity not on the basis of an economic merger of a political union with all the complications and psychological costs that the German experiences show; rather … they contribute through their participation in God's atonement and thus become reconciled with each other. This would include their not only being compassionate but merciful with each other in the light of their very different and complicated recent stories and so able to hear and confirm the apostolic message: 'In Christ, God was reconciling the world to himself … (2 Cor. 5.19–20)'.[54]

The 'cultural common memory' mentioned by Sauter is also echoed by Robert Schreiter, who has been working on the issue of reconciliation for many years. He sees that building shared identities is an important part of the process of reconciliation, and that healing memory and sharing narrative are essential parts of forming shared identities. For him, the shaping of the 'communities of memory' is important and he suggests several steps towards this: first, acknowledging loss, which does not mean abandoning the past, but rather building a new relationship to it; second, making connections, creating a situation where our relation to the past is no longer immediate but dialectical, where new

---

53 John de Gruchy, *Reconciliation: Restoring Justice* (London: SCM Press, 2002), p. 148.

54 Gerhard Sauter, 'What does Common Identity cost – not only economically and politically, but also spiritually and mentally? Some German experiences and provoking questions', in S. Kim, P. Kollontai and G. Hoyland (eds), *Peace and Reconciliation: In Search of Shared Identity* (Aldershot, Hampshire: Ashgate, 2008), pp. 21–33 at 32–3.

connections can begin to be made; third, taking action to bring a new dimension to the situation.[55] This process of forming shared identity for achieving reconciliation is further developed by Cecelia Clegg – it was the key she discovered in her research on the situation in Northern Ireland. She sees that if we look at the nature of group identities in conflict, identity is often distorted into 'negative identity', and this identity is formed over against the 'other' in such a way that the 'other' becomes a 'threatening other'. Therefore she suggests that there needs to be a 're-negotiation' of identity, and sets down three steps: empathy for the other, recognizing that others have also suffered, and admitting that one's own community has wronged the other. She concludes that reconciliation

> requires all parties to change; and in perceiving that call from God to change, to *metanoia*, we suddenly become aware that, in some paradoxical way, the other whom we perceive as threatening and whom we are invited to embrace is not only my Protestant or Catholic neighbour, it is Godself.[56]

The hope of reconciliation is also well expressed by the Taiwanese theologian C. S. Song who, basing his argument on the story of Sarah, Abraham's wife, sees the reconciliation God has brought to this world through the image of the womb.[57] He draws powerful pictures from poems from various Asian contexts to show the agony of the people, and yet he believes there is great hope for the future in the 'seed hidden within the mysterious womb of humanity' as a 'new life is in the making to succeed the life that has just passed out of the community of the living'. So, in his analogy, the despair of *han* of the Koreans, in turn, could be the seed in the womb that brings forth reconciliation. The process and practical implications of creating 'cultural common memory', shaping 'communities of memory' and the 're-negotiation' of identity is the ongoing task of Koreans seeking for lasting reconciliation.

---

55 Robert Schreiter, 'Establishing a Shared Identity: The Role of the Healing of Memories and of Narrative', in Kim, *et al.* (eds), *Peace and Reconciliation*, pp. 7–33.

56 Cecelia Clegg, 'Embracing a Threatening Other: Identity and Reconciliation in Northern Ireland', in Kim, *et al.* (eds), *Peace and Reconciliation*, pp. 81–93 at 92.

57 C. S. Song, *Third-Eye Theology: Theology in Formation in Asian Settings* (London: SCM Press, 1980), pp. 146–7.

Conclusion

The above public theologies of minjung theology, *kibock sinang* and reconciling theology, which struggle to answer the Korean problems of poverty, socio-political injustice and division, have each made a significant impact on Korean churches and society. It should be noted that the vast majority of the Korean churches are conservative evangelical churches, emphasizing revival, personal experience, eschatological hope, exclusive truth in Christ and the numerical growth of the Church. On the surface, they reject the three movements we have discussed, but in reality the life and practice of ordinary Christians is deeply influenced by these three movements. So in the case of the Korean church, Christian theology and thinking have permeated into the society and have been instrumental in bringing hope and justice in the context of injustice and division. This legacy may arguably be more important for Christian witness in Korea than the spectacular growth in numbers of Christians.

The Psalmist says, 'Grace and truth have met together; justice and peace have kissed each other.'[58] In the post-war South Korea, the twin problems of justice and peace have been the dominant concern for Koreans, who have responded through these three public theologies. In spite of their limitations and problems, these public theologies have challenged individuals, the church leadership and governments to seek justice and reconciliation in South Korean society and between the North and the South. The main conversation partners for public theology in this case were the state and the market, and the Church has provided some alternative approaches to the norms of society and government policies. In particular, the promotion of 'holistic blessing', justice for the farmers and factory workers, and development of a shared identity between the two Koreas by utilizing songs, arts, stories and poems, have proved effective ways to communicate theological insights to the public. The way in which the situation of the minjung demanded that the Church respond to the challenges and the way in which, in turn, together with minjung, theologians and church leaders have articulated these theological discourses, is a good example of how public theology is done. It has brought hope and aspirations to people who are struggling for a just and reconciled society.

58 Psalm 85.10 (CJB).

6

Global Economic Justice: Latin American Initiatives to Overcome Inequalities

Theology as critical reflection on historical praxis is a liberating theology, a theology of the liberating transformation of the history of humankind and also therefore that part of humankind – gathered into *ecclesia* – which openly confess Christ.[1]

At the beginning of the twenty-first century, we experience societies and nations coming closer than ever before; the world has become a 'global village'. But economically, the gap between rich countries and poorer ones is getting bigger in spite of the trends towards globalization.[2] The Christian Church is a global body, one that transcends national and cultural barriers. In our day we witness more and more Christian denominations and organizations 'internationalizing' or 'globalizing'. Consequently, the fact of global inequality poses a greater challenge than ever to the Christian Church.

Our world is one of gross inequality. This is increasingly apparent within national borders but it is equally obvious on a worldwide scale. After the demise of the communist bloc, the polarization of global affairs along an East–West axis, which has dominated world politics (and economics) for so long, has broken down to expose another, deeper division: the North–South polarization. The North–South axis represents the struggle between the rich or 'industrialized' countries of the North and the poor or 'developing' countries of the South. Though we are now accustomed to thinking of colonialism as a thing of the past, that era has very much shaped the world we live in today. The effect of colonialism – the impulse behind which from the beginning was trade – was to draw almost every nation of the earth into a global market. Early socialists correctly foresaw that this market would outlast the formal independence of colonies, resulting in 'neocolonialism'. That is, the world economic system created by colonialism would

---

1 Gustavo Gutiérrez, *A Theology of Liberation: History, Politics, and Salvation*, rev. edn (London: SCM Press, 1988), p. 12.

2 Ruth Leger Sivard, with Arlette Brauer and Milton I. Roemer, *World Military and Social Expenditures* (Washington, DC: World Priorities, 1989), p. 5.

continue to bind former colonies to their colonial masters long after 'decolonization'. So we see today that the countries of the South are largely the same countries that were colonized.

At the close of the Second World War, a new world order was drawn up by the superpowers. Politico-military decisions were made by Roosevelt, Stalin and Churchill at Yalta and an economic plan for the post-war world was formulated at Bretton Woods in 1944. The Bretton Woods meeting was attended by representatives of 44 independent countries; most of the non-industrialized were from Latin America. Most colonies were represented by their colonial masters, thus 'the re-structuring of the world economy was predominantly a First World affair'.[3] The economic structure laid out for the new world economy at Bretton Woods included four organizations still in existence today: the World Bank, the International Monetary Fund (IMF), the General Agreement on Tariffs and Trade (GATT; now the World Trade Organization) and the United Nations. In theory, the setting up of the UN was an opportunity for the less developed countries to influence the running of the international community. But in practice, involvement of the UN in economic affairs was opposed by the developed countries and so the Organization for Economic Co-operation and Development (OECD) – representing 25 developed countries and dominated by the USA – became 'the arbiter of trade and dominance in the world'.[4] It became increasingly apparent at the close of the twentieth century that economics took precedence over politics in international matters and that therefore those who hold the purse strings were also those who directed world affairs.

Since the end of the Second World War, the rich countries have remained rich and the poor have remained poor. The exception to this rule is a few countries in South East and East Asia who have joined the ranks of 'industrialized nations'. But particularly since 1980, the majority of Third World nations, especially in Africa and Latin America, have experienced falling wages, deterioration of infrastructure and lowered standards of living.[5] This state of affairs has led to the emergence since the 1960s of a doctrine of dependency: the underdevelopment of the South as the flipside of the development of the North, the so-called 'development of underdevelopment' position. These theories highlight the injustice and irrationality of world economic relations that perpetu-

3 Tom Hewitt, 'Developing Countries: 1945 to 1990', in Tim Allen and Alan Thomas (eds), *Poverty and Development in the 1990s* (Oxford: Oxford University Press, 1992), p. 223.
4 Hewitt, 'Developing Countries', p. 224.
5 Hewitt, 'Developing Countries', p. 232.

ate colonial relations.[6] Whether or not neo-Marxist explanations of neocolonialism and the dependency theory are accepted, there is no doubt about the continued one-sidedness of the world economy. The Age of Empire may be over, but our interdependent world economy continues to be an asymmetrical world economy. Real power remains in the hands of a decentred network of hegemonic actors in the OECD world economy; with the United States, the European Union, Japan and China; with the IMF, the World Bank and the private capital markets. The Third World, so-called, lacks a presence and lacks a voice.[7]

It must be said that the Church shares the responsibility for inequality when it is either silent on the issue or when it accumulates wealth at the expense of others. In this context of inequality, however, some Christians have raised their voices at both global and local levels. The concern of public theology presented by this context of global inequality is twofold. The first is to do with the relationship between the northern and southern churches. The second is with the difference between the global North and global South in economic terms, to which liberation theology has already made a significant contribution.

The global church as the body of Christ and the household of God

In the context of changing dynamics of societies, politics and religions, there is a great deal of uncertainty, which makes it very difficult to predict the future shape of Christianity worldwide. However, I believe that the future shape will not necessarily depend on whether the churches of the South and the North dominate one another, but rather on whether and how these two quite different forms of Christianity will share their resources, experiences and values with the other partner. In other words, the common quest for the theological and socio-cultural interaction between the two Christianities is a key to understanding the shape of the Christian Church. I would argue that the distinctive features of Christianity in a given context lie particularly in their theological approaches to socio-political and religious problems and not just in their sociological patterns of church growth and religious belief. In addition to analysing Christianity sociologically, observation of the engagement or interaction of theologians and church leaders with the context is vital to understanding contemporary Christianity in a particular part of the world and to predicting its future shape. The identity

6 Stuart Corbridge (ed.), *Development Studies: A Reader* (London: Edward Arnold, 1995), p. 5.
7 Corbridge, *Development Studies*, p. 334.

and mission of the Church needs to be understood in the context of global Christianity as the body of Christ or household of God.

It is a central affirmation of Christian faith that the Church of God is catholic, or universal. At the same time, because there is one God, there is one Church. As Christians, therefore, we are members of a world-wide, international, global entity – perhaps the first in history. What does scripture have to say about relationships in an international body? Three biblical themes seem particularly pertinent to this topic: the first two are images of the Church used in scripture applied to the global Church, and the third is the first global church project.

In his classic work, Paul S. Minear has drawn attention to the range of images used to refer to the Church of the New Testament.[8] The phrase 'body of Christ' is predominantly Pauline and richly expressive of the apostle's ecclesiology. Johannes Verkuyl observes that the apostle Paul did not see the local church at Corinth as *the* body of Christ since he never precedes the phrase by the definite article when he uses it to refer to the congregation.[9] The implication he draws is that 'the body of Christ' is an image that is properly applied only to the universal Church. The chief meaning of the image then is to express the unity or oneness of the Church of Jesus Christ throughout the whole earth. As Roland Allen puts it: the churches in Judaea, Macedonia, Achaia, Galatia, Syria, Cilicia and Asia 'were all alike members of a body which existed before they were brought into it'.[10] Application of the body image to the global Church implies:

1 any division between churches of different countries or continents is not acceptable since the unity of the Church is a confession of faith in Jesus Christ (1 Cor. 1.13; Eph. 4.4);

2 the Holy Spirit impartially bestows a variety of gifts on the different churches (Acts 10.35; Rom. 12.2–8; 1 Cor. 12.12–31) for the upbuilding of the universal Church (Eph. 4.1–16);

3 the 'weaker', 'less honourable', 'unpresentable' or 'inferior' parts have an honoured place in the worldwide Christian community (1 Cor. 12.22–24) as the old social relationships are transformed in Christ Jesus (Gal. 3.28);

4 since the head of the body is Christ, no member of the body can claim authority over the others (Eph. 4.16);

---

8 Paul S. Minear, *Images of the Church in the New Testament* (London: Lutterworth, 1961).

9 Johannes Verkuyl, *Contemporary Missiology: An Introduction* (Grand Rapids, MI: Eerdmans, 1978), p. 312.

10 Roland Allen, *Missionary Methods: St. Paul's or Ours?* (Grand Rapids, MI: Eerdmans, 1962; first published in 1912), p. 126.

5 but because the one Spirit fills the one body, we are bound together in love and can trust one another (Eph. 4.3, 15–16);

6 the global Church is a unity in diversity since each part has a distinctive contribution to make to the whole that complements the others (1 Cor. 12.15–26; Eph. 4.13);

7 the global Church is a begetter of an even greater unity through its example and its ministry of reconciliation (Col. 1.21–22; Eph. 1.9–10), its growth in mission towards the union of all things in Christ (Eph. 4.13,16).

The image of the Church as the household or family of God is particularly prominent in 1 Peter, where it is linked to the house of Israel and the house of David. The household image includes the pervasive image of believers as children of God. This in turn makes all Christians brothers (and sisters) (1 Pet. 2.17; 5.9). Christian fellowship in scripture emphasizes equality before God, shared life and possessions and solidarity – 'unity of spirit', 'suffering', 'sympathy', 'humility' (1 Pet. 3.8; 5.9). Since God is one, the household of God must be one. In this age there are other households, including 'all the families of the earth'. But God's covenant promise is to all these families, and thus in eschatological perspective, the household of God must encompass the whole inhabited earth.[11] It is in this sense that *oikoumene* has been taken up by the 'ecumenical' movement to express its mission of unity of the Church and humanity. Any household has an 'economy' or 'household law' (*oikos* + *nomos*) and so the household of God becomes a powerful metaphor for understanding how we bring theology and economics together in the modern world.[12] Some of the implications of this image for our theme are as follows:

1 the global Church is one entity governed by the same law, part of the same economy;

2 this law is founded on a principle of the equality of all believers and congregations;

3 the only central authority governing such a family rests with God (the Father) and not in any particular local church or part of the Church;

4 the global household/family of God shares resources and livelihood, has all things in common;

---

11 Minear, *Images of the Church*, pp. 170–1.

12 See, for example, M. Douglas Meeks, 'Global Economy and the Globalization of Theological Education: An Essay', in Alice Frazer Evans, Robert A. Evans and David A. Roozen (eds), *The Globalization of Theological Education* (Maryknoll, NY: Orbis Books, 1993), pp. 247f.

5 the global household/family of God shares the experiences of each member's life;

6 the global household/family of God stands together in solidarity against common enemies, supporting one another and suffering with one another.

As part of his missionary activity, the apostle Paul went to great pains to raise a collection from the Gentile churches to present 'to the poor among the churches of Jerusalem'. This collection is referred to in Galatians 2.9–10, 1 Corinthians 16.1–4, Romans 15.25–29, Acts 19.21 and 24.17, but is given extended treatment in 2 Corinthians 8.9. Paul's evident preoccupation with this matter over several years[13] and the risk he took in taking the gift raised to Jerusalem[14] indicate that this was more than a purely material concern. The collection was a way of demonstrating what was for Paul the central 'mystery of the gospel', that is, the unity of Jew and Gentile in Christ Jesus in the face of the Judaizers who would separate them.[15] In other words, this was a project that expressed Paul's convictions about the nature of relationships in the global Church. Some of these are as follows:

1 the churches of the world have a responsibility towards one another, especially towards the poorer and suffering members;

2 those who have the gospel owe a debt to those from whom they have received it (Rom. 15.25–27);

3 the grace of God inspires generosity – after the example of Jesus Christ – even among the poorest churches (2 Cor. 8.1–11);

4 the willingness to share is more important than the size of the gift (2 Cor. 8.12);

5 the aim is equality, the abundance of one supplying the want of the other (2 Cor. 8.13–15);

6 giving results in blessing for the giver, brings glory to God and demonstrates the truth of the gospel (2 Cor. 9);

7 giving results in a bond between giver and receiver (2 Cor. 9.14).

---

13 Paul Barnett, *The Message of 2 Corinthians*, The Bible Speaks Today Series (Leicester: InterVarsity Press, 1988), p. 139.

14 David J. Bosch, *Transforming Mission: Paradigm Shifts in Theology of Mission* (Maryknoll, NY: Orbis Books, 1991), p. 146.

15 See Bosch, *Transforming Mission*, p. 146; Barnett, *The Message*, p. 139.

The churches' responses to the problem of inequality

The problem of inequality between the North and the South is a reality that profoundly affects the Christian Church as a worldwide entity. Thus it also affects the way we do mission. It is an inescapable fact that during the colonial period the evangelization of the world was carried out by the same nations that also colonized it. While it would be unfair to the missionaries of this period to say that they simply 'followed the flag', we cannot avoid the conclusion that it was colonialism that made the 'Great Century' of Christian missions possible. It was colonialism that brought the nations of 'Christendom' into prolonged contact with their non-Christian nations, colonialism that (sometimes forcibly) opened up previously closed countries to missionary activity and colonialism that furnished the resources and technology for the missionary enterprise. In this sense, colonialism and mission went hand in hand.

In both the evangelical and ecumenical movements, the distinction between 'older' and 'younger' churches, 'sending' and 'receiving' countries, has been declared to be a thing of the past. Although the idea of 'mission in six continents' is accepted by most of us, in reality this is not fully implemented in mission today. There is considerable participation and involvement in leadership by the Two-Thirds World in any international missionary meeting, but missionary activities are still one-sided with the churches in the North sending money and missionaries to the churches in the South. Rene Padilla from Latin America states the problem:

> In many cases missionary work continues to be done from a position of political and economic power and with the assumption of western superiority... Many Christian churches, institutions, and movements in the Third World continue to operate in a 'colonial' situation, heavily dependent on foreign personnel and subject to foreign control.[16]

John Mbiti comments wryly, 'The church in Africa has been very much missionary minded, but only in terms of receiving missionaries and depending on them.'[17] And J. Rosario Narchison from India states:

> By and large, until recently Christian missions were for ecclesiastical expansion. They operated on a missiology of conquest, perpetuating in the process the power structures of the West ... Even today

---

16 C. Rene Padilla, *Mission Between the Times: Essays on the Kingdom* (Grand Rapids, MI: Eerdmans, 1985), p. 134.

17 Quoted in Padilla, *Mission Between*, p. 134.

the foreign missionary among the Protestants is a super-person with exorbitantly high money power.[18]

Allowing for generalization and overstatement in these comments – particularly the last – they do clearly indicate the problems of mission in the global Church. The Church has tried to solve the above problems in various ways. These include either moratorium – that is, a complete cut-off of finance and personnel from the North for a certain period – or perusing mutual interdependency.

A proposal for a moratorium on the Church and mission – that is, a cessation of foreign missionary work – was adopted by the Lusaka Conference of the All Africa Conference of Churches, 8–21 May 1974.

> The contribution of the African Church ... cannot be adequately made in our world if the Church is not liberated and has not become truly national. To achieve this liberation the Church will have to bring a halt to the financial and manpower resources – the receiving of money and personnel – from its foreign relationships ... Only then can the Church firmly assert itself in its mission to Africa and as a part of the ecumenical world.... Should the Moratorium cause missionary sending agencies to crumble, the African Church would have performed a service in redeeming God's peoples in the Northern hemisphere from a distorted view of the mission of the Church in the world.[19]

The proposal certainly brought a heated discussion among the participants and others, but the idea of a moratorium did not elicit positive reactions from churches and mission organizations in Africa. However, it does show a deep concern for self-expression, self-reliance and self-identity. In Asia, the moratorium idea was also put forward by three executives of the Christian Conference of Asia in a study document in 1974 entitled 'Let My People Go'. Here are some excerpts from that document:

> The word 'mission' denotes to us something foreign, something which came to us in western missionaries and resources, something we received and responded to, rather than our calling which requires of us both response and responsibility ... The missionary movement has been carried out with tremendous material resources ... Our pov-

---

18 J. Rosario Narchison, 'Mission in the Context of Religious Fundamentalism: A Few Questions from Asia', in Joseph Mattam and Sebastian Kim (eds), *Dimensions of Mission in India* (Bombay: St. Pauls, 1995), p. 42.

19 Quoted in Verkuyl, *Contemporary Missiology*, p. 335.

erty becomes what disqualifies us from participating in mission ... Our Asian churches need to dig our wells and draw our water in the life and the commitment of our local congregations ... Only a deeper identification with the responsibilities and priorities of mission will give clarity and freedom of judgement as to what the selfhood and mission of the Asian church requires.[20]

Both the AACC proposal and 'Let My People Go' reflect the problems of the churches in the South caused by the trends in mission of their particular time and context. These problems should not be overlooked and need careful consideration. However, the moratorium approach has serious shortcomings. First, theologically, our understanding of the global Church is as the total body of Christ and the household of God. Therefore, we cannot separate ourselves for any reason. However great the difficulties and problems may be, we must try to solve them together. Second, spiritually, giving and generosity are commended in scripture. A moratorium would deny an opportunity for giving. Instead, what is needed is the facilitation of and recognition of giving by the 'poorer' countries in non-material ways to other Christians. Third, ethically, if finance or personnel from the churches in the North stops, the first ones who suffer are the poor and weak. Those who are making the decisions would not suffer much. The people who are not directly affected by a moratorium have no right to deprive people in desperate need. Fourth, practically, any moratorium can only be effective if it is complete, and this requires the agreement of all parties. While churches are not united in mission, there will always be those who will see a moratorium by others as an opportunity to expand their own activities.

In the light of our studies on the issue, an alternative solution to the problems of global inequality and the Christian Church would be to recognize, promote awareness of and live out the mutual interdependence of the churches on both sides of the divide. Vinay Samuel challenges us, 'If the gospel is to be truly liberating in the contemporary world, we need to go beyond [global political] games to being "in Christ", where there is no East and West, North and South, yet all one in him.'[21] As the Christian community is the salt and light of the world, we must set an example to the people around us. As the first-fruits of the kingdom, we must begin with ourselves and become a model for society. But the

---

20 Harvey Perkins, Harry Daniel and Asal Simanjuntak, 'Let My People Go', in Gerald H. Anderson and Thomas F. Stransky (eds), *Mission Trends No 3: Third World Theologies* (New York: Paulist Press, 1976), pp. 192–210.

21 Vinay Samuel, 'Modernity, Mission and Non-Western Societies', in Philip Samson, Vinay Samuel and Chris Sugden (eds), *Faith and Modernity* (Oxford: Regnum Lynx, 1994), p. 320.

Church is more than a model, we are an agent of transformation, a catalyst for change. We expect that the leaven of the Christian Church will leaven the whole lump of global human society.

Ecumenical conferences on mission have consistently called for radical change in the relationships between churches. At Edinburgh 1910, V. S. Azariah led the way by decrying paternalistic relationships and asking the western churches to 'give us friends'. At Tambaram in 1938, Hendrik Kraemer urged a brotherly relationship between 'older churches' and 'younger churches':

> [The younger church] is the fruit of missionary labour, but not the possession of missions, and it is on the side of missions a serious and fatal misunderstanding of the nature of the Church to consider any indigenous Church in any stage of development to be in an inferior position because it receives financial support. This support given to one Church by another ... is no charity but fraternal help.[22]

This idea was developed at the following conference in Whitby in 1947 by the motto 'Partnership in Obedience'. Stephen Neill explains: 'The full spiritual equality of the younger Churches ... was now no longer a discovery: it was simply taken for granted as one of the postulates of thought.'[23] Furthermore, the theme for the Mexico Conference in 1963, 'Mission in Six Continents', indicated that there was no longer any distinction between sending and receiving churches or older and younger churches, but that mission is for every body of Christ. The Melbourne Conference Section Report on Good News to the Poor went on to affirm, 'The structures of mission and the church life still must be changed to patterns of partnership and servanthood.'[24]

In the words of David Bosch, 'we need new relationships, mutual responsibility, accountability, and interdependence (not independence!)'.[25] Mutual interdependence means there will be no one-sided approach and requires several presuppositions. First, we acknowledge the biblical images of the household of God and the body of Christ which is the global Church. Therefore, we share what we have with each other: financial resources, personnel and/or experiences. As Rene Padilla puts it, 'interdependence comes with a deeper understanding of the nature of unity in Christ and of the situation in which other mem-

---

22 Hendrik Kraemer, *The Christian Message in a Non-Christian World* (London: Edinburgh House, 1938), p. 426.

23 Stephen Neill, *The Unfinished Task* (London: Edinburgh House, 1957), p. 153.

24 Commission on World Mission and Evangelism, *Your Kingdom Come: Mission Perspectives* (Geneva: World Council of Churches, 1980), p. 178.

25 Bosch, *Transforming Mission*, p. 466.

bers of the body of Christ live'.[26] Second, both North and South should have an attitude of learning and accepting help from one another. Both must acknowledge that, in Christ, God has given gifts without partiality to all local expressions of the body of Christ, and so we need each other in order to experience full manifestation of the body of which Christ is the head. Third, we all have a responsibility to exercise those gifts and to create an environment in which others can exercise theirs. Fourth, both sides need to respect each other in their limitations and difficulties and try to build each other up, to be sensitive to the needs of the other and willing to respond to them. In order to implement the mutuality of obligations, both sides need to make a special effort to achieve a relationship that is theologically sound and practically builds up the body of Christ. As a result, 'Mission, then, becomes a two-way street, a constant exchange, a perennial learning', and, furthermore, 'mission awareness and mission cooperation are understood in terms of mutuality'.[27]

The second aspect of our study in this chapter is to do with global economic inequality. Here the ideas presented by liberation theology provide important insights for doing theology in the public sphere.

Latin American liberation theology and base communities

Liberation theology as a collective term and concept was formulated in Latin America in the context of political and economic injustice in 1960s and 1970s, when many of the Latin American countries were under military-backed governments and suffered economic hardships. Disillusioned with Christian democracy as the solution to the profound socio-economic problems of their continent, a new generation of Latin American priests sought answers by studying economics, sociology and political science in the Marxist-influenced atmosphere of 1960s universities. They did not have strong indigenous traditions to draw on as in Asia and Africa, nor could they engage in anti-western polemic since their culture is akin to that of Europe,[28] but Marxist analysis encouraged them to see the continent's problems in terms of unjust structures rather than individual failings, and to view economic underdevelopment as the consequence of the inequity of the prevailing global capitalist system, which rendered the Third World dependent on the developed

---

26 Padilla, *Mission Between*, p. 137.

27 Anthony Bellagamba, *Mission and Ministry in the Global Church* (Maryknoll, NY: Orbis Books, 1992), pp. 59–61.

28 Paul Freston, *Evangelicals and Politics in Asia, Africa and Latin America* (Cambridge: Cambridge University Press, 2001), p. 192.

world. In short, Latin American underdevelopment is the dark side of northern development.[29] At a national level they also identified vested interests that kept the poor in the situation of poverty, and theologically they began to redefine sin as a matter of the collective failure of society and not only of personal guilt.[30] As a result, they came to regard revolutionary change in society as necessary. In the mid-1960s bishops from the continent attended the Second Vatican Council. Because of the numbers of Catholics in Latin America they constituted more than 22 per cent of the total there – although this still left Latin American Christians underrepresented. At the Council it became clear that many of their concerns differed from those of the European bishops,[31] and as Adrian Hastings points out, the teaching of the Second Vatican Council with regard to social justice, empowering the laity, use of vernacular languages, encouragement of pluralism and concern for the poor offered a greater challenge to the church of Latin America than perhaps anywhere else.[32] The combined reflections of bishops and priests led to a unique response to the Second Vatican Council, which was to have worldwide influence. This came in three main ways: at the second meeting of CELAM (the Latin American Episcopal Conference), in liberation theology and through the 'base communities'.[33]

CELAM II in Medellín, Columbia, in 1968 was a momentous event in the history of the Latin American church in two ways. First, it was visited by Pope Paul VI – the first time a pope had ever set foot in the 'new world'. Second, the bishops took the extraordinary step of declaring the Church to be a 'poor church', against injustice and for the liberation of the poor as part of evangelization, and so rejected the socio-political order that had existed in Latin America since the sixteenth century.[34] The conclusions of Medellín were endorsed by all the episcopacies, and in the turbulent years of the 1960s and 1970s national churches took stances on behalf of the poor and against military regimes and other injustices in several different countries.[35] Eleven years later the 'preferential option for the poor' was reaffirmed at CELAM III in

---

29 José Miguez Bonino, *Doing Theology in a Revolutionary Situation* (Philadelphia: Fortress Press, 1975), pp. 26–7.

30 Gutiérrez, *A Theology of Liberation*, p. 102.

31 Enrique Dussel, *A History of the Church in Latin America*, trans. Alan Neely (Grand Rapids, MI: Eerdmans, 1981), pp. 139–40.

32 Adrian Hastings, 'Latin America', in Adrian Hastings (ed.), *A World History of Christianity* (London: Cassell, 1999), p. 359.

33 Hastings, 'Latin America', pp. 359–60.

34 Hastings, 'Latin America', p. 360. For documents, see Alfred T. Hennelly (ed.), *Liberation Theology: A Documentary History* (Maryknoll, NY: Orbis Books 1990), pp. 89–119.; for details, see Dussel, *A History of the Church in Latin America*, pp. 141–7.

35 For details, see Dussel, *A History of the Church in Latin America*, pp. 148–84.

Puebla, Mexico, despite conservative attempts to 'bury Medellín'.[36] The situation of the indigenous peoples and African Americans was described as abject poverty, which represented 'institutionalized injustice'.[37] For many Latin American Christians, like Enrique Dussel, these momentous events signalled a break of the Latin American church with the model of Christendom and the shift to a missionary stance.[38] The 'option for the poor' eventually became enshrined in Catholic social teaching in the encyclical of John Paul II, *Centesimus Annus*,[39] making clear the Church's position of solidarity with the poor in their struggles for justice, but not before it had caused major upheavals in theology in the region and worldwide.

The reverberations of the second response, 'theology of liberation', are still being felt around the world today. Frederick Pike sees in its emergence a number of currents in Latin American society and church: 'mystical Marxism, dependency analysis, an apocalyptic world-view extending back to pre-Columbian times, and utopianism, often verging on post-millennialism, of twentieth-century populist movements steeped in religious mythology'.[40] Peruvian priest Gustavo Gutiérrez was the first to articulate clearly 'a theology of liberation', which he defined as 'a critical reflection on Christian praxis in light of the word of God'.[41] Reading the story of the Exodus from Egypt, for example, he concluded that this liberation of Israel was 'a political action' and that this is foundational to the Judaeo-Christian faith.[42] This led him first to interpret Christian faith out of the suffering, struggle and hope of the poor, and second to criticize society and the ideologies sustaining it, and also the activity and theology of the Church, from the angle of the poor. Gutiérrez put 'orthopraxis' alongside 'orthodoxy' (right practice as well as right doctrine) as the test of faith.[43] This revolutionary movement demanded not only a theology of liberation but also 'the liberation of theology' from being 'the erudite theology of textbooks' to 'a theology arising out of the urgent problems of real life'.[44]

Constructively, liberation theology called for the reinvention and realignment of the Church from an institution that supported and

---

36 Dussel, *A History of the Church in Latin America*, p. 239.

37 For documents, see Hennelly, *Liberation Theology*, pp. 225–58.

38 Dussel, *A History of the Church in Latin America*, p. 255.

39 Para. 11.

40 Frederick B. Pike, 'Latin America', in John McManners (ed.), *The Oxford History of Christianity* (Oxford: Oxford University Press, 2002), pp. 437–73.

41 Gutiérrez, *A Theology of Liberation*, p. xxix.

42 Gutiérrez, *A Theology of Liberation*, p. 88.

43 Gutiérrez, *A Theology of Liberation*, p. 8.

44 Juan Luis Segundo, *The Liberation of Theology*, trans. John Drury, first published in 1975 in Spanish (Maryknoll, NY: Orbis Books, 1976), pp. 4–5.

mirrored the unjust structures of society to communities with char-ismatic ministries appropriate to the context.[45] The creation of 'base (ecclesial) communities' was a way of involving the laity in ministry, as instructed by the Second Vatican Council and utilized the encour-agement given by the Council for lay people to read and interpret the Bible. Unlike celebration of the Mass, reading the Bible was something they could do without a priest and so the communities can also be seen as a pastoral strategy to deal with the shortage of priests and also a response to the challenge of a growing Protestant movement. But in Recife in north-east Brazil, base communities took a new turn when, with the support of Archbishop Helder Camara, leader of the 'Move-ment for Moral and Liberating Influence', they were combined with the educational method developed by Paulo Freire. This involved 'conscien-tization', or awareness-raising, among the poor of the causes of their condition and of the ideologies used to perpetuate it to empower them to change their situation.[46] Groups of lay people were encouraged to read the Bible together (with priests participating only on an occasional basis), to reflect on it in the light of their social condition, to use it as the basis for community action and then to read the Bible again in the light of their experience, following the 'hermeneutic circle' explained by Segundo.[47] Perhaps as many as three million people were involved in the early 1980s, two-thirds of them in Brazil.[48] From this movement emerged a new way of understanding the Bible, which saw a message of social justice that could be applied directly to community life to bring about social change. Inspired by 'the crucified God', liberation theology turned attention to 'the crucified people'.[49] As it developed, liberation theology drew also on the resources of popular Latin American religi-osity to develop a spirituality of liberation.

Liberation theology encouraged a hermeneutics of suspicion that raised questions of power and vested interest in theology. Since it chal-lenged Church and state, liberation theology inevitably faced resistance from the authorities in Latin America and in Rome. Because of their work on behalf of the poor, and action to reduce the power of the land-owning elite, Catholic priests, nuns and church-workers suffered violent attack and persecution in the militarized societies of 1970s and

---

45 Leonardo Boff, *Ecclesiogenesis: The Base Communities Reinvent the Church*, trans. Robert R. Barr (London: Collins, 1986).

46 Paulo Freire, *Pedagogy of the Oppressed*, trans. Myra Bergman Ramos, first pub-lished in Portuguese in 1968 (New York: Seabury Press, 1970).

47 Segundo, *The Liberation of Theology*, pp. 7–38.

48 Pike, 'Latin America', pp. 437–73 at 467.

49 Jon Sobrino, 'The Crucified Peoples: Yahweh's Suffering Servant Today', in Leonardo Boff and Virgil Elizondo (eds), *1492–1992: The Voice of the Victims* (London: SCM Press, 1990), pp. 120–9.

1980s Latin America. El Salvador had perhaps the most highly charged atmosphere. In the late 1970s, where Marxists opposed a military junta (backed by the USA), six priests were assassinated and the Archbishop, Oscar Romero (1917–80), an advocate of the poor, was gunned down while celebrating Mass. Even at his funeral, attended by mourners from all over the world, a bomb went off and shots were fired. The violence continued to the end of the Cold War, and in 1989 six Jesuits were murdered in one incident in the same country.

Liberation theology in Latin America raises critical questions about who has the right to do Christian theology – the powerful or the powerless? It questions the ideological standpoint of any theology – does it support the status quo or does it represent the interests of the poor? And it encourages Christians not to stop at charity but to raise structural questions and engage in advocacy to change the structures of society for the better. As Las Casas had understood from reflecting on the book of Ecclesiasticus, 'It is of no use ... to pretend that one believes in the God of the Bible when one "lives ... on the blood of the Indians".'[50] There is no doubt that liberation theology has changed the theological landscape worldwide by attempting to bring the poor and poverty – rightly seen as central to Jesus' ministry – back into the centre of Christian concern and indeed of most religious communities.

When it comes to the question of globalization, the tendency of liberation theology was to oppose the system as evil and contrary to biblical principles. However, because Christianity, like other religions, is both an agent of globalization and a product of it,[51] this attitude needs to be reconsidered. There are major problems of economic globalization, such as unequal development and opportunities resulting in poverty in the South, overemphasis on consumption, which leads to waste of common sources, the tendency of some countries to monopolize the resources and means for production, and accumulation of wealth and power in certain elite groups and nations. However, while acknowledging these negative effects as problems of the system and also due to the greed of human nature, Max Stackhouse and other public theologians have proposed engaging critically with economic globalization in order to reform it because 'it is also possible that globalization reflects a more pervasive process than some of the protests comprehend, and that the moral dynamics behind it are at least more ambiguous, and

50 Gustavo Gutiérrez, 'Towards the Fifth Centenary', in Boff and Elizondo (eds), 1492–1992, pp. 1–10.

51 Sebastian Kim and Kirsteen Kim, *Christianity as a World Religion* (London: Continuum, 2008), pp. 11–13.

sometimes better, than critics allow'.[52] In particular, they point away from economic injustices to highlight the benefits of increased global interconnectedness – the multidirectional nature of globalizing forces and that Christianity itself has historically been a globalizing force – to show that globalization is a reality that also has many redeeming and positive features.[53]

Conclusion

The global economic inequalities between the North and the South have been a dominant concern for those in the South who wish to affirm self-reliance, justice and equal partnership in international relations. In this chapter the issue has been addressed by looking at the body of Christ and the household of God, and at the mutual interdependency of the North and the South. Furthermore, the rise of Latin American liberation theology and the base communities movement has had a lasting impact on approaches to this issue of the structural problems of the capitalist system and the protection of the poor and marginalized. While acknowledging the immense contributions of Latin American liberation theology and its different applications in other contexts and situations, public theology also seeks ways and means for reforming the system by changing the preconceived perceptions of the North and the South and the rich and the poor. This involves not only theologizing in academy and the Church but, like liberation theology, mobilizing wider society by using advocacy, demonstrations and education of the general public.

Among the best recent examples of the churches' efforts to seek equality and justice between the North and South were the Jubilee 2000 and Make Poverty History campaigns. The Jubilee 2000 campaign was, by and large, initiated and carried out by Christian churches and organizations. The very concept of jubilee comes from the Hebrew Bible and was recaptured by Jesus as he proclaimed a coming 'year of the Jubilee' to free the captives. It was an overwhelming experience when the participants were assembled along the main streets of Birmingham (in 1998), forming a huge human chain around the city, which they then broke to demonstrate the breaking of the bondage of the people of the poorest nations to the burden of debt. Christians took one of the most pertin-

---

52 Max Stackhouse, *Globalization and Grace: A Christian Public Theology for a Global Future* (New York: Continuum, 2007), vol. 1, p. 21.

53 Stackhouse, *Globalization and Grace*; see also Deirdre King Hainsworth and Scott R. Paeth (eds), *Public Theology for a Global Society: Essays in Honor of Max L. Stackhouse* (Grand Rapids, MI: Eerdmans, 2010).

ent (and yet perhaps most unimplemented) symbols of justice from the scripture and applied it to the contemporary context of global injustice. The Christian Church played the vital role of being a prophet in society and raised its voice in a collective and ecumenical way. Towards the end of the campaign there were 24 million signatures from 60 countries around the world and the campaign established the debt issue as one of the most important items on the global political agenda.

The Make Poverty History campaign, which succeeded Jubilee 2000, was highlighted in a demonstration on 2 July 2005 in Edinburgh. An estimated 225,000 people from all over Britain were wearing white T-shirts and holding placards with slogans such as 'Trade Justice Not Free Trade', 'Drop the Debt', 'More and Better Aid' and 'Fight Poverty Not War'. There was a sense of excitement and something of a carnival atmosphere, but those who took part in the demonstration experienced a sense of solidarity in being there with tens of thousands of others to make a point to those who make important decisions – especially to the leaders of the world's richest nations, meeting for the G8 summit in Gleneagles. It was a commitment to do something for the poor, particularly in Africa. Make Poverty History was a successful exercise in co-operation of over 500 organizations, which included secular NGOs and groups from various other religions. The initial campaign permeated into the wider society and the different interest groups were then integrated so that the whole Make Poverty History campaign could be owned by many ordinary people and organizations. It was especially encouraging to see that, among the participant organizations in Edinburgh, so many were Christian denominations, local churches, church-related organizations and other religious communities. It was clear that people felt that this was the place where the Church and other religious communities should be to share the concerns of the poor by showing our solidarity with them. The issues addressed were not only of debt release, but also to do with trade justice and more and better aid, which is an even greater problem for the modern globalized system of economy. Although the road to making poverty history is still long, the resulting announcement of the IMF's decision to cancel the debts of the world's poorest nations was welcome news indeed for those who had worked hard for many years in the campaign. The Christian contributions to the campaign and the overwhelming participation of the people of Britain made a deep impression on many in the public as an outstanding example of doing public theology.

7

Peace-Building: The Response of the Western Churches to the Iraq War

We bring faith into the public square when our moral convictions demand it. But to influence a democratic society, you must win the public debate about why the policies you advocate are better for the *common good*.[1]

In any international or regional conflict situation, there is no simple explanation for the causes and process of the conflict – social, economic, territorial, political, ethnic and religious factors play important roles in any conflict. It is, in most cases, a matter of degree. Religion is a contributing factor in many conflicts – past and present – for various reasons, and the critics of religion are right in pointing out that religious leaders and religious communities have contributed to some of the most devastating conflicts throughout history. In particular, religion has promoted the distinction between those who are in and out of their religious traditions:

> [T]oo often, religion has promoted an 'us versus them' attitude as with the Greeks and the barbarians, the Jews and the goyim, the Muslims and the infidels, the Christians and the pagans, the true faith and the heretics, the good people (us) and the bad (them).[2]

However, in spite of these negative effects of religions on the history of humanity, religion could and should be able to contribute in conflict situations by utilizing the strengths and positive aspects of religion. Religion both unites and divides[3] and 'promotes both intolerance and

---

1 Jim Wallis, *God's Politics: Why the Right Gets It Wrong and the Left Doesn't Get It* (New York: HarperSanFrancisco, 2005), p. 71.

2 Henry O. Thompson, *World Religions in War and Peace* (London: McFarland, 1988), p. xiv.

3 Eric O. Hanson, *Religion and Politics in the International System Today* (Cambridge: Cambridge University Press, 2006), p. 315.

hatred ... as well as tolerance of the strongest type – the willingness to live with, explore, and honour difference'.[4]

Public theology as peace-making

Appreciation of the importance of implementing religions in conflict resolution is based on some distinctive aspects of religion. First, peace-making is integral to the faith and practice of most religions. For many believers, 'peace-making is simply not a choice. It is a sacred duty',[5] and is part and parcel of what it means to 'fulfil the will of God or the gods or the spirit world'.[6] In this regard, religious enthusiasm and inspiration can be utilized to bring about peace and reconciliation in the conflict zones as well as encourage involvement in social justice for reasons of religious inspiration and activism.[7] That religious motivation for peace-making is a powerful tool in dealing with conflict situations is attested to, for example, in the volume *Peacemakers in Action: Profiles of Religion in Conflict Resolution*, which records how religiously motivated people have effectively contributed to peace and reconciliation. The core reasons for these contributions are, first, that the 'pursuit of justice and peace by peaceful means is a sacred priority' of religious traditions, and the 'hermeneutics of peace' drawn from one's own religious tradition (sacred texts, doctrines, and practices) acts for many believers as a guidance in implementing their commitment to peace.[8]

Second, religion offers critical understanding of the process of peace-making. Because religious traditions provide some of the fundamental explanations for and insights into both war and peace, utilizing these resources for peace is vital for peace-making.[9] As Daniel Smith-Christopher has argued,

> [I]f religious values and symbolism are potential weapons (as well as essential to understanding a conflict), then surely the resources for reconciliation must also come from a more creative analysis of the

---

4 Harold Coward and Gordon S. Smith (eds), *Religion and Peacebuilding* (Albany, NY: State University of New York Press, 2004), p. 2.

5 David Little (ed.), *Peacemakers in Action: Profiles of Religion in Conflict Resolution* (Cambridge: Cambridge University Press, 2007), p. 9.

6 Thompson, *World Religions in War and Peace*, p. xiv.

7 Coward and Smith (eds), *Religion and Peace Building*, 2; Daniel L. Smith-Christopher (ed.), *Subverting Hatred: The Challenge of Non-Violence in Religious Traditions* (Maryknoll, NY: Orbis Books, 1998), p. 2.

8 Little (ed.), *Peacemakers in Action*, p. 438.

9 Perry Schmidt-Leukel (ed.), *War and Peace in World Religions: The Gerald Weisfeld Lectures 2003* (London: SCM Press, 1989), p. 3.

religious cultural resources of the societies which are involved in the conflict itself.[10]

In the Christian tradition, for example, the concept of war and peace has been drawn out from both the Hebrew Bible and the New Testament. From this, the idea of 'just war' was initiated by Augustine of Hippo and then developed by Thomas Aquinas, and has been influential in the conduct and ethics of war, rightly and wrongly, in the West for centuries. At the same time the pacifist tradition, following certain teachings of Jesus, has also made a significant impact on peace movements both within and outside Christian traditions.[11]

Third, religious traditions possess unique authority and capacity among the followers of the particular religion to deal with conflicts, particularly by preventing conflict and making sustainable peace. Kofi Annan, former Secretary-General of the United Nations, insists that 'religious organizations can play a role in preventing armed conflict because of the moral authority that they carry in many communities'.[12] In the context of 'conflict transformation' – replacement of violent with non-violent means for settling disputes – religiously motivated people play a role as advocates, observers and mediators. Conflict transformation leads into 'structural reform' – efforts to build institutions and enhance civic leadership that will not only address the causes of the conflict but also develop long-term strategies for peaceful, non-violent relations in the society. In this process, religious people have served as educators and institution builders.[13] An example of a collective effort for peace is the World Council of Churches programme on the 'Justice, Peace and Integrity of Creation' (JPIC). This emphasizes the positive employment of the 'creative power' of God as empowerment for building communities of the poor and oppressed, and as the power of resistance for the sake of peace and justice. The group has pledged that community is the key aspect of this struggle for peace and justice since people gain inspiration from one another, share sufferings, and gain strength against any forms of oppression or conflict.[14]

---

10 Smith-Christopher (ed.), *Subverting Hatred*, p. 11.

11 See Lisa S. Cahill, *Love Your Enemies: Discipleship, Pacifism, and Just War Theory* (Minneapolis, MN: Fortress Press, 1994).

12 Kofi A. Annan, *Prevention of Armed Conflict: Report of the Secretary-General Kofi A. Annan* (New York: United Nations, 2002), p. 78.

13 David Little and L. Scott Appleby, 'A Moment of Opportunity? The Promise of Religious Peacebuilding in an Era of Religious and Ethnic Conflict', in Coward and Smith (eds), *Religion and Peace Building*, pp. 1–23.

14 Frederick R. Wilson (ed.), *The San Antonio Report – Your Will be Done: Mission in Christ's Way* (Geneva: World Council of Churches, 1990), pp. 37–51.

Fourth, religious traditions can be effective in practical ways, particularly in reconciliation. For example, in the case of Northern Ireland, in order to move beyond sectarianism, religious communities made significant contributions to the peace process by taking practical steps such as naming and exposing sectarian dynamics, breaking the cycle of antagonized division and developing a vision of reconciled community. One of the key tools for this was the renewal of the 'expanded and enlivened inner spirituality' of the people involved.[15] Discussing the importance of the way justice is done in the process of reconciliation in the case of South Africa, Russel Botman argues that the 'restorative justice' drawn from the biblical understanding of reconciliation involves memory, confession and forgiveness, and that the Truth and Reconciliation Commission has demonstrated this and 'invites people into a certain memory of the past that also frees them from it', and furthermore it 'frees people for the future, for each other, and for God'.[16] This is the conviction of Desmond Tutu, who led the Commission: 'God wants to show that there is life after conflict and repression – that because of forgiveness, there is a future.'[17] In both the above cases of Northern Ireland and South Africa, different forms of Christianity contributed significantly to the conflicts, but at the same time they have made important contributions to the processes of reconciliation. The relationship between religion and peace-making is ambivalent: religion has contributed to both conflict and peace, and scholars and practitioners are in agreement that religious resources have to be examined and utilized both in order to prevent conflict and in order to make a sustainable peace in a post-conflict situation.

Public debates on the Iraq War

The Iraq War (or Second Gulf War) started on 20 March 2003 with an invasion led by troops almost entirely from the USA and the UK. In addition to the human cost, the war has led to widespread destruction of the livelihoods of people in Iraq, as well as creating lasting damage to the relationship between the Muslim world and the USA and its allies. In the UK, there has been fierce criticism of the war, both within government and among NGOs, religious groups and other bodies. However, these criticisms were not effective either in preventing

15 Joseph Liechty and Cecelia Clegg, *Moving Beyond Sectarianism: Religion, Conflict, and Reconciliation in Northern Ireland* (Dublin: Columba Press, 2001), pp. 337–46.

16 H. R. Botman, 'Truth and Reconciliation: The South Africa Case', in Coward and Smith (eds), *Religion and Peace Building*, pp. 243–60.

17 Desmond Tutu, *No Future Without Forgiveness* (London: Rider, 1999), p. 230.

the war in the first place or in dealing with the subsequent situation. Many Christian groups in the UK, along with other religious groups, have condemned the war, but the question has to be asked whether the Church as a whole has played the role of prophet and catalyst for peace and reconciliation, or remained as a reluctant bystander who was hesitant to get involved. In order to answer that question, I shall examine documents produced by various denominations, as well as the writings of individual church leaders and theologians about the Iraq War.

The growing prospect of military action against the Iraqi government of Saddam Hussein became reality on 11 October 2002 when the US Congress authorized President Bush to invade Iraq. During the uncertain period that followed, in which the US and the UK governments were planning the invasion, people in both countries expressed serious doubts about engaging in such a war and showed their opposition in various ways, including organizing demonstrations. The climax of the collective anti-war demonstrations was the demonstration in London on 15 February 2003, where there was estimated to have been between 750,000 and two million people, which was the largest demonstration the city has ever witnessed. Between 15 and 16 February there were also demonstrations in other cities in the UK and in about 60 countries around the world, of which the one in Rome was the largest, attracting about three million people.[18] The demonstrations in the UK were organized by the Stop the War Coalition, the Muslim Association of Britain and the Campaign for Nuclear Disarmament, and the various groups and NGOs continued to engage with the issue right up to the beginning of the war. Many Christians also made clear their opposition to the war both individually and collectively by joining the demonstrations and campaigning in other ways.[19]

As far as collective responses to the proposed military action from the church in the UK are concerned, the earliest document on the possible Iraq War was 'Evaluating the Threat of Military Action Against Iraq' by the Archbishop's Council of the Church of England on 20 March 2002, exactly a year prior to the invasion.[20] The 16-page statement uses the just war tradition as its main moral basis for establishing 'principles, criteria and rules'. It has a very extensive account of the background in terms of UN resolutions since the Gulf War in 1991 and global political developments after 9/11. The document also raises the Church's concern for the humanitarian suffering due to the sanctions that had been imposed on Iraq for many years. On the issue of military

18 http://news.bbc.co.uk/1/hi/world/europe/2765215.stm (accessed 25 Mar. 2009).

19 Pew Forum, 'Religious Groups Issue Statements on War with Iraq', http://pewforum.org/PublicationPage.aspx?id=616 (accessed 19 Mar. 2009).

20 www.casi.org.uk/info/churcheng/020320coewar.pdf.

action, the document uses the just war theory for moral guidance, particularly on 'proper authority and right intent'. It also raises concern about the absence of a plan for post-war settlement and the possible damage to interfaith relationships between Christians and Muslims. The report concludes that the Iraqi government is seeking the end of sanctions and the survival of the regime, and suggests that 'the only way progress can be made' is by 'lifting the sanctions in return for letting weapons inspectors back in'. The document gives a thorough analysis of the situation, makes a clear assessment of the case against possible military action on Iraq on the basis of the just war theory, and presents a highly critical view of the foreign policy of the US government and the uncritical support of the British Prime Minister to the US-led 'war on terror'. There is less urgency in opposing the war in this document than in later ones, since the prospect was not entirely clear in the public mind at the time of publication, but the document exhibits awareness of the political situation and prepares the Church's responses to it.

In the later part of 2002 and the beginning of 2003, there were an increasing number of statements and articles issued by denominations and church leaders. The catchphrase of 'Disarm Iraq without War', which has often been used by church leaders, was coined by a joint statement of 42 US and 25 UK church leaders on 10 October 2002.[21] It starts with the passage from Isaiah 2.4, which says 'Nation shall not lift up sword against nation, neither shall they learn war any more.' The signatories state that they are 'compelled by the prophetic vision of peace' to speak out and urge that the two governments should pursue the matter with 'moral principles, political wisdom, and international law'. They call for alternative means to disarm Iraq, and argue that a 'pre-emptive war with Iraq is not a last resort', and that according to the just war principle, the war would be illegal, unwise and immoral. This document is significant not only because of the popular slogan of 'Disarm Iraq without War', which expressed the feelings of many Christians, and was later popularized by Jim Wallis through his article in *Sojourners* magazine,[22] but also because of its explicit usage of three points of objection to war – illegal, unwise and immoral – which were in line with just war theory and widely accepted by Christians who were against the war on Iraq.

In a wider context, on 5 February 2003, the World Council of Churches organized a gathering in Berlin of delegates from Europe, the Middle East and the USA, inviting also German Chancellor Gerhard Schröder. It made a statement cautioning that the current political

---

21 'Disarm Iraq Without War: A Statement from Religious Leaders in the US and UK', http://www.unitedforpeace.org/article.php?id=2837 (accessed 19 Mar. 2009).

22 Jim Wallis, 'Disarm Iraq ... Without War', *Sojourners* (Nov./Dec. 2002).

move by the US and UK governments 'creates an international culture of fear, threat and insecurity' and the participants cannot accept pre-emptive military strikes because they are immoral and in violation of the UN Charter. It concludes that 'God will guide those responsible to take decisions based on careful reflections, moral principles and high legal standards'.[23] Later in the month, the WCC Executive Commit-tee made clear its strong opposition to military action in Iraq during their meeting. The committee members were 'extremely concerned' and 'strongly deplore[d] the fact that the most powerful nations of this world again regard war as an acceptable instrument of foreign policy'. It criticized the Iraqi government for human rights violations and urged them to keep the UN Security Council resolutions. However, the state-ment insists that 'war is not an acceptable way to resolve conflict' and instead calls for public and international support of the UN. Reaffirm-ing the Berlin statement, the committee members declared that the war would be immoral, unwise and in breach of the principles of the UN Charter.[24]

From the Roman Catholic Church, Pope John Paul II made clear his opposition to military action towards Iraq on various occasions, but in his speech to the Diplomatic Corps on 13 January 2003 he voiced his strongest objection. He emphasized three vital aspects of public life: 'yes to life', 'respect for law', and the 'duty of solidarity', and declared that Christians should have the courage to say 'No': 'No to death', 'No to selfishness', and 'No to war'. 'War is not always inevitable ... but it is always a defeat for humanity', he insisted. Instead he put forward 'international law, honest dialogue, solidarity between states, noble exercise of diplomacy' as the right tools for resolving international con-flict. As he saw it, war is 'never another means that one can choose to employ for settling differences between nations': 'war cannot be decided upon – even when it is a matter of ensuring the common good, except as the very last option and in accordance with very strict conditions'.[25] In his *Angelus* address on Sunday 16 March 2003, the Pope empha-sized that the use of force should be the last recourse and asserted that 'there is still time to negotiate; there is still room for peace, it is never too late to come to an understanding and to continue discussions'. As he recalled his experience of the Second World War, he further chal-lenged his readers: 'We must do everything possible. We know well

23 http://www.nccusa.org/news/03news6.html (accessed 22 July 2010).

24 http://www.oikoumene.org/resources/documents/wcc-commissions/international-affairs/regional-concerns/middle-east/statement-against-military-action-in-iraq.html (accessed 22 July 2010).

25 http://www.vatican.va/holy_father/john_paul_ii/speeches/2003/january/documents/hf_jp-ii_spe_20030113_diplomatic-corps_en.html (accessed 22 July 2010).

that peace is not possible at any price. But we all know how great is this responsibility.'[26] Cardinal Joseph Ratzinger, in his interview with *30 Days*, also made his opposition to the war clear: 'it seems clear that the negative consequences will be greater than anything positive that might be obtained'. [27]

Between January and March 2003, many church leaders made strong statements, particularly in the UK and the USA.[28] The United States Conference of Catholic Bishops issued a statement on 13 November 2002, insisting that when it comes to the choice between war and peace, the choices are not just political and military ones but also 'moral ones because they involve matters of life and death'. The Conference therefore offered a 'series of concerns and questions' hoping to reach 'sound moral judgment', and called for an active pursuit of alternatives to war.[29] The National Council of the Churches in the USA made a strong statement, arguing that the war in Iraq is a 'failure of political and moral imagination' and declaring that:

> We encourage all people to protest the start of war by publically dissenting and disassociating themselves from the Bush administration's doctrine of pre-emptive attack. We support those who are called to participate in actions of conscientious objection, nonviolent civil disobedience, tax resistance, or other nonviolent acts of refusing consent to this war.[30]

In the UK, the House of Bishops of the Church of England (January 2003) stated that the war was 'ill-judged and premature' and 'could not be morally justified'. It warned that 'suffering on all sides could be immense, with widespread and unpredictable environmental, economic and political consequences'.[31] The Archbishop of Canterbury, Rowan Williams, and the Roman Catholic Primate, Cardinal Cormac Murphy O'Connor, made a joint statement on 20 February – 'war is always a deeply disturbing prospect' – and stressed the question of its

---

26 http://www.vatican.va/holy_father/john_paul_ii/angelus/2003/documents/hf_jp-ii_ang_20030316_en.html.

27 http://www.30giorni.it/us/articolo.asp?id=775 (accessed 22 July 2010).

28 See Pew Forum, 'Religious Groups Issue Statements on War with Iraq'; http://www.ncccusa.org/iraq/iraqstatements2.html; The National Council of Churches in the Philippines (NCCP), http://www.ncccusa.org/iraq/iraqstatements2.html (accessed 22 July 2010).

29 'Statement on Iraq', http://www.nccbuscc.org/bishops/iraq.shtml (accessed 22 July 2010).

30 *Sojourners* (20 March 2003), http://www.ncccusa.org/iraq/iraqstatements2.html (accessed 22 July 2010).

31 http://www.churchofengland.org/media-centre/news/2003/01/case_for_war_yet_to_be_made,_warns_house_of_bishops.aspx (accessed 22 July 2010).

'moral legitimacy' and the 'unpredictable humanitarian consequences' of a war with Iraq.[32] During this time, church leaders also visited politicians: some bishops in the UK met the Foreign Secretary,[33] the Papal Envoy made a visit to President Bush and made two points. On the one hand, the Iraqi government should keep the promise of human rights and disarmament under UN auspices, and on the other hand, the US government needs to continue to pursue the matter within the framework of the UN. War will cause suffering for the people of Iraq and military personnel, and bring 'a further instability in the region and a new gulf between Islam and Christianity'.[34] Although the churches did not explicitly support the anti-war demonstration on 15 February 2003, many individual Christians and church leaders participated in the demonstration in London and in other major cities around the country.

Unlike Europe and other parts of the world, there were opposing views from the churches in the USA, reflecting the divided opinion of the general public in the opinion polls. Although most of the smaller denominations made their opposition known, mainline evangelicals and Catholic churches were divided within. The best-known protagonists for the war were Richard Land, President of the Ethics and Religious Liberty Commission of the Southern Baptist Convention, and Richard John Neuhaus, the editor of *First Things*. Jim Wallis, the editor of *Sojourners* magazine, was the best-known voice against. In the letter to President Bush on 2 July 2002, over 40 evangelical Christian leaders, led by Wallis, alleged that at the heart of the issue was a distorted biblical interpretation that led to uncritical support for the Israeli government, and therefore aggression towards its Middle East neighbours.[35] Wallis also launched the 'Six-Point Plan', suggested by church leaders in the USA, and put forward a 'Third Way' between threat and war.[36] Wallis not only wrote articles engaging with his readers but also actively campaigned against the war by visiting politicians. On 18 February 2003, a group of US church leaders, along with leaders of churches in the UK, met with Prime Minister Tony Blair and Clare Short.[37]

Examining the documents, speeches and articles produced by the churches in the UK and the USA, there is no doubt that the churches not only made their opposition to war clear but also that they tried in vari-

---

32 http://www.archbishopofcanterbury.org/852 (accessed 22 July 2010).

33 http://www.cofe.anglican.org/news/church_leaders_meet_foreign_secretary.html (accessed 22 July 2010).

34 http://www.cm-ngo.net/PapalEnvoyvisitsPresidentBush.html (accessed 22 July 2010).

35 Wallis, *God's Politics*, pp. 185–6.

36 Jim Wallis and John Bryson, 'There is a Third Way', *Washington Post*, 14 March 2003.

37 Wallis, *God's Politics*, pp. 133–6.

ous ways to prevent their governments from going to war in Iraq.[38] The churches were not reluctant bystanders, but whether they were playing the active role of catalyst for peace is questionable. In retrospect, their efforts were not successful, the war did start, and the damage done to human lives involved in the war, the economic and social situation of Iraq, the relationship between the West and the Islamic world, and international law are immense. Except for the few politicians who led the war, hardly anyone argues that the war was the 'right thing to do', to use Tony Blair's phrase. In this context, the searching question of 'Could the war have been prevented?' comes to mind. Judging by the strength of opposition from the general public and religious communities, and also the seemingly clear arguments against the war, the decision could have been otherwise.

The limitations of just war theory

Both Bush and Blair are committed Christians, and one would predict they would listen to the voices from their churches, so we need to answer the question why they did not. It is relatively easy to find the answer to this question in the USA, because public opinion was quite equally divided immediately before the war,[39] and also the US President had very strong support from the more conservative sections of evangelical churches or the 'Christian Right', as was expressed in the letter sent to the President from Richard Land and other evangelical leaders on 3 October 2002, strongly endorsing the war on the basis of just war theory.[40] However, in contrast, there was no strong support for war in the UK from religious communities except from a handful of Anglican bishops. Tony Blair did secure the House of Commons's approval for the war by 412 votes to 149 due to the support of the Conservative Party (146 votes), and there was strong support for the war from the tabloid media, especially the *Sun* and the *News of the World*. However, from religious communities and the general public there was strong disapproval.[41] I would like to ask whether and how the churches could

---

38 Except some individual church leaders such as Michael Nazir-Ali, Bishop of Rochester. See *Church Times*, 20 February 2003. See also http://news.bbc.co.uk/1/hi/uk/2783435.stm (accessed 25 Mar. 2010).

39 According to CNN (18 Mar. 2003), 66 per cent of Americans supported Bush's decision to go to war: http://articles.cnn.com/2003-03-18/politics/sprj.irq.bush.poll_1_poll-iraqi-leader-saddam-hussein-ultimatum?_s=PM:ALLPOLITICS (accessed 25 Mar. 2010).

40 'Land Letter', http://erlc.com/article/the-so-called-land-letter/ (accessed 25 Mar. 2010).

41 According to a Gallup poll (January 2003), 68 per cent of British people opposed the war without UN support, 16 per cent opposed war even with fresh UN support.

have opposed the war more effectively. I will ask this question first about their argument, which was based on just war theory, and second about the way they engaged in the public sphere.

The most common argument from the Church was the idea that the war in Iraq was 'immoral, unwise and illegal' on the basis of the principle of the just war. Just war theory is divided into two categories: *jus ad bellum* (the right to go to war) and *jus in bello* (right conduct within war). The churches examined the first category, which includes just cause, legitimate authority, right intention, probability of success, last resort, and proportionality. According to just war theory, Christians argued that war against Iraq would be illegal because it would violate the UN Charter. Furthermore, war would not be a last resort since Iraq had not attacked, nor was it a direct threat to the USA and the UK, nor was there any evidence of Iraq's weapons of mass destruction (WMD). They also insisted that the war was unwise because the socio-economic and diplomatic consequences would be very damaging for the relationship between the West and the Muslim countries, as well as between western nations. They argued that the problem within Iraq had to be dealt with by the Iraqis themselves. Above all, they argued that the war would be immoral because of the human cost of innocent civilians and also of the attacking forces. Instead, it was argued that the international community should focus on supporting and rebuilding the Iraqi people who had been through hardship under Saddam Hussein and because of the sanctions imposed on them. Christians in the UK seemed to be united in opposing the war, on the basis of just war theory or pacifist tradition, and these seemed to be strong and convincing arguments.

However, the argument based on the just war principle was challenged by some Christian leaders who also used what they called 'time-honored criteria of Just War theory'. In the so-called 'Land Letter', the signatories praised President Bush as giving 'bold, courageous and visionary leadership' in this 'decisive hour' of the nation's history. They insisted that the President's policies against terrorism were both 'right and just' and argued in support of war in Iraq. First, they wrote, it is a just cause because, according to the theory, defensive war is admissible, and in view of Saddam Hussein's record of aggression towards neighbouring nations and his own people, disarming Hussein would be 'to defend freedom and freedom-loving people from state-sponsored terror and death'. It also stood the test of 'just intent' from the theory because 'liberty for the Iraqi people is a great moral cause'. On the question of the 'last resort', the signatories claimed that all the efforts to disarm Iraq of WMD had been exhausted. On the issue of legitimate authority, though it is 'wise and prudent' to obtain the UN Security Council's endorsement, the drafters of the letter considered that the 'legitimate authority to authorize the use of US military force is the government of the United States' and 'the authorizing vehicle is a declaration of war or a joint resolution of the Congress'. They also discussed the question of proportionality. Citing the reluctance of the western allies to deal with Hitler's ambition when he illegally reoccupied the Rhineland in 1936, they insisted that 'the cost of not dealing with this threat now will only succeed in greatly increasing the cost in human lives and suffering' in the future.[42]

Another strong supporter of the war was Richard John Neuhaus, who saw the role of government as to protect its people from perceived threat and 'the Church's competence and responsibility is to set forth the pertinent moral principles'. 'In the absence of *tranquillitas ordinis*', he argued, 'war may sometimes be a moral duty in order to overturn injustice and protect the innocent.' The cause must be just, but in this case the disarmament of Iraq, he believed, constituted a just cause.[43] In response to criticism of the pre-emptive strike, he responded that 'war, if it is just, is not an option chosen but a duty imposed', and in the case of Iraq, it was the response to its aggression towards Kuwait, defiance of the terms of disarmament, and support for (or involvement in) terrorism. Furthermore, he argued, to wait too long before acting would make leaders 'guilty of negligence', for which they would be held 'morally accountable'. And if the UN did not take action, he insisted that the 'credibility and future usefulness of the UN will be gravely undermined'. Regarding the question of proportionality for the civilian casualties, he answered that the consequences are 'unknowable and therefore unknown, except to God'.[44]

Intellectual and theoretical support for the war was forcefully presented by George Weigel, Senior Fellow of the Ethics and Public Policy Center in Washington. In his view, the USA is already engaged in a war on terror and against terrorists who, since 9/11, he regarded as combatants. He argued that the just war tradition must be developed to meet the demands of present contexts; that in the context of terrorist threats, a pre-emptive strike is 'not only morally justifiable but morally imperative', and that states 'do not require the permission of others to defend' themselves.[45] In his view, the tradition should be understood as 'a kind of ethical calculus', to be combined with 'moral reasoning and rigor-

---

42 'Land Letter', http://erlc.com/article/the-so-called-land-letter/ (accessed 25 Mar. 2010).

43 *First Things* (May 2003).

44 'Father Richard Neuhaus on the Iraqi Crisis', ZENIT (March 2003), http://www. catholiceducation.org/articles/religion/re0627.html (accessed 20 July 2010).

45 George Weigel, 'Reality of Terrorism Calls for Fresh Look at Just-War Tradition', *The Catholic Difference*, 20 September 2001.

ous empirical analysis', in order to give guidance to public authorities. Furthermore, he regarded the 'pursuit of justice' as the moral compass for statecraft when applying the just war tradition, and argued that to begin with a 'presumption against violence' would be to 'empty the just-war tradition of its moral power'. Weigel criticized his opponents' usage of the theory, which was anchored in their interpretation of the 'presumption against war', and contended that the theory is a tradition of morally serious statecraft primarily meant for statespersons, which begins with 'the moral obligation of legitimate authorities to defend the security of those for whom they have assumed responsibility'.[46] He further argued that *bellum* is the 'use of armed force for *public* ends by *public* authorities who have an obligation to defend' the public, and in this context war, or use of armed forces, should not be subject to moral judgement, since they are a necessary part of carrying out justice for the people of the state.[47]

Along similar lines, Brian Stiltner, writing immediately after the start of the war, argued that the USA, the UK and their allies have 'rightly arrived at war on Iraq as a just and necessary last resort'. He argued that just war theory is 'an exercise in prudential judgement-making'. He pointed out that just war theory is both a strength and a weakness for the Christian community: its strength lies in the possibility of influencing public policy but its weakness lies in the 'possibility of not offering anything new and spiritually powerful to moral debate'.[48] He is right on this point. He argues that just war theory does not call for avoiding war at all costs but only that 'all reasonable attempts must be made to seek a just resolution of a pending conflict'. The stress on the words 'reasonable' and 'just' should not encourage leaders to 'compromise the justice of the outcome simply to secure peace'. 'Staying with the path of peace is always more attractive, especially for a follower of Jesus. But there are times when peace must give away to the struggle for justice that will establish a more lasting peace.'

The arguments both for and against war presented by Christians heavily relied on just war theory. Those who were against the war concentrated on *jus ad bellum*, whereas the supporters of the war focused on issues related to *jus in bello*, by arguing, as Weigel did, that the USA was already at war. When it comes to the legality of the war, the key issues were whether it is legitimate for the USA and the UK to engage in war without the UN's approval, whether a pre-emptive strike is accept-

---

46 'What is the Just War Tradition For?', *The Catholic Difference*, 4 December 2002.

47 'Moral Clarity in a Time of War', *First Things* (December 2002).

48 Brian Stiltner, 'The Justice of War on Iraq', http://www.elca.org/What-We-Believe/Social-Issues/Journal-of-Lutheran-Ethics/Issues/March-2003/The-Justice-of-War-on-Iraq.aspx (accessed 25 March 2010).

able, and whether the situation in Iraq is a domestic or an international affair. The anti-war camp used just war theory to support their argument but the theory does not cover the modern situation of the UN, international law and WMD, and so opponents were able to produce counter-arguments. Furthermore, there is ambiguity when we discuss just cause, right intention, last resort and proportionality, and the anti-war protagonists were standing on weak ground here. Traditional just war theory does not cover these complex situations in which it is not one nation against another, but conflict in an international setting. As we have seen, the supporters of the war also had their justifications based on just war theory, and they were quite convincing and reasonable, as far as the argument went. Therefore the moral argument against the war on the basis of just war theory is difficult to sustain. The vital argument of the protagonists for war was on the basis of 'protection' of the people in Iraq from oppression, of their democratic values, and also of neighbouring countries and indeed the world from the threat of possible attack. And this argument eventually persuaded many politicians to vote for war.

Effective modes of engagement in the public sphere

As we saw in the above discussion, in their arguments the churches held on to the tradition of just war theory. But not only did this fail to provide a fresh vision for the public, it also turned out to be quite easily disputed by counter-arguments on the basis of the same theory. So the argument based on just war theory could persuade neither the general public nor the politicians. However, the weakness of the argument was not the only reason the churches could not effectively oppose the war. Church leaders appeared to be lacking in their determination against the war and in persuading even their own constituencies on an issue that they believed to be moral, just and in the cause of peace, which is in line with the central Christian message. The key issue here is the strategic engagement of the churches with a public issue. It seems the churches either did not have the courage of their convictions or did not possess the appropriate tools for engagement. There was lack of leadership and passion for the cause.

The protagonists of the war, on the other hand, brought the case with strong passion and powerful appeal to the public. This was quite clear in both the speeches of President Bush and Prime Minister Blair. In his speech in the General Assembly of the UN on 12 September 2002, President Bush appealed to the members of the UN:

The United States has no quarrel with the Iraqi people. They've suffered too long in silent captivity. Liberty for the Iraqi people is a great moral cause and a great strategic goal. The people of Iraq deserve it. The security of all nations requires it ... We must choose between a world of fear and a world of progress. We cannot stand by and do nothing while dangers gather. We must stand up for our security and for the permanent rights and the hopes of mankind. By heritage and by choice, the United States of America will make that stand. And, delegates to the United Nations, you have the power to make that stand, as well. [49]

And to the members of Parliament, Blair made his points with great passion on 18 March 2003:

To retreat now, I believe, would put at hazard all that we hold dearest, turn the UN back into a talking shop, stifle the first steps of progress in the Middle East; leave the Iraqi people to the mercy of events on which we would have relinquished all power to influence for the better ... This is not the time to falter. This is the time for this house, not just this government or indeed this prime minister, but for this house to give a lead, to show that we will stand up for what we know to be right, to show that we will confront the tyrannies and dictatorships and terrorists who put our way of life at risk, to show at the moment of decision that we have the courage to do the right thing.[50]

In other words, the two political leaders made passionate appeals for war, arguing that it was the right thing to do, that it was in a greater cause and that the sacrifice would be necessary and worthwhile for a better world. They made a kind of religious appeal to the public and the message prevailed, in spite of a lack of hard facts and the problem of not having the support of the UN. In contrast, religious leaders made very little impact on the decision-making apart from on their own immediate constituencies. Of course, it is not fair to judge their impact compared to both political leaders, who had the advantages of media attention and their political positions. Nevertheless, a lack of clear leadership from church leaders is also apparent. Throughout the several months prior to launching the war, the Church as a whole did not engage in an explicit campaign nor did church leaders make a strong appeal to the Christian churches – not to mention to the general public. In the UK, the two archbishops of the Anglican and Roman Catholic Churches did

---

49 http://news.bbc.co.uk/1/hi/world/middle_east/2254712.stm (accessed 25 July 2010).

50 http://www.guardian.co.uk/politics/2003/mar/18/foreignpolicy.iraq1 (accessed 25 July 2010).

issue a statement, but the message was rather weak and did not raise a prophetic voice to the general public. In the USA, on the other hand, though Jim Wallis and others passionately campaigned against the war, the Christians and the general public were more or less equally divided over the interpretation of the just war theory. The Pope did make a strong objection to war in January 2003, but it was to a small group of diplomats. He never mentioned Iraq in his New Year address, which was listened to not only by Catholics around the world but also by the general public. Through the Jubilee 2000 and Make Poverty History campaigns, the churches and church-related organizations made a deep impact on people's attitudes towards the debt issue and affected policy-making. But on the issue of the Iraq War, the churches did not play as active a role as they could have done in persuading policy-makers to take a different course rather than engage in war. It was a failed opportunity for church leaders to make a strong stand for peace.

In a recent publication, Tom Frame has fiercely criticized Archbishop Rowan Williams on the issue of war and peace. Although Williams has frequently criticized the conduct of the Iraq War by the British government, Frame argues that his theology does not 'return to the world in which conflict needs to be managed and tensions resolved' and often his comments do not 'touch nor transform the political order'. In his public statements, Frame writes, Williams needs to be 'more specific about what needs to be done' if he (and the Anglican Communion he leads) is to be heard by those outside the Church 'in the hard-headed, argumentative, and intellectual world of strategic studies'. The Archbishop needs to speak not only with conviction but also with clarity.[51] Perhaps this is rather a harsh and unfair criticism of Dr Williams' approach since he cannot be an expert on every political and social issue; nevertheless he could have used his position as the most senior religious figure in the country and a key member of the House of Lords to convey the desire of most Christians and other religious communities and persuade politicians for an alternative solution to engaging in war. Although intellectually convinced, he and other church leaders failed to convert their conviction into passionate and convincing political action.

Conclusion

In this chapter we have examined the response of the western churches to the prospect of war in Iraq and the public theology they developed on the side of peace. We have questioned whether they could have done

---

51 Tom Frame, 'Rowan Williams on War and Peace', in Matheson Russell (ed.), *On Rowan Williams: Critical Essays* (Eugene, OR: Cascade Books, 2009), pp. 163–85.

more to prevent war. There are two other reasons why the churches were not as effective as they might have been in opposing the Iraq War. The first is that though they raised objections to the Iraq War using just war theory, they themselves were divided about its application in this case. Furthermore, just war theory was also co-opted by political leaders in support of war. In light of this, there is an urgent need for the churches to re-evaluate the just war tradition and further develop their capacity for discernment in this area. The second reason is that those who did formulate a theological objection to the war were not able to translate this into mobilizing public opinion or stimulating further reflection and action among Christians. Reflecting on the Iraq War and the 'war on terror', the British Methodist Church and the United Reformed Church produced a resource book, *Peacemaking: A Christian Vocation* in 2006. In a self-critical manner it says that there have been many times when 'prophetic judgement has been deficient or absent': 'Too often, we react too late, jump on the bandwagon, or satisfy ourselves with less than fully-informed comment ... Too often, the Church and its members have influence but do not know how to use it.'[52] The churches need to find effective means of engagement on these issues, otherwise the Church will remain increasingly isolated from contemporary debate in the wider society.

On the issue of the Iraq War, the churches may not be accused of being reluctant bystanders but at the same time neither did they play the role of catalyst for peace in a concrete way. The churches, in spite of being convinced of the folly of war and possessing resources for peace, failed to convey the message and will bear the consequences for years to come. Two issues should be discussed here. One of the key reasons for this failure was anchoring their argument on the just war theory and, as we have discussed above in the case of the USA, this was not effective in persuading the general public. Just war theory, articulated by theologians – and we could say as a public theology – has been immensely influential not only among Christians but also the general public as a guide for peace-keeping and the ethics of war. But it has to be constantly revised to meet the modern and more complex situation of international politics. Similarly, we could argue that any public theology has to be constantly revised and shaped by new ideas and new situations otherwise it will cease to be an authentic public theology.

---

52 http://www.methodist.org.uk/index.cfm?fuseaction=opentogod.content&cmid=1866 (accessed 25 July 2010).

PART 3

Public Theology in Europe

8

Interactive Pluralism in a Multicultural Society: Rowan Williams' Lecture on Sharia Law

There is a position – not at all unfamiliar in contemporary discussion – which says that to be a citizen is essentially and simply to be under the rule of the uniform law of a sovereign state, in such a way that any other relations, commitments or protocols of behaviour belong exclusively to the realm of the private and of individual choice.[1]

The Church has been struggling to find appropriate models and approaches to engage in public affairs with the authorities and the wider public, and this is not a new problem. But it is particularly problematic for church leaders who are regarded as public figures, when expectations from the general public differ in changing contexts. This is especially so in Britain in the new situation of religious pluralism, which is relatively unfamiliar to the leaders of the traditional churches. Rowan Williams is acknowledged as an 'outstanding theological writer, scholar and teacher',[2] and possesses 'intellectual prowess and unpretentious piety'.[3] He is regarded as combining 'highest scholarly erudition with a profound commitment to the theologian's responsibility to the church and the world',[4] and also as being a 'uniquely gifted Christian leader'.[5]

Williams is particularly concerned with secularism and with the position of minority groups – gay people in the Church and Muslims in society. On the relationship with the Church, with other religious groups and civil society, he sees the significance of the Church as 'in

---

1 Rowan Williams, 'Civil and Religious Law in England: A Religious Perspective', http://www.archbishopofcanterbury.org/1575 (accessed 12 Feb. 2010).

2 http://www.archbishopofcanterbury.org/73 (accessed 30 Mar. 2010).

3 John Dart, 'Rowan Williams Named Anglican Leader', *Christian Century* (31 July–13 Aug. 2002), p. 12.

4 Todd Breyfogle, 'Time and Transformation: A Conversation with Rowan Williams', *Cross Currents* (Fall 1995), pp. 293–311 at p. 293.

5 Tina Beattie, 'Rowan Williams and Sharia Law', http://www.opendemocracy.net/article/faith_ideas/europe_islam/sharia_law_uk (accessed 12 Feb. 2010).

keeping alive a concern both to honour and to justify the absolute and non-negotiable character of the human vision of responsibility and justice that is at work in all human association for the common good'. He argues that the Church 'asks the freedom to remind the society or societies in which it lives of their own vulnerability and their need to stay close to some fundamental questions about the nature of the humanity they seek to nourish', and that 'the Church is most *credible* when least preoccupied with its security and most engaged with the human health of its environment'.[6] However, his pursuit of 'credible' approaches to the various complex issues both within and outside the Church have brought him heavy criticism, particularly on the issue of homosexuality and on sharia law, to which we shall now turn.

The Archbishop's lecture on sharia law

During February 2008, Britain witnessed an unprecedented debate over a lecture given by the Archbishop of Canterbury (on the evening of 7 February) on 'Civil and Religious Law in England: A Religious Perspective' at the Royal Courts of Justice.[7] The Archbishop had chosen the topic of sharia law as the key topic for his sophisticated and complex lecture. However, he was heavily criticized by the media, politicians and other church leaders for his seemingly naive and positive suggestion that sharia law should be adopted into the British juridical system. The debate had already started when he was interviewed by BBC Radio 4 during the afternoon, when he answered it 'seems unavoidable' to a question of whether the application of sharia law could be considered 'in certain circumstances'.[8] After the initial reactions from the public, the ensuing discussions have been more sombre and reflective. Many commentators admitted that the initial harsh criticism was quite unfair and in many cases was the result of a misreading of (or failure to read) his lecture. Here, a brief summary of his lecture is necessary.

In his lecture, Williams starts with the growing challenge in British society for public or legal recognition and provision for religious groups. He states clearly that the aim of his lecture is to 'tease out some of the broader issues around the rights of religious groups within a secular state, with a few thoughts about what might be entailed in crafting a just and constructive relationship between Islamic law and

---

6 Rowan Williams, http://www.archbishopofcanterbury.org/745 (accessed 20 Feb. 2010).

7 http://www.archbishopofcanterbury.org/1575 (accessed 12 Feb. 2010).

8 17,000 viewers contacted BBC's online message board: *The Sunday Times*, 10 February 2008.

the statutory law of the United Kingdom'. He then discusses the concept of sharia law, briefly arguing that sharia is a principle and not a fixed code, which still requires legal interpretation, and that he is not talking about two 'rival systems'. He emphasizes that *our social identities are not constituted by one exclusive set of relations or mode of belonging*', and on the basis of that thesis he questions the secular government's assumption of a 'monopoly in terms of defining public and political identity'. He argues that this causes two problems: first, under the rule of the uniform law, 'other relations, commitments or protocols of behaviour' are pushed into the 'realm of private and of individual choice'; second, this situation disadvantages believers because the law of the land discounts the rationale of the believers based on their convictions.

Very much aware of the difficulties of his suggestions for integrating sharia law into the British system, he then cautiously examines three possible objections to his proposal. First, the concern that this may lead into a higher level of attention to religious identity and communal rights. The Archbishop argues that this can be prevented through distinguishing serious matters of faith and discipline from religious prescription, and through an enhanced and sophisticated version of the sharia court with checks and balances. Second, the suspicion that the recognition of 'supplementary jurisdiction' might lead to reinforcing 'repressive or retrograde elements', especially towards women. The Archbishop recognizes the difficulties of this problem, but insists that no 'supplementary' jurisdiction should have power to deny or prevent their rights; that both parties, citizens and believers, should have open access to British law and should not be denied access to either system. Third, he raises the question of legal monopoly:

> So much of our thinking in the modern world, dominated by European assumptions about universal rights, rests, surely, on the basis that the law is the law; that everyone stands before the public tribunal on exactly equal terms, so that recognition of corporate identities or, more seriously, of supplementary jurisdictions is simply incoherent if we want to preserve the great political and social advances of Western legality.[9]

He sees the chief contribution of the Enlightenment as removing monopolistic religious authority and upholding 'open reasoned argument' and the 'successful provision of ... liberties for the greatest number', leading to 'equal levels of accountability for all and equal levels of

---

9 http://www.archbishopofcanterbury.org/1575 (accessed 12 Feb. 2011).

access for all to legal process'. Therefore, in the Enlightenment spirit, he challenges the current legal monopoly of the state. He restates his argument:

> [A] defence of an unqualified secular legal monopoly in terms of the need for a universalist doctrine of human right or dignity is to misunderstand the circumstances in which that doctrine emerged, and that the essential liberating (and religiously informed) vision it represents is not imperilled by a loosening of the monopolistic frame-work.[10]

He explains that members of modern society possess 'multiple affiliation' and in that case the present arrangement is

> a damagingly inadequate account of common life, in which certain kinds of affiliation are marginalized or privatized to the extent that what is produced is a ghettoized pattern of social life, in which particular sorts of interest and of reasoning are tolerated as private matters but never granted legitimacy in public as part of a continuing debate about shared goods and priorities.

He sees the need for accountability to prevent monopolistic claims by specific communities, or by secular government, as established by a 'non-negotiable human dignity' so that 'each agent ... could be expected to have a voice in the shaping of some common project for the well-being and order of a human group'. To prevent the 'sterility of mutually exclusive monopolies', he claims, this 'market' element in applying the law seems 'unavoidable'. As he put it, it is 'interactive pluralism'.

In sum, his lecture is divided into three sections: first, an overall discussion of the rights of religious groups within a secular state, especially the meaning of sharia law for the Muslim community in the UK, and their implications; second, a questioning of the validity of the legal monopoly of the secular state in the context of contemporary plural societies, arguing that this in fact goes against the spirit of the Enlightenment and also does injustice to communities and individuals who hold various affiliations and commitments; and third, he deals with three perceived objections to his proposal and suggests that the key perspective should be the promotion of what he sees as 'interactive pluralism' in which a 'complementary' legal system helps in the promotion of human dignity for all members of society by allowing the full expression and exercise of their aspirations.[11] Although this idea of

---

10 http://www.archbishopofcanterbury.org/1575 (accessed 12 Feb. 2011).

11 For good discussions of the lecture, see Mike Higton, 'Rowan Williams and Sharia: Defending the Secular', *International Journal of Public Theology* 2/4 (2008), pp. 400–17;

implementing various complementary legal systems has been discussed by scholars and implemented in various global contexts and in the UK, the suggestion by the most senior member of the Church of England of incorporating sharia law into the British legal system brought much controversy. A reporter asked, 'How could one speech have united against him the liberals, the conservatives, most Muslims, most Christians, all secularists, all the political parties … ?', but the issue the Archbishop raised was a far from simple matter, nor did it bring about the unified opposition as the reporter suggested.[12]

Responses to the lecture

The main opposition came from the media – both conservative and liberal – who were particularly critical of Williams' lecture and interview, as some of the headlines indicate: 'Craven counsel of despair', 'An unholy mix of law and religion', 'A defender of the faith needs better judgement',[13] 'Williams is dangerous. He must be resisted.'[14] 'Archbishop, you've committed treason',[15] 'How law and faith war broke out', and 'Wrong, Dr Williams, but the debate is right',[16] not to mention the very harsh comments made by the tabloid newspapers. It was described as 'catastrophic in terms of social cohesion'[17], as 'cultural and legal apartheid',[18] and as 'moral cowardice dressed up as worthy celebration'. The lecture was even described as the 'rivers of blather', a 'liberal mirror image' of Enoch Powell's 'rivers of blood' speech given 40 years before.[19] It was also seen as an 'attack on multiculturalism'.[20] Even former Archbishop George Carey and Cardinal Murphy O'Connor appeared to be critical of the lecture.[21] The criticisms were expressed in several ways. First, the positive assessment of sharia law was challenged by many in the media. Sharia means, Andrew Brown insists, 'something atavistic, misogynistic, cruel and foreign', and reminds the public and the media of fatwas, hangings in Iran and stonings in Afghanistan. It

Jonathan Chaplin, 'Legal Monism and Religious Pluralism: Rowan Williams on Religion, Loyalty and Law', *International Journal of Public Theology* 2/4 (2008), pp. 418–41.

12 Andrew Brown, *Guardian*, 9 February 2008.

13 *Sunday Telegraph*, 10 February 2008.

14 *The Times*, 9 February 2008.

15 *The Times*, 10 February 2008.

16 *Observer*, 10 February 2008.

17 David Blunkett in Janes Sturcke, *et al.*, *Guardian*, 8 February 2008.

18 Sayeeda Warsi, *Sunday Telegraph*, 10 February 2008.

19 Matthew d'Ancona, *Sunday Telegraph*, 10 February 2008.

20 Johann Hari, *Independent*, 11 February 2008.

21 http://www.dailymail.co.uk/news/article-513351/Two-powerful-clergy-Britain-launch-stinging-attack-Archbishop-sharia-row.html (accessed 20 Feb. 2010).

was argued that the real victims of this controversy would be British Muslims, despite the Archbishop's apparent support for them. There was also a fear that Muslim advocates for sharia law would want to see full implementation of it in the UK.[22] The second area of criticism was that the lecture was not clear, and failed to specify why and how sharia law should be adopted into the British legal system.[23] Furthermore, the Archbishop was regarded as showing an 'intellectual arrogance common to many of Britain's liberal elite' and 'out of touch with modern Britain', which 'characterizes the otherworldliness that still pervades the inner sanctums of the Church of England'.[24] Third, the Archbishop was seen as promoting more autonomy for faith communities who insist on levels of commitment that make it extremely difficult for their members to make a choice between religious and civil law, especially women and other vulnerable members. It was regarded as 'legal apartheid and moral cantonisation'.[25] Fourth, its radical suggestion of legal pluralism was seen as a direct challenge to modern democracy and the vital importance of equality under the law: 'The speech itself was characteristically learned, philosophical and tightly nuanced, but there was no getting away from its radical message.'[26] Minette Marrin goes further:

> To seek to undermine our legal system and the values on which it rests, in a spirit of unnecessary appeasement to an alien set of values, is a kind of treason. It is a betrayal of all those who struggled and died here, over the centuries, for freedom and equality under the rule of law and of their courage in the face of injustice and unreason.[27]

Support for the lecture came from church members, theologians and church leaders. Most of them complained that the media and general public unfairly treated the Archbishop and condemned his lecture without careful examination. First, they criticized the media: they believed the incident revealed the 'chauvinistic' attitude of the media combined with 'ignorance and prejudice'.[28] Or it showed 'ill-informed, sensationalist and polemical' reporting, which left 'permanent scorch marks on the British debate about the place of religion in public places'.[29]

---

22 Andrew Brown, *Guardian*, 9 February 2008. See also Yitzchok Adlerstein and Michael Broyde, http://www.forward.com/articles/12733/.

23 Minette Marrin, *The Sunday Times*, 10 February 2008.

24 Ruth Gledhill, *The Times*, 11 February 2008. See also Joan Smith, *Independent*, 10 February 2008.

25 Matthew d'Ancona, *Sunday Telegraph*, 10 February 2008.

26 Andrew Anthony, *Observer*, 10 February 2008.

27 Minette Marrin, *The Sunday Times*, 10 February 2008.

28 Beattie, 'Rowan Williams and Sharia Law'.

29 Jonathan Chaplin, 'Legal Monism and Religious Pluralism', p. 419.

Media behaviour was described as 'ill-informed hysteria' about a topic that needs to be addressed through reasoned and civil public discussion, and the response was criticized as 'one of immediate distortion, disbelief, dismissal and disdain' towards the Archbishop.[30] Second, they supported the Archbishop's effort to find the place of religious communities in secular society: the lecture was regarded as an 'invitation to the legal establishment to consider the challenges posed to the abstract universalities of a post-Enlightenment concept of law by the traditional values and identities associated with religious communities'.[31] Andrew Goddard insisted that the lecture provided 'a vision of how to enable order, cohesion and belonging in a single political society which seeks to embrace multiple religious and other communities under the rule of law'.[32] Another saw it as an invitation for religious communities to accept accountability in their engagement in the wider society for a healthier interaction. Third, they suggested the argument was about legal monism and 'interactive pluralism': it was regarded as a 'thoughtful exploration' of 'how legal monism can cope with religious pluralism', and the Archbishop was said to offer 'serious theological grounds for the notion that religious minorities should receive a degree of public recognition'.[33] The fundamental issue here was seen to be the relationship between 'the law of the land and the religious conscience of the citizen':

> For 200 years it has been assumed that these operated in separate spheres: the law regulates my public life, faith or religion operates in private. This was always a dangerous half-truth, since many of the great world faiths, including Christianity itself, actually claim that all of life is included within religious obedience.[34]

Issues relating to public engagement of the Church

Examining the above debate, I would like to draw out four major issues for our consideration: the legitimacy or appropriateness of the Archbishop's intervention on the matter; the role of the media in the public debate; the question of legal monopoly and 'interactive pluralism'; and the issue of the implementation of sharia law in the UK.

---

30 Andrew Goddard, 'Islamic Law and the Anglican Communion: Is there a Common Vision?', http://www.fulcrum-anglican.org.uk/page.cfm?ID=274 (accessed 20 Feb. 2010).

31 Beattie, 'Rowan Williams and Sharia Law'.

32 Goddard, 'Islamic Law and the Anglican Communion'.

33 Chaplin, 'Legal Monism and Religious Pluralism', pp. 420, 423.

34 Tom Wright, 'Letter to Durham Clergy on Law and Public Life', http://www.fulcrum-anglican.org.uk/page.cfm?ID=277 (accessed 20 Feb. 2010).

Rationale for the involvement of the Church in public affairs

The question was raised whether the Archbishop, a religious leader, should discuss matters related to the legal system of the country, or whether it is appropriate for a Christian leader to discuss a matter that does not concern his own constituency but speak on behalf of Muslims. A religious leader addressing any issue in the public sphere is much scrutinized in secular contexts, but the Archbishop gave a strong defence during his Presidential Speech at the General Synod a few days later, arguing that it is entirely appropriate for a pastor of the Church of England 'to address issues around the perceived concerns of other religious communities, and to try and bring them into better public focus'.[35] This idea of a vicarious role of the leadership is not unfamiliar to the vicars and bishops of the Church of England. This stems from their unique position in British society and politics as fulfilling both the private and public role of the Church.

To examine further the Archbishop's views on the public engagement of the Church, we will need to look at some of his recent writings. In his first press conference, he asked himself about 'how to speak of God in this very public position' in a context 'generally sceptical of Christianity and the church although there is some nostalgia, fascination and even hunger for the spiritual'. He said he wished to see Christianity having a 'proper confidence' to 'capture the imagination of our culture, to draw the strongest energies of our thinking and feeling into the exploration of what our creeds put before us'. Furthermore, in his interview with the *Guardian* editor, Alan Rusbridger, responding to a question about 'the public role of the Archbishop' and church leadership, he stated it was, 'setting some kind of tonal vision for the church ... [to] crystallise ... a moral vision that's communicable to the nation at large'. When pressed further on this point, he gave the example of William Temple as an 'attempt to make a responsible contribution to public debate where appropriate'.[36]

When we examine Williams' writings, we see that he has been increasingly drawn to address social and political issues, and his main concern has been the place of faith communities in the public sphere. In his lecture on 'Secularism, Faith and Freedom', Williams discussed the question of the public engagement of faith. He criticized the secularists' notion of 'public reason' – freedom, equality, reasoning and evidence – and the idea that fair and open argument in public are only possible when specific commitments of a religious or ideological nature are

---

35 'Presidential Address', *Church Times*, 15 February 2008.
36 http://www.guardian.co.uk/world/2006/mar/21/religion.uk (accessed 15 Mar. 2010).

barred. He sees that this is based on the false assumption that 'the public expression of specific conviction is automatically offensive to people of other (or no) conviction' and argues that such 'secular' freedom is not enough; 'this account of liberal society dangerously simplifies the notion of freedom and ends up diminishing our understanding of the human person'; it is not at 'all self-evident that people can so readily detach their perspectives and policies in social or political discussion from fundamental convictions that are not allowed to be mentioned or manifested in public'.

> I am arguing that the sphere of public and political negotiation flourishes only in the context of larger commitments and visions, and that if this is forgotten or repressed by a supposedly neutral ideology of the public sphere, immense damage is done to the moral energy of a liberal society ... The struggle for a right balance of secular process and public religious debate is part of a wider struggle for a concept of the personal that is appropriately robust and able to withstand the pressures of a functionalist and reductionist climate ... without this dimension, the liberal ideal becomes deeply anti-humanist.[37]

Similarly, to the question of the place of religion in modern democratic society, he responds by defending the role of Christianity in the public sphere, saying that 'the voice of faith should be heard clearly in the decision-making processes of society', not seeking for 'political control' but for 'public visibility – for the capacity to argue for and defend their vision in the public sphere, to try and persuade both government and individuals of the possibility of a more morally serious way of ordering public life'. He insists that a healthy democracy is the 'one in which the state listens to the voices of moral vision that spring from communities that do not depend on the state itself for their integrity and meaning – above all the communities of faith'.[38]

Coming back to the lecture, despite the criticism of the media that he should be confined within the boundary of the Church and the 'private' sphere, I believe the Archbishop is right in asserting the public role of the Church. In response to the question of religion and public life, Bhikhu Parekh argues convincingly that the secularist's notion of the strict separation of religion and politics, and the idea that political debate and deliberation should be conducted in terms of secular reason alone, is problematic because secular reason is not 'politically and culturally neutral' since 'reasons are public not because their grounds are

---

37 http://www.archbishopofcanterbury.org/654 (accessed 15 Mar. 2010).
38 http://www.archbishopofcanterbury.org/495 (accessed 15 Mar. 2010).

or can be shared by all, as the secularist argues, but because they are open to inspection and can be intellectually discussed by all'.

> [The secularist agenda] discriminates against religious persons and violates the principle of equal citizenship. It is undemocratic and ignores the wishes of a large body of citizens and even perhaps the majority. It is impractical for there is no way of enforcing it. It is counterproductive as it is likely to alienate religiously minded citizens from the political system and create a crisis of legitimacy. It is unwise because it deprives political life of both the valuable insights religion offers and the moral energies it can mobilize for just and worthwhile causes.[39]

In contrast, in spite of its many weaknesses, Parekh argues that religion provides a 'valuable counterweight to the state', offers 'an alternative source of morality and allegiance', and reminds us that 'human beings are more than citizens'.[40] This is a powerful reminder of Jürgen Moltmann's assertion that theology must publicly maintain the universal concerns of God's coming kingdom because there is 'no public relevance without theology's Christian identity', and conversely, 'there is no Christian identity without public relevance'. Theology, Moltmann insists, should exhibit 'general concern in the light of hope in Christ for the kingdom of God' by becoming 'political in the name of the poor and the marginalized in a given society', by thinking 'critically about the religious and moral values of the societies in which it exists', and by presenting 'its reflections as a reasoned position'.[41] In short, on this issue, the Archbishop has firm grounds, both by secular reason and by Christian theological thinking, for his insistence on speaking on other than just 'spiritual matters' and also speaking on behalf of different sections of the society, especially for the marginalized and the vulnerable.

The role of the media in public discussion

The role of the media in public discussion needs to be examined as the controversy seems to have been enflamed by the media, and most of the criticisms from the supporters of the Archbishop have been anchored on the role of the media. The initial response to the lecture from the media was very critical and unsympathetic. Reporters even questioned

---

39 Bhikhu Parekh, *Rethinking Multiculturalism: Cultural Diversity and Political Theory* (New York: Palgrave, 2000), pp. 323–4.

40 Parekh, *Rethinking Multiculturalism*, pp. 328–30.

41 Jürgen Moltmann, *God for a Secular Society: The Public Relevance of Theology* (London: SCM Press, 1999), pp. 1–3.

whether Williams should continue to hold his post, and some called for his resignation. But in retrospect the treatment by the media was seen as out of proportion and rather reactionary:

> It is also a reminder – if such reminders are needed – that this is a woefully anti-intellectual society, fed on a daily diet of the tabloid press and reality television, and apparently incapable of engaging in intelligent public debate about significant issues ... They have also revealed again just how chauvinistic the media in Britain can be, in this case by preying on public perceptions of Islam as a misogynistic and barbaric religion.[42]

Even those who oppose the Archbishop's lecture acknowledge that the reaction was inappropriate and that the media was much to blame for it.

> [W]hile Britain needs this debate, it appears to lack the discipline to conduct it in a civilised way. The scale of the backlash, some of the language used and the haste with which some opponents of the archbishop have reached for crude stereotypes of Islam is dispiriting. It is unedifying to see the majority culture turn with near unanimous scorn on a minority. It suggests that secular Britain is deeply insecure about the durability of its own culture ... It is a contest that reveals just as much about modern Britain as any treatise on faith. It is the contrast between reasonable, sensible exposition of an idea, whatever its merits, and unthinking, poisonous, prejudiced reaction.[43]

In many ways, Williams himself has been very critical of the media. In particular, in his lecture on 'The Media: Public Interest and Common Good', he strongly asserts that the pursuit of public interest should be in line with the notion of the common good if it is to serve active democracy. He writes:

> We need to deflate some of the rhetoric about the media as guardians and nurturers of democracy simply by virtue of the constant exposure of 'information', and we need to be cautious about a use of 'public interest' language that ignores the complexity and, often, artificiality of our ideas of 'the public' ... we need a form of self-regulation that admits provisionality and provides means of assessment. We need journalistic work that equips its own critics.[44]

---

42 Beattie, 'Rowan Williams and Sharia Law'.
43 Leader, 'Wrong, Dr Williams, but the Debate is Right', *Observer*, 10 February 2008.
44 Rowan Williams, 'The Media: Public Interest and Common Good', http://www.archbishopofcanterbury.org/992 (accessed 20 Mar. 2010).

He pointed out that members of the national media in the UK are drawn from specific groups, are largely London-based, and hence may posses 'a strong tribal identity', and that this needs to be constantly checked if the media is to pursue 'mature democracy'. He argues, 'in respect of religious communities of all kinds', the ignorance of the press 'seems endemic'. He further sees that the common good requires public space, which is more than a market driven by profit-seeking: 'a space that doesn't demand that every speaker before entering the discussion, be reduced to an abstract member of the public, a consumer of general information'. One might suspect that this critical view of the media doesn't help in a situation like this.

The supporters of the Archbishop heavily criticized the media for a chauvinistic attitude and for not carefully examining or reading the lecture itself. However, the media objected to this criticism. Responding to the accusation of misreading the lecture, Andrew Brown accused the Archbishop of being 'elitist' without appreciating the consequences of applying sharia law in the British context.[45] Some argued that the lecture showed that he is out of touch with the reality of British life,[46] and his argument was seen not only as 'incoherent' but even showing 'disingenuousness' because he 'failed to say why and how' to implement sharia law into the British legal system.[47]

The problem for the Archbishop appears to be that although he brought a vital issue to the public forum, he did not provide concrete suggestions, for the media and the general public. As Tina Beattie puts it, the lecture was an 'invitation' for consideration rather than a 'series of prescriptions or propositions'.[48] Perhaps it is a tendency of his approach that he is reluctant to make concrete suggestions but rather makes some theoretical suggestions. For this tendency he often receives criticism for not being clear in his position. As I noted in Chapter 7 (see page 169), in a recent publication Tom Frame has fiercely criticized Williams on the issue of war and peace. Although Williams has frequently criticized the conduct of the Iraq War by the British government, Frame argues that his theology does not 'return to the world in which conflict needs to be managed and tensions resolved' and often his comments neither 'touch nor transform the political order':

To my mind, the principal problem with Williams' work is that it does not deal adequately with the world and its problems, nor provide a sufficiently clear set of principles that are needed to regulate

---

45 Andrew Brown, *Guardian*, 9 February 2008.
46 See also Minette Marrin, *The Sunday Times*, 10 February 2008.
47 Matthew Parris, *The Times*, 9 February 2008.
48 Beattie, 'Rowan Williams and Sharia Law'.

the use of force while promoting a vision of non-violence that is practically workable ... if Williams is not prepared to be more specific about what needs to be done, he (and the Anglican Communion he leads) will not be heard by those outside the church in the hard-headed, argumentative, and intellectual world of strategic studies where decisions affecting whole nations are made and human lives are held in the balance ... Williams has spoken with conviction but not with clarity.[49]   *discussion of the media's need for answers!*

Part of the reason for this lack of clarity, as Frame points out, is that Williams may not have a 'good grasp of strategic concepts, international diplomacy, national security or military strategy'. Perhaps this is rather a harsh and unfair criticism of his approach since he cannot be an expert on every political and social issue. Nevertheless, on the issue of this particular lecture, he outlined a vital principle but failed to make it more 'media friendly' or approachable by the general public, by providing some practical and workable suggestions.

When it comes to the question of the media, the forum for public debate needs to be explored if we wish to continue a healthy and meaningful debate. The various forms of media provide this space for the public, and this is the strength of liberal democracy. Indeed, that strength relies on free and fair access to information and debate through the media. However, in this particular case, the media often played the role of judge, asserting their own verdict rather than allowing the public to engage in a healthy debate. For healthy debate, the provision of a forum for a critical dialogue is vital. Comments such as 'we [media] are the only instrument with which a sculptor of public opinion can work',[50] even in the midst of debate taking place, exhibits a certain arrogance from those who are involved in the media, and for this the Archbishop's criticisms of the media are highly relevant. The media should play the role of providing a platform for a healthy dialogue among people from various understandings and perspectives, and not just insist on one agenda, as Bhikhu Parekh has warned: 'the secularist mistake lies in pushing the separation [of religion and public life] further than is warranted.'[51]

Although its main concern has been for the relationship between Christians and people of other faiths, the Christian theology of dialogue may provide methodologies and working models for such a complex situation of religious and secular conflict. Dialogue between different

49 Tom Frame, 'Rowan Williams on War and Peace', in Matheson Russell (ed.), *On Rowan Williams: Critical Essay* (Eugene, OR: Cascade Books, 2009), pp. 163–85.
50 Andrew Brown, *Guardian*, 9 February 2008.
51 Parekh, *Rethinking Multiculturalism*, p. 327.

religious communities is for mutual knowledge and critical engagement, which leads to the correction of prejudices towards others. In the case of Britain, we find an urgent need for such dialogue between religious and secular groups. This process should be a beacon of a democratic society where both the secular and religious identities are respected and also critically assessed. Religious and secular communities need to listen to each other, and be prepared to be shaped by each other's differing values, none of which should be regarded as absolute, and each of which needs to be negotiated in the context of contemporary society through open and critical dialogue.

'Secular legal monopoly' versus 'interactive pluralism' in a multicultural society

The critics and the supporters are in agreement that the Archbishop's lecture touched on more than the matter of sharia law. Yes, the main focus of the lecture was indeed the meaningful relationship between sharia law and the law of the land, and he spent most of his time on the theoretical and practical implications of his proposal. While the initial reaction from the general public and most of the tabloid media focused on the issue of sharia law, the articles with in-depth analysis addressed the wider issue of the application of the law in multicultural and multireligious contexts. It is a misreading of the Archbishop's intent to think that he was only defending Muslims; he naturally had the interests of the Christian community also in mind. Therefore, Williams advocates that the law should accommodate the public involvement of all religious communities.

However, some who rightly perceived this also strongly contended against it, on the grounds that religious people have questionable loyalties. So the *Guardian* leader argues that 'sometimes, religious believers will be forced to choose whom they obey, a religious judge or a civil one. They must choose the latter every time. Democracy and the rule of law demand it.'[52] On the same point, Matthew Parris accused the Archbishop of being 'profoundly conservative' on this issue and of promoting 'communitarianism', which is 'repressive and reactionary':

A religion is more than a collection of rules and habits: it is a complete moral and philosophical system with deep claims upon the inner and outer life of the adherent, from cradle, through schooling, and beyond. The rules it lays down – the private laws – are of a more commanding kind than the rules of Scrabble or the High Peak Hunt

---

52 Leader, 'Wrong, Dr Williams, but the Debate is Right'.

because they are morally joined-up: joined with a loyalty beyond the State; joined within an overarching faith and its explanations of the Universe. Dr Williams knows this. He preaches it. It is the reason he wants more autonomy for faith communities. And it is the reason we should resist him.[53]

The above commentators are critical of Williams as challenging the hard-earned British democracy, which is based on equality before the law.[54] However, some of the supporters present the positive aspects of this multiple approach to law and public life, and see that the debate was to do with 'the challenges posed to the abstract universalities of a post-Enlightenment concept of law by the traditional values and identities associated with religious communities'.[55] The heart of the issue here is in what way religious allegiance and secular ideology meet in public life. Bishop Tom Wright welcomes the lecture as exhibiting the Archbishop's 'sensitive and intellectual rigour'. He supports the idea of 'interactive pluralism' and argues:

> the question of how we live together as a civil and wise society while cherishing different faiths is a deep and serious one and can't be pushed away just because people take fright at certain misunderstandings. His point was precisely that neither the secular state nor any particular religion should 'monopolize' the legal system.[56]

Mike Higton goes further, saying that the lecture was focused on public accountability and public scrutiny from both secular and religious sections of society so that it not only defended the 'pluralist public conversation of our society' but in contrast to many secularists' argument, the lecture was in fact defending secular ideology. Higton argues that to achieve this, 'interactive pluralism' will provide freedom of religious voices to contribute to the public life *and* also bring religious communities into the 'world of accountability'. He challenges the notion that the state should exercise a rigid form of law applied to all citizens, arguing that 'the role of the state is instead to listen, negotiate and find constructive ways of doing justice to and for the different people who make up the state'.[57] Higton sees that 'secularity without freedom of

53 Matthew Parris, *The Times*, 9 February 2008.
54 Theo Hobson, 'Rowan Williams: Sharia Furore, Anglican Future', http://www.opendemocracy.net/article/rowan_williams_sharia_furore_anglican_future (accessed 25 Mar. 2010).
55 Beattie, 'Rowan Williams and Sharia Law'.
56 Wright, 'Letter to Durham Clergy'.
57 Higton, 'Rowan Williams and Sharia', p. 412.

religion is failed secularity' and argues that what Williams is asking for is a 'means of bringing this religious community more fully into public conversation'.

> In other words, Williams is putting forward a model for a pluralist, liberal, state, governed by the impartial rule of law, which preserves the heritage of the Enlightenment. Williams does not think that the model he is proposing is a step away from universality, the Enlightenment or the freedoms we have so painfully won over the last few centuries. Indeed, he thinks the model he is proposing is more accountable, transparent and realistic about how freedom is preserved than any model of unqualified secular monopoly. It is more serious about binding religious citizens fully into publicly accountable conversation as religious; more serious about working against the creation of cultural and religious ghettos isolated from the mainstream of public discourse ... It is a vision of society as religious and secular; a defence of religious freedom that is at the same time an interpretation and defence of secularity.[58]

Some scholars wish to connect the notion of interactive pluralism in relation to multicultural discussion. For example, Tariq Modood argues that multicultural citizenship is a continuous dialogue and contains a 'right to not just be recognised but to debate the terms of recognition'. He further expands:

> Citizenship consists of a framework of rights and practices of participation but also discourses and symbols of belonging, ways of imagining and remaking ourselves as a country and expressing our sense of commonalities as well as differences in ways in which these identities qualify each other and create inclusive public spaces. Change and reform do not all have to be brought about by state action, laws, regulation, prohibitions etc. but also through public debate, discursive contestations, pressure group mobilisations, and the varied and (semi-) autonomous institutions of civil society ... the absolute and dogmatic separation of citizenship and religion appears to be an obstacle to pluralistic integration and equality ... For secularism pure and simple is not what exists in Britain or indeed in any democratic country.[59]

---

58 Higton, 'Rowan Williams and Sharia', p. 417.

59 Tariq Modood, 'Multicultural Citizenship and the Anti-Sharia Storm', http://www.opendemocracy.net/article/faith_ideas/europe_islam/anti_sharia_storm (accessed 15 Mar. 2010).

Similarly, Andrew Goddard criticizes the 'inability' of our secular society to engage in serious discussion on the matters of public life and 'inability to understand the importance of religious commitments and communities in and for our public life', and argues we have an urgent 'need to address this through reasoned and civil public discussion'.[60] Going even further, Jonathan Chaplin criticizes secular approaches to the issue: by issuing unqualified declarations of loyalty to the legal system, 'the commentators are inadvertently undermining the possibility of any arguments, religious or secular, for resisting an authoritarian conception of the state; this is why Christians must resist them'. This position, he argues, has 'a logic consistent with the deepest currents of Christian political conviction'. He suggests that the lecture may be an invitation 'to the church to regain the political courage from which its early missionary confidence derived', and 'to the secular state to acknowledge the limits of its pretensions'.[61]

The argument for 'interactive pluralism' has two dimensions of mutual accountability: one explicit and one implicit. It calls for the acknowledgement of the potential contributions of religious communities, the obligation on the state to provide this possibility in the public sphere and the challenge to the state's holding the monopoly over the conduct of the law. The other dimension is to do with bringing religious communities into the public discussion. Interactive pluralism helps religious communities to be more open for scrutiny by the public and hence encourages them to integrate into the wider society. This should be welcomed as the two dimensions would mutually benefit both religious communities and wider society, as I have discussed above concerning the public engagement of the Church. Indeed this is already taking place in that religious people are engaged in public life and contribute to decision-making individually and collectively. The question that should be asked in the process of public decision-making is what are the most appropriate ways and means to be engaged in matters wider than their own interests.

I would like to support the Archbishop's notion of 'interactive pluralism' and challenge the state monopoly in public life, arguing that the state should be open to scrutiny of its conduct of law by various groups, including religious communities. Religious communities could make a vital contribution to mutual accountability in a wide range of issues in the public life of contemporary Britain. However, how do the religious communities and secular society interact when it comes to law? I would

60 Andrew Goddard, 'Prudence and Jurisprudence: Reflections on the Archbishop's interview and lecture', http://www.fulcrum-anglican.org.uk/page.cfm?ID=275 (Accessed 25 Mar. 2010).

61 Chaplin, 'Legal Monism and Religious Pluralism', p. 441.

suggest that this is not through the incorporation of current forms of religious law into secular law, but by allowing the principles and values of religious communities to permeate into the existing law so that it can benefit all and not be confined to a religious community. This suggestion has been brought out by some commentators. Theo Hobson saw the controversy as due to Williams' attempt 'to defend the rights of all faith communities' by challenging secular liberalism, but in doing so, he argues, Williams rejected that liberal Protestantism of the majority of the British people who hold the opinion that Christianity and secularism are pretty much compatible. This understanding of the compatibility of secular and Christian views of public life in general and the law in particular has been further elaborated by Roger Scruton, who insists that the idea that the law should be a secular institution, founded in human decisions and not on 'divine command', is in fact a Christian contribution to the legal system and secular democracy. This is illustrated by Jesus' response to the question of tax, which suggests a complementarity between obligations to Caesar and to God, and also in the writings in St Paul in relation to the Roman law.[62]

Their argument is in contrast to Williams' seemingly dichotomist approaches to secular and religious identities. When it comes to democracy and the rule of the law, Christianity and secular ideology are compatible, they argue, because Christianity has made a fundamental contribution to the establishment of modern democracy. They argue that the British justice system, which offers the 'best guarantee of fairness', and equality before the law as the 'most meaningful form of equality',[63] has been strongly shaped by Christianity and is in line with its principles and values. Religious values are therefore already implied in the formation of the present form of democracy, and they do not see any need to supplement British law with any religious law. Although they may overstate the foundational role of Christian theology in the formation of the legal system, I would tend to agree with Hobson and Scruton that Christianity is compatible with British law because it has influenced its development. So I would like to see values and principles of sharia law influencing British law rather than bracketing it as a supplementary part of the system. I have a further reason for resisting the incorporation of sharia courts: I doubt whether it would benefit the wider society and whether it is practical. In the next section, I shall discuss the basis of these doubts.

62 Roger Scruton, 'Islamic Law in a Secular World', http://www.opendemocracy.net/article/faith_ideas/europe_islam/secular_world (accessed 25 Mar. 2010).

63 Mathew d'Ancona, *Sunday Telegraph*, 10 February 2008.

Sharia law and women's rights

The question of the adoption of some aspects of sharia law into existing British law requires much thinking through in its legal, political, socio-cultural and religious implications, and this cannot be done in isolation from what is happening around the world, and particularly from the issue of the treatment of women in Islam, as many commentators pointed out. More recently, the Lord Chief Justice of England and Wales, Britain's most senior judge, gave a speech in July 2008, in support of the Archbishop, saying that 'it is not the case that for a Muslim to lead his or her life in accordance with these [sharia] principles will be in conflict with the requirement of the law in this country'.[64] However, in a liberal democracy this also needs to be examined carefully and in an informed manner, as in the case of the Archbishop's lecture. Matthew Parris made a strong point here that religion makes profound claims on people of faith in every area of their lives, hence he questions the idea of consent and opt-out when the supplementary option is implemented, which he believes is in many cases impossible for a member of a religious group to do. With sharia courts recognized in British law,

> it would be a Britain in which the individual Muslim – maybe female, maybe ambitious, maybe gay, maybe a religious doubter – would lose their chances of rescue from his or her family or community by the State. The State, not family, faith or community, is the guarantor of personal liberty and intellectual freedom, and it will always be to the State, not the Church, synagogue or mosque, that the oppressed individual needs look. [65]

This uneasiness with women's situation under sharia law is expressed by many,[66] and it was even suggested that the Archbishop is in 'near-total disconnection from the reality of Muslim women's lives'.

> Multiculturalism was formed with good intentions as a counter-reaction. But it has become a mirror-image of this old racism, treating Muslim women – and others – as so different that they do not deserve the same rights as the rest of us. As the European-Iranian feminist Azar Majedi puts it: 'By creating different laws and judicial

---

64 Lord Philips, Lord Chief Justice, 'Equality before the Law', 3 July 2008, http://www.judiciary.gov.uk/docs/speeches/lcj_equality_before_the_law_030708.pdf (accessed 13 July 2008).

65 Matthew Parris, *The Times*, 9 February 2008.

66 Beattie, 'Rowan Williams and Sharia Law'; Mary Ann Sieghart, *The Times*, 14 February 2008; Joan Smith, *Independent*, 10 February 2008.

systems for each ethnic group, we are not fighting racism. In fact, we are institutionalising it.'[67]

In particular, on this issue, Jytte Klausen's analysis of women and sharia law is very helpful. In his fascinating study on the politics and religion of Muslims in western Europe, he observes that many Muslim leaders believe that it would be a 'serious mistake to grant statutory status to Islamic religious law' in Europe. He asked Muslim women the question: 'Should secular civil law respect religious law and allow imams and Islamic legal scholars to decide on legally binding decisions for Muslims living in country X?' Interestingly, in Denmark (9.4), Sweden (14.3), France (8.3), Germany (10.3) and Holland (13.0) the 'yes' responses were very low, whereas in the UK 70 per cent said 'yes' to the question. He sees the reason for this as largely due to ethnic origin in that those who have South Asian origin tend to be more con-servative or familiar with the Indian situation of separate civil code for Muslims, than those of North African or Turkish background.[68] This explains some of the reasons for the favourable attitude to the imple-mentation of sharia law among British Muslims. On the question of whether members of the Muslim community should be able to choose either the sharia court or the British civil court, Klausen categorically rejects that notion as it would 'violate principles about the equal appli-cation of the law'. He further explains his objections: first, it will cause a split between traditional and modernist Muslim leaders; second, even female leaders who hold traditional views oppose the idea and support accommodation between Islam and the European legal norm; third, it 'empowers unelected traditional elites and, in the case of gender relations, disadvantages women'; fourth, it is 'exceedingly difficult to manage', and would lead to 'a codification of minority cultural prac-tices that is detrimental to the objectives of enhanced pluralism and flexible adjustment'.[69]

Klausen's rationale for the objection to implementing sharia law in the UK is convincing. Williams raised a significant issue in challenging the legal monopoly of the state, but by relating it to the implementation of sharia law in the UK he not only failed to convey his profound chal-lenge to state policy, but also, perhaps, damaged a healthy interaction between Muslim communities and the secular media in the UK. The

67 Johann Hari, *Independent*, 11 February 2008; Sami Zubaida, 'Sharia: Practice of Faith, Politics of Modernity', http://www.opendemocracy.net/article/faith_ideas/europe_islam/sharia_politics_of_modernity (accessed 30 Mar. 2010).

68 Jytte Klausen, *The Islamic Challenge: Politics and Religion in Western Europe* (Oxford: Oxford University Press, 2005).

69 Klausen, *The Islamic Challenge*.

intended debate was diverted in such a way that it only confirmed the wide gap between secular and religious views in the eyes of the public. One of the problems of dealing with introducing religious law into the secular law of the land is that, apart from the problems mentioned above, it hardly helps the healthy interaction between religious community and the wider society. The law in the UK, though not perfect by any means, has developed throughout centuries to represent all sections of the society and not to privilege certain groups. The notion of equality under the law is vital since secular law should be open to scrutiny by all members of the society, whereas any religious law will have limits in its application and interpretation to a religious community and will not benefit the wider society.

One way to move this forward could be by distinguishing law and ethics: the law draws the minimum boundaries of an individual's conduct in relation to others, whereas ethics considers much detailed and personalized behaviour and is often informed by various cultural, social and religious affiliations. It would be advisable to leave the issue of sharia law, and any other religious laws and principles, in the realm of ethical code rather than pushing it into formalizing as law. I would argue that the making and implementation of secular laws has not been entirely in the hand of secular ideologies. The legal system has been profoundly influenced by religious values and principles, as in the case of the Declaration of Human Rights, and this should be cherished and acknowledged by both secular and religious communities. The debate on sharia law is somewhat misleading, because it is perceived as if the law of the land and religious law are in competition with each other and secular ideology and religious values are in opposition. This is not the case, and the public engagement of the Church does not mean fighting against secular ideology nor reclaiming public space, but rather reaffirming the contributions of religious thought in everyday public life and continuing to make further progress on it by working with all members of society, especially with those who hold a secular ideology.

Conclusion

The examination of the Archbishop's lecture helps us in our search for appropriate ways and means for the churches to engage in the public sphere, especially in a secular but multicultural society. Linell E. Cady argues that theology should not only address itself to the wider social and political issues, but it must 'appropriate a form of argumentation that is genuinely public'. She further argues that to achieve a public form of argumentation, theologians must make changes on two fronts:

on the one hand they must 'unmask the impossible pretensions to neutrality and universality that underlie the Enlightenment understanding of public, and the public exercise of reason, while on the other hand respecting 'the Enlightenment distinction between open inquiry and dogmatic citation, and work to combat the authoritarian traces that linger on in contemporary theology'.[70] In other words, the fact that theology is not 'neutral' does not disqualify it from participation in public discussion; on the contrary, because of its distinctive perspective, theological findings can make an effective contribution to public issues. Rowan Williams is right in insisting that the Church and other religious communities should be able to contribute to public issues other than religious matters, and the state should not only respect the resources but also welcome the richness these interactions would bring to the wider society. He is also right in challenging what he calls the 'legal monopoly' of the state that maintains a rigid and static understanding of law, and in calling for providing the members of communities with the opportunity to demonstrate their 'full expression' and 'aspirations'. However, from the point of view of the Church and other religious communities, on the issue of law, public engagement will require the exploration of *permeation* rather than introducing a separate supplementary form, as we have discussed above.

The unfortunate outcome of the lecture on sharia law was that the Archbishop was seen to be challenging the clear and uncompromising divide between secular and religious entities in contemporary society, but I do not believe that this was his intention. It is an obvious fact that Christians, individually and collectively, have made enormous contributions to the establishment of liberal democracy in the UK in general and the formation of law in particular, and this should continue to be a vital aspect of the Christian contribution to the formation of a healthy society. The public engagement of the Church can take many forms, for example, political and social action, caring for the poor and marginalized, and protesting and challenging unfair systems of the state. The approach of 'permeating presence' could be one way to engage in the public sphere, but the question of how we are to implement this idea in contemporary society, where religious voices are often suppressed or regarded with suspicion, has never been more pertinent to the Christian Church and to individual Christians.

---

70 Linell E. Cady, *Religion, Theology and American Public Life* (Albany, NY: State University of New York Press, 1993), pp. 64–5.

9

Freedom of Expression Versus Respect for Faith: The Danish Cartoon Controversy

[I]f a believer demands that I, as a nonbeliever, observe his taboos in the public domain, he is not asking for my respect but for my submission. And that is incompatible with a secular democracy.[1]

It is about power, domination and demonisation ... it was an exercise to demonstrate power, and to illustrate that European liberal secularists have a superior right to define and determine how Islam should be seen and how Muslims observe their faith.[2]

In recent years, no incident so dramatically illustrates the conflict between two differently held values than the controversy around the publication of the Danish cartoons (2005–06) and the debates and protests from Muslims around the world. The incident clearly demonstrates the differing concept of religious and secular values as both communities felt that they were pushed to the limit and reacted in an inappropriate way. The incident has to be understood in the light of the socio-political situations in Denmark, Europe and the Middle East. A number of things have been blamed for the conflict: the initial mishandling of the situation by the Danish government; the right-wing political pressure towards the minority Muslim community in Denmark; the provocative dossier compiled by the imams and their role in the whole situation; the political manipulations of the governments in the Middle East to divert people's frustration from their own domestic problems; and the continuing suspicion between the West and Muslim communities, especially in the aftermath of 9/11, that this is a part of wider political conflicts between the two civilizations.

Although these factors are important to consider, the main cause of the argument seems to lie in the conflict of different values. The

---

1 Flemming Rose, *Washington Post*, 19 February 2006.
2 Ziauddin Sardar, 'A "freedom" whose Home is the Jungle', *Independent*, 5 February 2006.

purpose of this chapter is to consider the issue further by examining the debate for and against the cartoons; discussing the two apparently competing values of 'freedom of expression' and 'respect for faith'; and then investigating further to find a common place for mutual respect of both secular and religious values.[3] This will lead us to draw conclusions about the dual engagement of public theology with both sides of the argument.

Arguments for and against the publication of the cartoons

The controversy started when Kåre Bluitgen, a Danish writer, in an interview with a reporter from the newspaper *Politiken* (17 September 2005), complained that he could not find an artist who could draw cartoons of Muhammad for his children's book on the life of Muhammad. Flemming Rose, culture editor of the daily newspaper *Jyllands-Posten*, took this as an issue and commissioned Danish cartoonists to draw Muhammad and then published 12 cartoons under the heading 'The face of Muhammad' on 30 September 2005. There were immediate reactions from Muslim communities in Denmark, whose concerns were expressed in a letter sent to Prime Minister Anders Fogh Rasmussen from 12 ambassadors of Muslim nations on 12 October. Later a group from the Muslim community in Denmark filed a case against the newspaper, on 27 October 2005.[4] As there was growing anger among the Muslim community because of the lack of response from the political leaders of the country, a group of imams compiled the 'Akkari-Laban dossier', which included additional and more disturbing cartoons,[5] and in the latter part of the year toured the Middle East to present their case. As Muslims in the Middle East started to demonstrate against the cartoons, boycott Danish products and otherwise put pressure on the Danish government and the newspaper, so growing numbers of newspapers in Europe published the cartoons as a way of expressing their solidarity with the newspaper. During the months of January and Feb-

---

3 For some of the best accounts of the cartoons controversy, see Jytte Klausen, *The Cartoons that Shook the World* (New Haven and London: Yale University Press, 2009); Risto Kunelius, Elisabeth Eide, Oliver Hahn and Ronald Schroeder (eds), *Reading the Muhammed Cartoons Controversy: An International Analysis of Press Discourses on Free Speech and Political Spin* (Bochum/Freiburg: Projektverlag, 2007), p. 10.

4 The Regional Public Prosecutor found no evidence of the editor breeching the constitutional code (6 Jan. 2006). See the Letter from the Danish Government on 23 January 2006, http://www.um.dk/NR/rdonlyres/ooD9E6F7-32DC-4C5A-8E24-FoC96E813Co6/o/ 060123final.pdf (accessed 26 Mar. 2006).

5 The additional cartoons were apparently sent to some Muslims in Denmark and not published in the public domain.

ruary 2006 the situation worsened as several Danish embassies in the Middle East were attacked and the cartoonists received death threats from various Muslim groups. In the UK, though the incident was much debated in the public media, the media did not show the cartoons as it would have been a deliberate provocation of the Muslim community in the country.[6] However, it was in the UK that a demonstration by some Muslim groups in London on 3 February 2006 drew much attention and serious criticism from the public.[7] The whole incident seemed to have calmed down by March 2006 as a result of the efforts made by diplomatic, civil and religious groups in Denmark and elsewhere.

Arguments for the publication of the cartoons

Flemming Rose, culture editor of *Jyllands-Posten*, who was at the centre of the controversy, justified his actions by saying:

> I commissioned the cartoons in response to several incidents of self-censorship in Europe caused by widening fears and feelings of intimidation in dealing with issues related to Islam ... Our goal was simply to push back self-imposed limits on expression that seemed to be closing in tighter ... if a believer demands that I, as a non-believer, observe his taboos in the public domain, he is not asking for my respect but for my submission. And that is incompatible with a secular democracy.[8]

He further argues that by treating Islam in the same way as other religions and also the royal family in Denmark, the cartoons are 'including, rather than excluding, Muslims' as a part of Danish society and that the portrayal of the prophet with the bomb-shaped turban is not intended to indicate that the prophet is a terrorist but shows that 'some individuals have taken the religion of Islam hostage by committing terrorist acts in the name of the Prophet', and calls on others to agree that 'this is a topic that we Europeans must confront, challenging moderate Muslims to speak out'.[9]

---

6 See http://news.bbc.co.uk/newswatch/ukfs/hi/newsid_4670000/newsid_4678100/4678186.stm (accessed 26 Mar. 2006).

7 There was a counter-demonstration in London organized by moderate Muslim groups on 10 February 2006.

8 *Washington Post*, 19 February 2006.

9 See also his editorial in *Jyllands-Posten*, 30 September 2005. 'The modern, secular society is rejected by some Muslims. They demand a special position, insisting on special consideration of their own religious feelings. It is incompatible with contemporary democracy and freedom of speech, where you must be ready to put up with insults, mockery and ridicule. It is certainly not always attractive and nice to look at, and it does not mean

In the same manner, in his response to the ambassadors' letter, Anders Fogh Rasmussen, the Prime Minister of Denmark, while expressing the importance of religious tolerance and of equal standards for all religions, emphasized that 'freedom of expression is the very foundation of the Danish democracy' and said that he had no intention of interfering in the matter in relation to the press.[10] In addition to this, in his New Year's speech, he further insisted on the importance of freedom of speech in Danish society:

> In Denmark, we have a healthy tradition of putting critical questions to all authorities, be they of a political or religious nature. We use humour. We use satire. Our approach to authorities is actually rather relaxed. And to put it bluntly: it is this unorthodox approach to authorities, it is this urge to question the established order, it is this inclination to subject everything to critical debate that has led to progress in our society. For it is in this process that new horizons open, new discoveries are made, new ideas see the light of day while old systems and outdated ideas and views fade and disappear. That is why freedom of speech is so *vital*. And freedom of speech is *absolute*. It is not *negotiable*. [italics are mine][11]

Later, Carsten Juste, editor-in-chief of *Jyllands-Posten,* made a statement to the 'honourable fellow citizens of the Muslim world' in which he said that the cartoons were not intended to be offensive but recognized that they 'have indisputably offended many Muslims, for which we apologize', and called for further dialogue with Danish Muslims.[12] The arguments of the protagonists for the publication of the cartoons soon shifted to criticism of the violent demonstrations in Muslim nations. This, they saw, 'proved' the newspaper's point that they were under pressure to curb freedom of speech.

This feeling of pressure from a religious community was also expressed in various articles. For example, in the *Sunday Telegraph*: 'the problem is that militant Islam is not seeking a level playing field – equality before law, for instance – but special treatment ... What is

---

that religious feelings should be made fun of at any price, but that is of minor importance in the present context ... we are on our way to a slippery slope where no-one can tell how the self-censorship will end.'

10 Letter from the Prime Minister to the Ambassadors (21 Oct. 2005), http://gfx-master. tv2.dk/images/Nyhederne/Pdf/side3.pdf (accessed 28 Apr. 2006).

11 The speech was delivered on 1 January 2006. The text is quoted in the government response to the letter from UN Special Rapporteurs on 23 January 2006, http://www. ambdamaskus.um.dk/NR/rdonlyres/337D2B4D-A68A-4832-AFB0-7A6BF6779E7B/0/ PMsNewYearAddress2006.pdf (accessed 28 Apr. 2006).

12 http://www.jp.dk/meninger/ncartikel:aid=3527646 (accessed 28 Apr. 2006).

completely unacceptable is that this debate should be carried out in a climate of fear.'[13] Furthermore, there was a growing concern that the religious values and customs of Muslim communities were being imposed on European citizens, that Muslims were therefore pushing the limits of tolerance in a democratic society, and that the cultural norm – which was now perceived as secular – should be respected in the matter of the conflict of differing opinions. Europe has witnessed violent attacks on individuals who either criticize Islamic faith (or other faiths, for instance, in the case of the Sikh community in Birmingham, UK) or portray religious figures in an unconventional manner. These were seen as religion challenging the hard-won freedom of expression, which is regarded as the core value of western democracy. Criticism of the violent aspects of Muslim protests was also made by many Muslim writers: 'some Muslims have once again managed to exchange their role from being a victim (to be felt sorry for) to becoming the culprit (spreading fear of Islam).'[14] Others, who were against publication of the cartoons, made a similar point:

> The people who knowingly provoke Muslim rage are hugely enter-tained by religious people making fools of themselves, and it serves their cause well to have yet more evidence that religious people are all fanatics who are moved not by the tangible injustices and crimes represented by world poverty ... but only by pride, competitive aggression, and hurt feelings at the desecration of symbols which mean little or nothing to the majority of people in a secularised soci-ety.[15]

Arguments against the publication of the cartoons

The opposition to the publication of the cartoons came from all sections of the Muslim community, both in the Middle East and else-where, although the form of reaction differed. The very portrayal of the Prophet at all, which is prohibited in Muslims' religious practice (though there are exceptional cases), was provocative. Furthermore, that this was done in a manner disrespectful of and insulting to the prophet, and also of the followers of their faith, caused deep resent-ment within the Muslim community. In the letter to the Prime Minister of Denmark, the Muslim ambassadors wrote that the incident not only

---

13 'Democracy has a Gun Held to Its Head', *Sunday Telegraph*, 5 February 2006.

14 Murad Hofmann, 'Sliding Towards the Clash', *Emel* (Mar. 2006), p. 44.

15 Jeremy Henzell-Thomas, 'Cartoon Wars: The Challenge from Muslims in the West', *Emel* (Mar. 2006), p. 42.

went against 'the spirit of Danish values of tolerance and civil society', but also showed 'a very discriminatory tendency', and that the 'Danish press and public representatives should not be allowed to abuse Islam in the name of democracy, freedom of expression and human rights, the values that we all share'.[16] There were stronger criticisms from Muslim leaders, scholars and the general public in Muslim countries. Among other articles and statements, the 'Declaration on Behalf of Muslim Religious Leaders', signed by 41 Muslim scholars from various parts of the world, was widely cited by many Muslim organizations. It stated that the events in Denmark represented an 'entirely unacceptable crime of aggression that has violated the highest sanctities of the Muslim people' and insisted:

> We call upon the Danish government and the Danish people to yield to the large number of objective and sincere voices emanating from within their society, by apologizing and condemning and bringing an end to this attack. This is to ensure that Denmark is not isolated from the global community, a community that upholds the kind of freedom that prevents it from attacking and desecrating religious symbols or provoking animosity and antagonism towards any religion or race.[17]

The declaration also appeals to Muslims to exercise 'self-restraint in accordance with the teachings of Islam' as the signatories 'reject countering an act of aggression by acts not sanctioned in Islam' since violent reactions 'can lead to a distortion of the just and balanced nature of our request'. It further called upon the Organisation of Islamic Conferences, Muslim countries, governments and the international community to press the United Nations to issue 'a declaration criminalizing any insult to Muhammad, Jesus or Moses or to any other revered prophetic figure'.[18]

Even moderate Muslims and commentators in the media, though strongly condemning the violent attacks in the Middle East and the Muslim demonstration in London on 4 February, criticized the cartoons as the 'worst kind of arrogance'[19] and examples of 'western double

---

16 The letter was written on 12 October 2005. See http://www.filtrat.dk/grafik/Letter fromambassadors.pdf (accessed 28 Apr. 2006).

17 http://www.guidancemedia.com/downloads/articles/declaration.pdf (accessed 29 Apr. 2006).

18 http://www.guidancemedia.com/downloads/articles/declaration.pdf (accessed 29 Apr. 2006).

19 Fareena Alam, 'Why I Reject the Anarchists who Claim to Speak for Islam', *Guardian*, 12 February 2006.

standards'; they warned that without action 'this depressing cycle will continue'.[20] It was regarded as 'a deliberate provocation', a move 'to push further the limits of insult and ridicule' and a 'calculated attempt to paint all Muslims the same way'.[21] And it was, in contrast to the Danish government's insistence, not a matter of legality or right, but of 'civic responsibility and wisdom'. In particular, the re-publication of the cartoons was seen as 'a deliberate power struggle, a test of wills to see who will get the upper hand'.[22] Representing the Muslim sentiment, Ziauddin Sardar strongly asserted his opinion that the issue was not one of 'freedom of expression':

> It is about power, domination and demonisation ... The Muslims of Denmark, France, Germany and Holland are among the most mar- ginalised, unrepresented and voiceless of communities ... 'freedom of expression' becomes an instrument of oppression ... it was an exer- cise to demonstrate power, and to illustrate that European liberal secularists have a superior right to define and determine how Islam should be seen and how Muslims observe their faith ... It is time for mindless 'freedom of expression' to realise that the kind of absolute freedom they seek belongs only in the jungle. In a civilised society, freedom always comes with responsibility.[23]

The churches' response has been similar in that they have condemned the publication of the cartoons as well as the violent reactions from Muslim communities. The Vatican issued a comment that 'these forms of exasperated criticism or derision of others manifest a lack of human sensitivity and may constitute in some cases an inadmissible provoca- tion ... [yet] violent actions of protest are equally deplorable'.[24] The Methodist Church 'recognizes that immense hurt has been caused to Muslims' but was also 'saddened' that a 'minority of Muslims have responded with violence in word and deed'.[25] In particular, the General Assembly of the World Council of Churches, which met in Brazil on 14–23 February, called for genuine dialogue between secular and reli-

---

20 Humera Khan, 'The Bad News: British Muslims have been let down, and Extremism is the Result', *Independent*, 12 February 2006.

21 Faith Alev, 'The Cartoons were the Last Straw', *Emel* (Mar. 2006), p. 44. Alev is a Danish columnist for the daily *Politiken*.

22 Henzell-Thomas, 'Cartoon Wars', p. 41.

23 Sardar, 'A "freedom" whose Home is the Jungle'.

24 http://www.zenit.org/english/visualizza.phtml?sid=83985 (accessed 23 Mar. 2006).

25 'Methodist Church statement regarding offensive cartoons and inter-faith rela- tions', 6 February 2006, http://www.methodist.org.uk/index.cfm?fuseaction=news.news Detail&newsid=108 (accessed 20 Mar. 2006).

gious communities and a working towards justice for minority groups in the context of dominating cultures:

> As people of faith we understand the pain caused by the disregard of something considered precious to faith. We deplore the publications of the cartoons. We also join with the voices of many Muslim leaders in deploring the violent reactions to the publications … By the publication of the cartoons, freedom of speech has been used to cause pain by ridiculing peoples' religion, values and dignity … The real tension in our world is not between religions and beliefs, but between aggressive, intolerant and manipulative secular and religious ideologies. Such ideologies are used to legitimise the use of violence, the exclusion of minorities and political domination. The main victims of these types of controversies are religious minorities living in a context of a different majority culture.[26]

On the other hand, the European Evangelical Alliance issued a press release expressing their view that religious communities should understand the situation of a largely secular Europe, where criticism of faith is common in the media, and stating that they strongly support 'the principle of freedom of speech and an independent media' and condemn all the violence and incitement to violence; they called for both parties to engage in an 'open and sensitive dialogue'.[27]

Freedom of expression versus respect for faith

In spite of the justification put forward by Flemming Rose and other editors for the publication of the cartoons, the publication came under heavy criticism. Moreover, re-publication of the cartoons was regarded as unnecessary provocation of a sensitive and often vulnerable section of society. At the same time, the verbal and physical violence demonstrated by some Muslim groups was criticized both within and outside Muslim communities as incompatible with their faith and discrediting their argument. While considering the vital importance of the socio-political circumstances, certain issues require further investigation. The arguments of most advocates and commentators have been based on

---

26 http://www.wcc-assembly.info/en/theme-issues/assembly-documents/plenary-presentations/committee-reports/public-issues-committee/final-report/7-minute-on-mutual-respect-responsibility-and-dialogue-with-people-of-other-faiths.html (accessed 28 Apr. 2006).

27 http://www.europeanea.org/documents/PublicationofDanishCartoonsFeb2006.doc (accessed 25 Apr. 2006).

the concepts of 'freedom of expression' and 'respect for religious faith'. These two concepts are entwined with, and need to be understood in the light of, each other because they are not necessarily in opposition; in fact, in the course of the debates, these two areas of concern overlapped. In spite of the damage done by both sides, some valuable lessons can be drawn as we move into a multicultural, multireligious and globalized world.

Freedom of expression

Individual Muslims and Muslim communities around the world have been deeply hurt and have expressed their anger in various ways. The suggestion that political manipulation by the political and religious leaders of the nations in the Middle East could be a factor exacerbating the situation missed the whole point Muslims were making about their faith. Respect for the Prophet is a central tenet of the faith of Muslims. It forms a core value in their sense of identity, and the cartoons intruded on their private life and their community, and they were genuinely hurt. In the context of the marginalization of Muslim communities in western Europe, the Israel–Palestine conflict, the Iraq War and terrorist acts perpetrated in the name of Islam, Muslims are struggling with their own identity as a faith community and as a part of wider communities in Europe and elsewhere. The 'self-censorship' described by the editor of the Danish newspaper that the Muslim community appears to impose on secularized Europe needs to be understood as a way of making boundaries for their faith and community. Needless to say, freedom of expression cannot be absolute. The media imposes self-censorship. For instance, refraining from printing pornographic pictures of children and close-up pictures of dead bodies respects the privacy of the person involved and protects vulnerable individuals. It is a constant struggle to choose between 'respect' and 'freedom', and the newspaper in this case chose to side with 'freedom' at the expense of 'respect'. In doing so, the secular media stepped into an area that is 'taboo' for a religious community. Though Flemming Rose and Joan Smith in the *Independent*[28] convincingly argued that they as non-believers should not be asked to observe 'taboos' set by a religious community and that they have 'freedom' to express their views, their freedom in fact violated a private area of life and therefore did not exhibit the 'respect' required in a civil society. The resentment from Muslim communities in Europe was not because they objected to the 'freedom' promoted by the secular media but because the publication of the cartoons was disrespectful of the

---

28 *Independent*, 5 February 2006.

founder of their faith and therefore insulted them as a community. Furthermore, it was not done by negotiation but imposed on them – and this they saw as a violation of the respect required in any civil society.

The importance of freedom of expression, as it was repeatedly expressed by the supporters of the cartoons, is indeed a cornerstone of liberal democracy and should continue to be a beacon of civil society. However, freedom of expression should include freedom for *religious* expression as well. The secular media, by promulgating their version of freedom of expression, have consciously marginalized religious expression to the extent that any statement of religious conviction is regarded not as a matter of freedom of expression but as an issue of 'self-censorship' towards non-believers. The arguments for the publication of the cartoons were on the basis of this secular freedom, but by exercising this freedom, the editors in turn limited the freedom of expression of the Muslim community to cherish and uphold their Prophet as they wish him to be understood and portrayed. As Sadar and Alam have argued, it is 'arrogance' that the secular media determines how the Muslim community should observe the Muslim faith. As was rightly pointed out, freedom cannot be exercised in an atmosphere of fear, so the manner and area of freedom should not be determined by a particular section of society, even if they are the majority, but needs to be constantly negotiated in the public sphere with the minorities.

It is quite clear that the editors of the Danish newspaper and other newspapers in Europe felt that the issue of 'freedom of expression' was an area where they were pressurized by a religious group who hold certain religious and cultural values, and wished to assert what they regard as 'non-negotiable' values in a civil democracy. The publication of the cartoons in a Danish newspaper was justifiable in that it made clear to the public and to the religious communities that, in the secular context of Europe, a religious group cannot impose their religious beliefs and practices on the wider public. Though the prohibition on depicting the Prophet is limited to the Muslim community, it turns out that there is an atmosphere of fear that compels non-Muslims to follow the rules set by this religious community, as on several occasions in Europe we have witnessed physical attacks on those who dare to criticize Islam or misrepresent the Prophet Muhammad. And in this sense, the editor was justified in his defiance of what he saw as an encroachment on the freedom of expression. However, publishing a cartoon that depicted Muhammad with bomb-shaped turban and other derogatory illustrations went beyond the limits of freedom of expression, particularly in the contemporary context of terrorist attacks by Islamic fundamentalist groups. It has touched a very sensitive nerve within the Muslim community by directly associating the Prophet with suicide bombers. In this sense, Flemming Rose's opinion that some individuals have taken the religion of Islam hostage in the name of the Prophet and that 'the bomb comes from the outside world and is not an inherent characteristic of the Prophet' is not convincing since the majority Muslims see it otherwise. Furthermore, in spite of Muslim protests, the re-publication of the cartoons in many other European nations went further than mere freedom of expression. The protagonists of the freedom of expression have to consider its boundaries, especially when the people represented strongly object to the nature and contents of the expression. Claiming the 'tradition of satire' in European culture is not sufficient to justify bringing the very sensitive matter of religious faiths and practices into the public arena in this way. Freedom of expression must be accompanied by respect for others' beliefs and values, and it was on this that the Muslim communities and the opponents of the publication of the cartoons hinged their argument.

Respect for others' faith and values

Freedom of expression has been cherished as a beacon of western democracy. This is a result of a long struggle in the history of Europe and should rightly be respected and guarded at great cost. In this struggle, religious leaders (or religious people) often placed major obstacles by trying to impose their censorship upon the people by various kinds of doctrines, beliefs and codes of conduct that determined the life of the people. Until recently, in the history of western Europe, Christianity enjoyed unparalleled prestige over any other form of institution, and this legacy has been deeply resented by people of other faiths or no faith. The reaction of people of a secular leaning to anything encroaching on freedom of expression has to be understood in this context. In response, they hold on to what they regard as a core value in the face of religious orthodoxy that threatens liberal democracy. Therefore, the publication of the cartoons should be understood as self-defence rather than an exhibition of 'arrogance' or 'power, domination and demonisation' or 'discrimination'. Although the way this opposition was presented, in a form portraying the Prophet in such a disrespectful manner, was not appropriate and was rightly condemned by many, the whole action should not be understood as the majority community imposing its own values upon other minority communities. The majority community, realizing that certain values from a religious community were being imposed upon their values and were becoming the social and cultural norm, felt their own identity was challenged, and that the religious community was determining the values of the wider community.

Muslim communities throughout the world hold a strong sense of identity based on a distinctive religious faith and practice, which is a strength of community and should be respected. However, when this comes into conflict with other religious or secular communities, they also need to exhibit the 'respect' they require from others. Secular values in Europe hinge on the freedom to challenge authority, including religious authority, and the resentment people hold towards religion is not much to do with religion per se, but more to do with the unchallenged authority Christianity has held for many centuries. This freedom from any form of misuse of power or authority, particularly in the form of religious doctrine, is something Europeans find it hard to compromise on. Unlike many parts of the world, and particularly the Muslim world, religion and religious figures do not occupy much importance in the public sphere in contemporary western Europe, and this fact is something Muslims need to appreciate when they encounter secular Europe. Often Muslim religious leaders have expressed deep suspicion of European secular values, moral conduct and the marginalization of religion in the public sphere. In this regard, Frareena Alam's argument is convincing: she points out that, for a British Muslim, 'religion matters' and 'religion can be a powerful tool for social cohesion and good citizenship'. However, she asserts that in the context of secular Britain, 'if religion is to have relevance, it must strive towards a higher moral ground where provocative insult and retaliatory violence are unacceptable'. In other words, the very concepts they deplored in the cartoons – portraying Islam as inherently violent and somehow related to terrorism – were dramatically exhibited through the actions of some Muslims in protest at them.

Though Muslim anger over the cartoons is justifiable, translating that anger into physical and verbal violence was something the general public in Europe found it hard to understand. In retrospect, using the tool of boycotting Danish goods and calling off diplomatic relations with Denmark was far more effective than using violence in this matter. The Muslim argument was based on 'respect' for their religion, but they have failed to exhibit their 'respect' for the European understanding of civil society. Furthermore, they portrayed the action of one daily newspaper as that of the whole of the nation of Denmark while at the same time asking non-Muslims not to identify the acts of terrorists with the whole of the Muslim community or with the Prophet. When violence is committed in the name of religion, Europeans do not regard it as simply a religious matter; it brings to mind the history of the dominance religion once exercised over the whole society, and non-religious people find this 'non-negotiable'. In the context of modern and postmodern Europe, religious communities need to 'respect' European understanding of religion and society. I am not suggesting that religious communities should compromise with the secular agenda to sideline anything religious in the public sphere. The protest of the Muslim community on this matter is a legitimate one, though the method of violence was not acceptable in any civil society. When core values are in direct conflict with each other, according to Flemming Rose, the 'respect' the Muslim community are asking for can be interpreted as requiring 'submission' by the secular media to their religious values and, particularly when there is a context of fear, it causes strong reactions. Respect is of vital importance in a society where conflicting values are encountered in everyday life; it cannot be demanded of others – and certainly not by crossing another's identity boundary – rather it has to be earned by finding mutual ground for negotiation. This brings up the question of finding a common space for both religious and secular values in the context of modern and postmodern Europe.

In search of a common space of mutual respect

As I have argued in the previous sections, these two values of freedom and respect are not necessarily mutually exclusive and, while keeping its own distinctive values, any community needs to explore ways and means to appreciate other values and accommodate them into its own identity. Creating a common space is a vital aspect of living in any multicultural society, where the values have to be constantly negotiated through mutual tolerance. The problem of the controversy over the cartoons was that one section of society tried to impose its values on others in an 'aggressive' manner, and the others reacted to this by demonstrating in violent ways. The scope and limit of tolerance is hard to define, especially on religious issues. According to Bernard Williams, the idea of tolerance developed to deal with religious conflicts throughout the centuries, in which context it has been described as both 'necessary and impossible' and as required 'only for the intolerable'. Tolerance is a tension between the elimination of people's 'desire to suppress or drive out the rival beliefs' and the 'commitment to their own beliefs, which is what gave them that desire in the first place'.[29] Often the attempt to solve the problem of intolerance becomes either capitulation or indifference. David Heyd, dealing with this dilemma, suggests that tolerance requires a 'perceptual shift', that is, a 'shift of attention rather than an overall judgement', in which one perceives the other as a human being

---

29 Bernard Williams, 'Toleration: An Impossible Virtue?', in David Heyd (ed.), *Toleration: An Elusive Virtue* (Princeton: Princeton University Press, 1996), pp. 18–27.

and not merely 'the subject of certain beliefs or the agent of a particular action'. Tolerance involves 'respect, involving restraint', but it does not result in 'any weakening of certainty, confidence, or commitment to our own beliefs and values'.[30] This idea of a 'perceptual' shift of 'respect and restraint' is of vital importance in untangling the conflict between different religious communities.

In India, due to the complex nature of communal conflicts between different religious traditions, this idea of tolerance is much discussed. S. Radhakrishnan, the prominent Indian philosopher, portrayed toler-ance as a hallmark of Hinduism and a sign of maturity, and insisted that it should be adopted 'not as a matter of policy or expediency but as a principle of spiritual life' and a 'duty' rather than a 'conces-sion'. He saw tolerance as based on the belief that 'every community has inalienable rights which others should respect', which results in 'equal treatment for others' views'.[31] Following this Hindu notion of tolerance, Ashis Nandy raised the question of religious tolerance in the Indian politics of secularism in the context of communal violence, particularly between Hindus and Muslims. In his vigorous attack on secular ideology, he put forward the importance of 'religion as faith' over against 'religion as ideology', and claimed that the Indian secular state had failed to acknowledge the importance of the former since it was easier to deal with the latter. Furthermore, he found that, by regarding communal clashes as the result of socio-economic problems, the supporters of secularism had failed to realize the deeper problem of 'conflicting interests and a philosophical encounter between two meta-physics'. He insisted that because Indian secular politics suppressed the public role of religious faith, it was not able to meet the needs of a people 'to whom religion is what it is precisely because it provides an overall theory of life, including public life, and because life is not worth living without a theory, however imperfect, of transcendence'.[32] While Nandy's critics accused him of naivety about post-colonial India and political leaders (including Gandhi), and of an over-reactionary attitude to secular politics,[33] he nevertheless drew attention to the impossibility of marginalizing religion from society in India. He suggested that the

---

30 David Heyd, 'Introduction', in Heyd (ed.), *Toleration*, pp. 11–17.

31 S. Radhakrishnan, *The Hindu View of Life* (New Delhi: HarperCollins, 2009, first published in 1927), pp. 21–36; 'Hinduism', in A. L. Basham (ed.), *A Cultural History of India* (Delhi: Oxford University Press, 1975), pp. 70–2; S. Radhakrishnan, *Eastern Religions and Western Thought*, 2nd edn (Oxford: Oxford University Press, 1940), pp. 313–17.

32 Ashis Nandy, 'The Politics of Secularism and the Recovery of Religious Tolerance', *Alternatives* XIII/2 (Apr. 1988), pp. 177–94.

33 See Rajeev Bhargava (ed.), *Secularism and Its Critics* (Delhi: Oxford University Press, 1998), especially the article by Rajeev Bhargava, 'What Is Secularism For?', pp. 486–542.

solution ought to include exploration not only of 'tolerance of religions but also tolerance that is religious'.[34]

Coming back to the encounter between secular and religious values, one has to find a shared common place whereby two parties can acknowledge each other's identity. Here I would suggest that in Europe this common place has to be within secular democracy and civil society. This does not mean that a religious community should lose its religious identity, but rather, as Thomas suggested, it should become 'truly religious without being communal' by consciously moving out to interact with the values of the wider society. Of course, in the context of Muslim countries where Islamic laws are practised, the secular ideology has to find its common place within the wider society that holds the Islamic religious values. Both parties need to negotiate their own values within these contexts and accommodate the other's. This is not an easy option and it requires a constant effort to respect one another's values. For example, in the case of Muslim communities in Europe, not all the rules and norms practised in Islamic nations are observed and Muslims have to accept the value of the wider society; similarly, non-Muslims in the Middle East have to observe the norms of Muslim society. In this respect, in the case of Europe, the portrayal of the Prophet has to be in the area of freedom of expression, and the Muslim community needs to be reconciled to this as a part of their integration in the society, while the secular media has to observe respect for faith by sensitively listening to minority communities.

These suggestions are not on the basis of Muslims in Europe being a minority nor being 'outsiders', nor because religious faiths need to yield to secular ideology since Europe is supposedly a secular society, but rather because a religious community must contribute its values by sharing in a common space within the context it is in. Jeremy Henzell-Thomas, Chair of the Forum Against Islamophobia and Racism (FAIR), put this well:

> The wisdom given to us in the Islamic revelation is not the exclusive, inward-looking and parochial property of Muslims, to be jealously defended and set apart from all other formulations, or retreated into as a sullen refuge for a victimised minority, but is a universal gift to all [hu]mankind. Muslims need to offer this gift with an open hand for the benefit of the wider community. Islam has something precious to give to the West again. It once gave to the West an intellectual enlightenment. It can now offer the greater prize of spiritual enlightenment, and by so doing it can restore to the West the connection

---

34 Nandy, 'The Politics of Secularism', p. 192.

between the intellect and the spirit which Western science, despite its achievements, has lost sight of. It can help to feed the unconscious spiritual hunger of so many people in our society.[35]

This, I believe, is to be achieved not by making converts for Islamic faith nor by visioning the Islamicization of Europe, but rather, as M. M. Thomas (see Chapter 4) would have put it, by the permeation of Islamic values into the wider society for the greater benefit, and it is possible when the Muslim community in Europe appreciates the values of the wider society. Permeation therefore requires understanding and respecting the most important value of freedom of expression, including freedom to criticize religion.

As the sticking points of the controversy over the cartoons have been the twin issues of freedom of expression and respect for faith, so too the solutions to the problem seem to be on the same issues of freedom and respect. As I have discussed in the previous section, these two aspects of the life of communities in contemporary society are not simply divided into European and Muslim communities respectively, but, rather, are complicatedly entwined within their identities and constantly interact with one another. The key to our investigation could be in the concept of mutual respect for one another's values, while liberating members of society to express their opinions freely. The two values are always in tension, but this tension is necessary in that both secular and religious values are essential in forming a society where there should not be intimidation from others for holding any particular view strongly. The issue is not a matter of right or wrong but of emphasis, and this will be determined by context. The issue of the cartoons was regarded as a clash of western and Islamic cultures, or a clash of secularists and religious fundamentalists, but it also can be seen as a conflict between religious and secular values. Though certain modes of action by both parties were inappropriate, and therefore we witnessed unprecedented conflicts, both made their points by asserting their own most cherished values – freedom of expression and respect for faith. But as we have seen, these two are not necessarily mutually exclusive – they have to be in constant negotiation. There is no easy solution to the prevention of similar conflict, but the cartoon incident of 2005–06 clearly demonstrates an urgent need for both secular and religious communities to appreciate and learn from each other and find a common space of mutual respect.

---

35 Henzell-Thomas, 'Cartoon Wars', p. 43.

Conclusion

By way of conclusion, I would like to return to the question of the public engagement of theology: what could be the guiding principle in dealing with a complex situation such as we have discussed? A Scottish theologian, John Baillie, in his book *What is Christian Civilization?* pointed out that Christianity has two sides to it: 'it is *pistis* and it is also *koinonia*. It is a faith and it is a fellowship.' He goes on to explain that 'The two are inseparable parts of the same whole. And neither has ever flourished while the other has languished.' He further argues that these two dimensions of Christianity have played a vital role in its public engagement within the wider society.[36] It is very true that when we talk about the public engagement of theology, we are constantly reminded that Christian theology negotiates these two dimensions of faith or religions, on the one hand, and fellowship – community, society and nations – on the other.

If I expand further on Baillie's thought, I would argue that the public engagement of theology constantly requires moving beyond a Christian audience to engage public opinion by standing in the gap – the gap of religious, socio-economic and political differences – and trying to provide an alternative view so that the differences will not lead to confrontation or conflict. In the multireligious context, the gap could be between Christianity and other religions; church and other communities; religious and secular communities; and between various different religious communities. Doing public theology means being engaged with both sides of the gap. It is seeking to represent the one to the other, and also asking critical questions of both. Public theology takes the role of mediating in the gap with critical solidarity. It recognizes the religious dimensions of social questions, particularly the relationship between faith and identity and, at the same time, the social implications of a particular religious stance. It questions secularism that does not respect faith, and religion that sets itself against freedom of expression. And it does so in a way that promotes critical understanding and peaceful relations between different communities. By mediating in the gap with critical solidarity, public theology contributes to the formation of a community of communities in which the religious dimensions of identity are better understood and religious bodies are encouraged to work for the interests of the wider society.

---

36 John Baillie, *What is Christian Civilization?* (London: Christophers, 1947), p. 36.

10

Community Identity and Critical Dialogue: The Racial and Religious Hatred Bill

Dialogue ... challenges the sense of self-sufficiency, the smugness of unexamined claims, the narrow boundaries of one's own community, the aggressiveness of insensitive proclamation.[1]

Anthony Giddens discusses in his book *Modernity and Self-Identity* (1991) the nature of the close interconnection between globalizing influences and personal dispositions, which has been caused by modernity. He characterizes the key aspect of the effect of modernity as the reorganization of time and space, which in turn transforms our daily social life and defines 'self-identity' as not something that is given but as 'something that has to be routinely created and sustained in the reflexive activities of the individual'.[2] While agreeing with this notion, I believe that in the modern and postmodern situation of a society like Britain, the question of identity has to be looked at in the context of various groups, including religious communities. Despite the predictions of sociologists and historians that religion would become far less significant in contemporary societies, the present context shows otherwise and the growth of religious fervour and the rise of fundamentalisms are apparent. Community identity formulated out of religious commitment tends to be far deeper and more consolidating than that from any other source. Religion is, for many communities, a vital source of identity. It is not difficult to understand the extent to which people of some traditions anchor their identity in religion and will maintain it at great cost. It is therefore vital for contemporary scholarship to examine the source and mechanisms of community identity in a particular religious community and its interaction with other communities in order

---

1 Stanley J. Samartha, *Courage for Dialogue: Ecumenical Issues in Inter-Religious Relationships* (Geneva: World Council of Churches, 1981), p. 52.

2 Anthony Giddens, *Modernity and Self-Identity: Self and Society in the Late Modern Age* (Cambridge: Polity Press, 1991), pp. 52–3.

to understand how religious allegiance plays in relation to the wide spectrum of individual and community life.

Though the diversity of religious traditions and their aspirations are welcomed, the interaction between different communities sometimes causes conflicts and misunderstanding and, in extreme cases, violence, for example, the verbal and physical attacks on the Muslim community after the terrorist attack in the USA in 2001. As a response to attacks on Muslims by extremists, the UK government proposed a Racial and Religious Hatred Bill, provoking a public debate on freedom of expression and respect for faith. Examining this will give us some insights for our investigation of community identity in contemporary Britain, and, furthermore, it is revealing because the arguments for and against are equally convincing depending on one's own understanding of religion, community and identity. In this chapter I will examine the contents of the Bill, government documents and commission reports, the debates in both Houses, articles that appeared in the national media, and documents produced by various groups. By way of conclusion, I shall further discuss the differing concepts of the identity of secular and religious communities in contemporary Britain as revealed in the debates, and shall suggest theological engagement in critical dialogue as a way forward for mutual understanding.

The Racial and Religious Hatred Bill – government and supporters' positions

In the aftermath of September 11 2001, the British government introduced the Anti-Terrorism, Crime and Security Bill in November 2001,[3] which includes a measure to deal with the problem of incitement to hatred on the grounds of religion in line with the law against 'racial hatred' in the Public Order Act 1986. This attempt initiated heated debates both in public and in Parliament, and the intended proposal was defeated in the House of Lords in December 2001. In early 2005, the Home Office put forward the Racial and Religious Hatred Bill,[4] but it was again dropped due to opposition from the Lords and also because

---

3 House of Commons, 'Anti-Terrorism, Crime and Security Bill' (12 Nov. 2001), http://www.publications.parliament.uk/pa/cm200102/cmbills/049/2002049.htm (accessed 18 Aug. 2005).

4 Home Office, 'Racial and Religious Hatred Bill' (9 June 2005), http://www.publications.parliament.uk/pa/cm200506/cmbills/011/2006011.pdf (accessed 20 Oct. 2005); House of Lords, 'Religious Offences in England and Wales – First Report' (10 Apr. 2003), http://www.publications.parliament.uk/pa/ld200203/ldselect/ldrelof/95/9501.htm (accessed 10 June 2005).

of lack of time before the General Election. In their third attempt, the government presented the Bill again in June 2005, and this time the Bill completed its Commons stages in July. The House of Lords passed its amendment on 25 October 2005,[5] and in spite of the government's attempt to have the amendment rejected, the government lost by a margin of one on 31 January 2006.[6]

In response to the Bill presented to the House of Lords in 2001, the House launched a Select Committee on Religious Offences in England and Wales to 'consider and report on the law relating to religious offences' in May 2002, and the report was published in April 2003.[7] The questions addressed in the Committee were whether the 'Blasphemy Law' should be abolished and whether a new offence of incitement to religious hatred should be created and, if so, how. The Committee members, in their investigations, stated that they particularly considered the role of religion in the twenty-first century and the large increase of the number of adherents to non-Christian religions. The Committee received more than 500 submissions, among which Christian churches and Muslim communities made significant contributions. The Muslim community particularly expressed their grievance that there was fear in relation to their own religious identity. For example:

> I would simply make the point that it is very difficult to encourage open and free dialogue, involving people of faith communities who may feel insecure and may actually have a sense of fear in relation to their own religions identity. Dialogue and mutual understanding can be developed much more successfully in a society where it is absolutely clear that people of different faiths have a legitimate place, that their place is respected, and that they will not be subject to ill treatment and abuse.[8]

Similarly, the Commission for Racial Equality recognized that for many minority ethnic communities there is a close relationship between race and religion and that identity through faith is as important as identity through racial origin.[9]

5 House of Lords, 'Racial and Religious Hatred Bill' (amendment: 20 Oct. 2005), http://www.publications.parliament.uk/pa/ld200506/ldbills/015/amend/amo15-e.htm (accessed 3 Nov. 2005).

6 See the 'Racial and Religious Hatred Act 2006', http://www.opsi.gov.uk/acts/acts2006/20060001.htm (accessed 4 Feb. 2007).

7 House of Lords, 'Religious Offences in England and Wales – First Report (10 April 2003)', http://www.publications.parliament.uk/pa/ld200203/ldselect/ldrelof/95/9501.htm (accessed 10 June 2005).

8 House of Lords, 'Religious Offences in England and Wales – First Report'.

9 House of Lords, 'Religious Offences in England and Wales – First Report'.

The Committee insisted that the existing law breached Article 9 combined with Article 14 of the European Convention on Human Rights,[10] and many Muslims believed that the law treated them as second-class citizens of British society. The Committee concluded that there is an increasing role and multi-faith dimension of religion in the lives of people in Britain. In this context, they expressed their agreement that there 'should be a degree of protection of faith' and that 'in any further legislation the protection should be equally available to all faiths' and that there is 'a gap in the law as it stands'.[11]

The 2005 Bill was presented to 'make provision about offences involving stirring up hatred against persons on racial or religious grounds', and for this purpose the offence is described as 'hatred against a group of persons defined by reference to religious belief or lack of religious belief'.[12] Section 18(1) states:

> A person who uses threatening, abusive or insulting words or behaviour, or displays any written material which is threatening, abusive or insulting, is guilty of an offence if – (a) he intends thereby to stir up racial or religious hatred, or (b) having regard to all the circumstances the words, behaviours or material are (or is) likely to be heard or seen by any person in whom they are (or it is) likely to stir up racial or religious hatred.[13]

If a person is found guilty, the punishment is up to seven years of imprisonment. In addition to the Bill, the Home Office prepared 'Explanatory Notes', insisting that the Bill is meant to protect 'all groups from having religious hatred stirred up against them, regardless of whether members of that group share a common ethnic background'; the Home Office does not define religion or religious beliefs but wished the court to

---

10 See Article 9 (Freedom of thought, conscience and religion): '1. Everyone has the right to freedom of thought, conscience and religion; this right includes freedom to change his religion or belief and freedom, either alone or in community with others and in public or private, to manifest his religion or belief, in worship, teaching, practice and observance'; '2. Freedom to manifest one's religion or beliefs shall be subject only to such limitations as are prescribed by law and are necessary in a democratic society in the interests of public safety, for the protection of public order, health or morals, or for the protection of the rights and freedoms of others.' See also Article 14 (Prohibition of discrimination): 'The enjoyment of the rights and freedoms set forth in this Convention shall be secured without discrimination on any ground such as sex, race, colour, language, religion, political or other opinion, national or social origin, association with a national minority, property, birth or other Status.'

11 House of Lords, 'Religious Offences in England and Wales – First Report'.

12 Section 17A, Home Office, 'Racial and Religious Hatred Bill'.

13 Section 18, Home Office, 'Racial and Religious Hatred Bill'.

determine this; the term is meant to be a broad one, including people who hold Atheist and Humanist views. The offences are designed to include 'hatred against a group where the hatred is not based on the religious beliefs of the group or even on a lack of any religious belief, but based on the fact that the group do not share the particular religious beliefs of the perpetrator'. Furthermore, 'what must be stirred up is hatred of a group of persons defined by their religious beliefs and not hatred of the religion itself'.[14]

The debates were focused on the meaning of equal treatment of religious communities, the definitions of the terms for religious belief, the issue of freedom of speech and expression, and the ambiguity of the distinction between 'religious belief' and a 'religious person'. The Bill, as government and supporters argued, may be necessary for affirming solidarity with particular religious communities suffering abuse from right-wing political groups, but it seemed to have far-reaching implications for community life.

The supporters of the Bill included the Association of Chief Police Officers, the Crown Prosecution Services, the Commission for Racial Equality and Justice, some major church denominations and civil rights organizations, many minority religious groups and most Muslim organizations. The arguments of the government and supporters were:

- the necessity to protect all religious communities from aggressive attack by right-wing political groups;
- it is a preventive measure to warn those who abuse the loophole of the current law rather than actual implementation of a new law;
- it is meant to protect religious communities and individual believers rather than belief itself since the latter is open to criticism and debate;
- as in the case of the law in relation to inciting racial hatred, freedom of speech and expression is not an absolute right and there must be a limit to this fundamental right;
- the new legislation will eventually become the accepted norm.

As the government presented the Bill, it argued:

It is widely accepted that individuals in our society are stirring up hatred against particular religious groups. This may take the form of publications distributed by extremist groups which equate a particular religion with mass murder or rape, or speeches at public

---

14 Home Office, 'Racial and Religious Hatred Bill'. See also http://www.homeoffice. gov.uk/comrace/faith/crime/frq.html (accessed 10 June 2005).

meetings that use inflammatory language and exhort people to make life unbearable for those of a certain religion.[15]

Where this type of incitement to religious hatred exists, it has a 'disproportionate and corrosive effect on communities, creating barriers between different groups and encouraging mistrust and suspicion'.[16] The government also asserted that the legislation would have prevented the riots in northern towns in 2001.[17] In addition, it pointed out that the new legislation would not prevent people from criticizing the beliefs, teachings or practices of a religion or its followers, for example by claiming that they are false or harmful, proselytizing one's own religion or urging followers of a different religion to cease practising theirs. The government further argued that the Bill was rather for 'declaratory purpose and deterrent effect'.[18]

The Bill was very much promoted by the Muslim community along with other religious communities, and this was well expressed in the extensive document presented by the Forum Against Islamophobia and Racism (FAIR) in October 2002. It included systematic discussion on the various laws relating to the 'incitement of religious hatred', such as the Criminal Libel Act 1819 and the Public Order Act 1986. The document insists that far-right groups in Britain 'deliberately incite hatred towards Islam and Muslims':

> It is our view that an offence of incitement to religious hatred is not only necessary to provide equality of protection from incitement across religious groups but critical to avoid 'the shifting focus of bigotry' we have witnessed in the UK from race to religion. In this shifting focus, the target remains the same, only the marker changes – 'not because he is Pakistani but because he is Muslim' or 'not because she is Chinese but because she is Buddhist'. Unless the new offence of incitement to religious hatred is introduced, in our view, it leaves a loophole in the law that could potentially make a mockery of the current offence of incitement to racial hatred.[19]

---

15 Home Office, 'Racial and Religious Hatred Bill – Frequently Asked Questions', http://www.publications.parliament.uk/pa/cm200506/cmbills/011/en/06011x--.htm (accessed 26 Aug. 2005). See also http://old.homeoffice.gov.uk/docs/racerel1.html (accessed 19 Aug. 2005).

16 Home Office, 'Racial and Religious Hatred Bill – Frequently Asked Questions'.

17 *The Times*, 9 June 2005.

18 Home Office, 'Racial and Religious Hatred Bill – Frequently Asked Questions'.

19 The Forum Against Islamophobia and Racism (FAIR), 'The Religious Offences Bill 2002: A Response', www.fairuk.org/docs/rof2002.pdf (accessed 31 Aug. 2005). See also the statement from the Association of Muslim Lawyers (UK) at http://www.muslim-lawyers.net/news/index.php3?aktion=show&number=168 (accessed 31 Aug. 2005).

In the appendix, it gives various examples of aggressive slogans towards the Muslim community such as: 'Islam Out of Britain'; 'Islam a Threat to Us All'; 'The Truth about Islam: Intolerance; Slaughter; Looting; Arson; Molestation of Women'; 'Muslim Extremists plan to turn Britain into an Islamic Republic by 2025 ... They must be stopped!'; 'An Islamic Britain: A Cross to Bear?' The document convincingly argued that the British National Party was fully aware of the current loophole in the legislative framework, and called for new legislation. It further asserted that the legislation not only provided 'equality of protection from incitement across religious groups' but was also critical to avoid merely replacing the category of race with that of religion.[20]

In support of the legislation, a joint statement was delivered by religious leaders in April 2004. It argued that 'there is significant overlap between racial and religious identity, with communities sometimes targeted on the basis of their religious, as much as any racial, identity', that it is a 'highly desirable addition to the range of existing legal measures designed to ensure that our society is able peacefully to contain a wide range of strongly held beliefs and opinions'.[21]

Opposition to the Bill

Opposition to the Bill was from the media, both the Conservative Party and the Liberal Democratic Party, much of academia and some Christian groups.[22] The arguments included the following:

- the law will lead down the road to censorship;
- though there are various safeguards for its implementation, it would have a great effect on people's expression of faith and practice;
- since religion is not clearly defined and cannot be defined, like race, it opens the way to the abuse of the law to assert any form of social practice to obtain protection from healthy criticism;

---

20 FAIR, 'The Religious Offences Bill 2002: A Response'.

21 http://www.ekklesia.co.uk/content/news_syndication/article_050118hatred.shtml (accessed 10 June 2005). It further argues that 'the hostility towards some religious communities will not easily be reduced while the international situation remains as it is, particularly if the media continue to talk up terrorist threats and directly or indirectly relate them to these communities.'

22 See Neil Addison, 'Faith Doesn't Need a Bodyguard of Lawyers', *Church Times*, 24 February 2006; Polly Toynbee, 'What's at Stake is the Right to Insult and Cause Offence', *Guardian*, 31 January 2006; Polly Toynbee, 'My Right to Offend a Fool', *Guardian*, 10 June 2005; *Guardian*, 10 June 2006; 'A Bill Built on Flimsy Foundations', *Daily Telegraph*, 10 June 2005; 'Religion and the Law', *The Times*, 10 June 2005.

- it is open to religious extremists to use the law to silence any opposing opinions on their faith and practice;
- the present laws cover these the problems and should be implemented strictly rather than creating new legislation.

Journalists and those who are in the public entertainment sector very much feared the restrictions on the freedom of speech the Bill was perceived to impose on them. The main objections were:

- 'religious hated' is as subjective as 'religious belief itself', therefore it is impossible to discern what is 'likely to' stir up hatred from what is merely hostile anti-clericalism, and what is a simple joke at the expense of religion;
- a strong suspicion of politics behind the measure – as one commentator insisted, a Bill put forward for 'such unprincipled [political] reasons, and built on such flimsy foundations, should not become law';[23]
- it is extremely difficult to create an adequate distinction between what would constitute legitimate criticism of faiths and what would constitute a 'stirring up' of 'religious hatred' without 'diminishing free speech', and therefore government is urged to 'greater focus on means to improve [the Muslim community's] economic position';[24]
- the Bill 'owes far more to politics than to justice ... far from calming fears of prejudice, this law could actually exacerbate fear, as fundamentalists of all sorts demand police action against their critics'.[25]

Some Christian groups were concerned with the implications of the law for preaching the Christian message.[26] The Lawyers' Christian Fellowship argued that it was *inappropriate*, because: first, unlike race, a religious belief can be wrong and it is 'in society's interests that such debates are as free as possible without fear of prosecution'; second, protecting a particular religious minority does not justify enforcing such a law at the expense of freedom of expression; third, it is almost impossible to separate vilification of a certain belief from vilification of the person who holds that particular belief and so it is inevitable that criticism of others' religious beliefs will be taken to be insulting. Furthermore, they argued that the legislation was *impractical* since

---

23 'A Bill Built on Flimsy Foundations', *Daily Telegraph*.
24 'Religion and the Law', *The Times*.
25 'A Foolish and Unnecessary Bill', *Independent*, 10 June 2005.
26 BBC, 11 July 2005, http://news.bbc.co.uk/2/hi/uk_news/4671605.stm (accessed 18 Aug. 2005).

the definitions of religion and incitement to religious hatred are too vague and open to misuse by various groups. They insisted that 'the law would be punishing the most tolerant and protecting the least tolerant in society'. In addition, the legislation would be *counterproductive*, because 'it could be abused to try and stifle the teaching of fundamental beliefs that go against the teaching of other religions' (thus curtailing freedom of religion) and also to 'stifle criticisms of other's [sic] beliefs and practices' (thus curtailing freedom of expression).[27]

In similar vein, the Christian Institute argued that it would contravene both Article 9 (Freedom of thought, conscience and religion) and Article 10 (Freedom of expression) of the European Convention of Human Rights. It believed the government attempt to legislate would take the law into 'vast uncharted territory' and that 'in the name of protecting religion, the Attorney-General and the court would have unprecedented powers to adjudicate on Jewish and Sikh beliefs as well as all other beliefs ... including ... even Satanism.' It further argued:

> Religion is all about ideas, beliefs and philosophies. Religion (and irreligion) governs the choices people make between doctrinal, philosophical or moral alternatives. Race and national origin, on the other hand, are immutable characteristics. Arguments take place between people of different beliefs where people try to convince one another of their point of view. Attempts are made to convince people to change or abandon their religion. Such arguments are not possible over race – because no one can change their race. Bracketing together race and religion fundamentally misunderstands the difference between the two.[28]

After extensive discussion, the House of Lords amended the Bill to include:

> 29B: Use of words or behaviour or display of written material
> (1) A person who uses threatening words or behaviour, or displays any written material which is threatening, is guilty of an offence if he intends thereby to stir up religious hatred [omitting the words, 'abusive' or 'insulting' but keeping the word 'threatening'].

---

27 The Lawyers' Christian Fellowship (2005), 'Incitement to Religious Hatred' (Jan. 2005), http://www.religionlaw.co.uk/reportba.pdf (accessed 8 June 2005).

28 The Christian Institute (2001), 'Why a Religious Hatred Law would Harm Religious Liberty and Freedom of Speech' (Nov. 2001), http://www.christian.org.uk/incitement2005/incitement_aug05.pdf (accessed 31 Oct. 2005).

29J: Protection of freedom of expression
Nothing in this Part shall be read or given effect in a way which pro-
hibits or restricts discussion, criticism or expressions of antipathy,
dislike, ridicule, insult or abuse of particular religions or the beliefs
or practices of their adherents, or of any other belief system or the
beliefs or practices of its adherents, or proselytizing or urging adherents of a different religion or belief system to cease practising their
religion or belief system.[29]

In this amendment there is a considerable addition to the Bill to safeguard the freedom of expression.

Religion, legislation and identity

As we have heard from both sides of the argument, I would now like
to examine two areas that I believe are important to understanding the
nature of the debates – one is the issue of the place of religion in contemporary society, and the other is the understanding of the identity of
a religious community.

Britain: secular or multireligious society?

In the course of the debates there was a strong argument against the Bill
from liberal sections of the media and academia, mainly on the basis
of freedom of expression and also the anticipated misuse of the legislation by some fundamentalist groups. This is a valid caution, and there
have already been some cases in Australia, in Pakistan and in the USA,
though the nature and context of their legislation is different from that
in Britain. The underlying assumption of the opponents to the Bill was
that Britain is a secular society and therefore should be treated as such.
In particular, in her argument against the Bill, Polly Toynbee, expressing her dislike of anything religious, strongly asserted that 'this most
secular state in the world, with fewest worshippers at any altars, should
be a beacon of secularism in a world beset by religious bloodshed'.[30]
In this understanding, for the well-being of society, religion should be
regarded as a private matter and should not be on the agenda in the
public sphere. This view is coupled with many sociologists' arguments
that religion has become irrelevant in British society, which is perceived
to be secular.

---

29 House of Lords, 'Racial and Religious Hatred Bill' (amendment 20 Oct. 2005).
30 Toynbee, 'My Right to Offend a Fool'.

It is a commonly accepted view that Christianity in Britain has been experiencing rapid decline, and that this was most pronounced in the 1960s. Hugh McLeod identifies this period as a 'cultural revolution' and argues that the cause of this change was the search for greater individual freedom, which led to rejection of moral and doctrinal codes and authority. This was aggravated by social changes such as rapid decline in rural cultures, weakening of the sense of 'respectability' and loss of association of social identity with the Church. As a result, 'religious community was ceasing to be a necessary source of identity and support' to the people of western Europe.[31] This idea is taken further by Callum Brown, who insists that though Christianity had endured the challenge of the Enlightenment and modernity, the decisive decline in church attendance in the 1960s was because 'respectability' was supplanted by 'respect' and the traditional moral code was replaced by toleration and greater individual freedom.[32] In a similar argument, about the issue of the impact of modernity on religion in Britain, Steve Bruce observes that modernity changes the world-view of the people, bringing 'rationality' and 'subtly altering the way we think about the world so as to make religious beliefs and rituals ever more irrelevant'.[33]

However, on the other hand, other religions in Britain have been gradually increasing since the 1960s, mainly through migration and natural growth of the members of religious communities, and, as a result, Britain has become a multireligious society. The report of the House of Lords' Select Committee on Religious Offences in England and Wales (2003) raised the question of whether religion still played an important role in the formation of morals and values and whether this new phenomenon will lead to the transformation to a secular society. The Committee concluded that 'religious belief continues to be a significant component, or even determinant, of social values, and plays a major role in the lives of a large number of the population'. It emphatically stated that 'beyond doubt Britain is a multi-faith society' and that 'the United Kingdom is not a secular state'. In fact, if we go further than looking at church attendance and the decline of church membership, we see a different picture from the notion of the sociologists above. The 2001 census showed that 77 per cent of respondents claimed that they were part of 'Christian tradition and identity'.[34] Britain, in contrast

---

31 Hugh McLeod, *Religion and the People of Western Europe 1789–1989* (Oxford and New York: Oxford University Press, 1997), pp. 141–3.

32 Callum Brown, *The Death of Christian Britain* (London and New York: Routledge, 2001).

33 Steve Bruce, *Religion in Modern Britain* (Oxford: Oxford University Press, 1995).

34 http://www.statistics.gov.uk/CCI/nugget.asp?ID=460&Pos=1&ColRank=1&Rank=326 (accessed 20 Oct. 2005).

to Toynbee's argument, has a distinctive combination of secularism and modernity, on the one hand, and religion and spirituality, on the other, each occupying a different arena of people's life in society, and in this sense, using Grace Davie's terminology, Britain is an 'exceptional case'.[35] In fact, one has to question Toynbee's perception of the reality of British society. Yes, British society cherishes and has been the beacon of secular and parliamentary democracy, but not in the absence of religion. Yes, religions have been the cause of and factors in conflicts, but faiths in Britain have neither been simply pushed away by secularism nor have they ceased to contribute to the betterment of society.

In this context, the argument of the government is right that the state needs to protect vulnerable religious communities on equal terms without showing any impartiality. Secularism has two meanings – one has to do with the state keeping a distance from religions, the other is to do with the state treating all religious groups equally. The government's intention, in this case, was to choose the latter option since the first option is not realistic in contemporary British society. In spite of the secularists' assertion and many sociologists' arguments that Britain is a secular society in the sense of the demise of religion in the public sphere, the debate brought out the reality that Britain is a multireligious society. Many religious communities are not embarrassed that their identity has a religious dimension.

During the course of debates on the Bill, the Muslim community expressed that, in their treatment not only by far-right groups but also by the general public, their religious identity had been severally questioned as if the problem lay intrinsically in Islam as a faith. The Muslim community as a whole should not be judged by the actions of fundamentalist groups within them, and they deserve protection from aggressive campaigns against their community and their faith. This requires a sense of respect and appreciation of others' beliefs from the wider community since their faith is part and parcel of self and community identity. It is the strength of Britain that it has worked to maintain an open society where people are welcomed and share their values and aspirations. This effort has to be an ongoing one and should extend to the 'religious' dimensions of life as well as the cultural in order to create shared identities. This process requires the participation of both the majority community and the minority religious communities. Therefore, the protagonists of the Bill sought to demonstrate solidarity with vulnerable sections of society. This should be respected. However, whether enactment of legislation is the appropriate way to improve

---

35 Grace Davie, *Europe – The Exceptional Case: Parameters of Faith in the Modern World* (London: Darton, Longman & Todd, 2002), pp. 2–8.

their situation is in question exactly because of the issue of the integrated identity of religious communities.

Religious belief versus religious person – the integral identity of religious community

In response to opposition criticism that the legislation would infringe
the freedom to make healthy criticism of or jokes about religion, the
government insisted that the Bill is intended to protect religious people
and not religious belief itself. However, the separation of religion and
religious people is arbitrary if not impossible when it comes to many
religions and religious communities. The identity of many religious people is drawn from their faith, and this includes its doctrines, founders,
particular religious practices and the religion as a whole. Therefore it is
impossible to make a distinction and, in many cases, it is more insulting
to criticize the religion or religious figure than the believers themselves.
It is precisely because of this that some religious communities find it
very hard to tolerate the insults of right-wing groups. Therefore, the
new legislation was viewed by religious groups as a preventive measure
to protect their beliefs from being ridiculed or criticized.

That religion is, for many communities, a vital source of their identity is often overlooked by those who oppose the Bill when they argue
that there is an important distinction between race and religion: that
is, one cannot criticize or ridicule someone on the basis of race because
this is an accident of birth, whereas religion is a matter of choice. However, just because religion can be accepted by people of their own free
will, this does not mean that all people of religion are so because of
choice. For many, their religion is determined by their origin and is
central to their identity. Religion is not something you can change – it
is against the will of Allah for Muslims and against *dharma* for Hindus,
for example. It is important to understand the extent to which people
of some traditions anchor their identity in religion and will maintain it
at great cost. This is why many religious traditions object to the notion
of conversion. For them the freedom of religion is to do with freedom
to keep and practise one's faith, whereas often in the West freedom of
religion is understood as freedom to propagate one's religion or freedom to change one's religion.

The question then comes whether we should criticize a religion that
forms people's identity. Since many believers regard their religion as
an integral part of their self-identity, should we not then treat religion
as we treat race and bar it from criticism? On the contrary, we cannot
treat religion as we treat race in this regard. The argument against

racial abuse is correct: it is not acceptable to ridicule or make rude comments on the basis of skin colour or racial background, and legislation should be enforced in the case of incitement of hatred towards an individual or a community on the basis of their race. However, though religion forms the core identity of many believers, religious ideas and faith have to be open to critique by both insiders and outsiders, otherwise a religious tradition or community can easily be corrupted and become dogmatic. We have seen this throughout the history of western Christendom, Islamic fundamentalism and the Hindu nationalist movement in India. Religious beliefs as well as believers themselves need constantly to be reformed – and the only way to maintain this is by openness to criticism. Any aspect of religious faith – doctrines, rituals, authority, scriptures, institutions, religious leaders – should be open to scrutiny. It is vital for civil society that no individual, community, belief or ideology should stand above the criticism of the public, and religious belief is no exception to this principle.

In response to the criticism of the Racial and Religious Hatred Bill, the Home Secretary said that the legislation would be like a 'line in the sand', that it would be a warning to those who misuse the loopholes in the current law and would therefore contribute to the improvement of community relations.[36] However, rather than promoting harmony between communities, it may be used to maintain boundaries, and therefore have the opposite effect. The grievance of the Muslim community is a reality and the aggression of far-right groups against this community would not seem to evaporate easily. The legislation may prevent verbal or written attacks on minority religious communities from hate campaigns, but the negative consequences seem to be far greater than the immediate protection of a religious group. It would be regrettable to find that by drawing a 'line in the sand' we end up digging a 'ha–ha' (sunken fence) that divides communities so that healthy interaction may no longer be possible and legal intervention is the only recourse.

Differing concepts of identity and the need of critical dialogue

I have argued in my previous section that Britain is a multireligious society and also a secular society. During the course of debate it was highlighted that the arguments hinged on the issue of identity. As I have discussed, the protagonists for and against the Bill were not simply religious groups versus secular groups; it was much more complex,

36 *The Times*, 9 June 2005.

and indeed we witnessed an unusual alliance between some evangelical/ fundamentalist Christian groups and secularists on this 'religious' issue, each asserting their own reasons against the Bill. Though I have argued against the Bill on the basis of healthy and open interaction of religious beliefs and communities with the wider community, this does not mean that there are any single criteria for us to work with on disputes on religious matters. As we witnessed in the 'clash of cultures' over the Danish cartoon issue, the secular assertion of freedom of expression irrespective of any religious sensitivity is rather exhibiting the attitude of ignorance and arrogance towards 'otherness', though the Muslim reaction to the situation is equally unacceptable. This situation is not necessarily a conflict between Muslims and non-Muslims, but a conflict between fundamentalists, each claiming that they are representing the whole group.[37] This clash of secular and religious agendas is far more complex, since they also relate to political and economic undercurrents between the Muslim and the western world. The limits of the scope of this chapter do not permit me to go further, but this illustrates the urgent need for open dialogue on religious issues and that neither the enforcement of law nor suppressing the issues will be the appropriate response to the problem. Meaningful dialogue between religious communities and secularists, and between various groups within communities, is urgently needed, particularly on this issue of conflicting identities.

The Christian theology of dialogue, although its main concern has been between Christians and people of other faiths, may provide methodologies and working models for this complex situation of religious and secular conflict. Dialogue can be defined as commitment to one's faith and openness to that of others with genuine respect. Dialogue involves a desire to understand those of another faith better and learn from one another, an attitude that leads to an ongoing reflection on one's own faith and practice. It is also for mutual knowledge and friendship that leads to the correction of prejudices towards others. It is a relatively recent paradigm in the field of contemporary theology and has especially come to the fore as discussion on religious pluralism has developed.

Though the theoretical concept of dialogue has been developed in the field of systematic theology in the West, the philosophical and experimental experience of dialogue has been articulated most clearly among Indian theologians. Due to the vast diversity of religious and cultural

---

37 See Timothy Garton Ash, 'Our Media Must Give Muslims a Chance to Debate with Each Other', *Guardian*, 9 February 2006; Fareena Alam, 'Why I Reject the Anarchists Who Claim to Speak for Islam', *Guardian*, 12 February 2006.

communities, one of the most difficult public issues in India has been the problem of communal conflicts. Through these experiences, Indian theologians have developed a pragmatic approach to living together and a philosophical concept of finding truth and goodness in each other. They regard plurality as a blessing rather than an obstacle to harmony, and argue that active engagement in dialogue with others with respect is part and parcel of, if not essential to, any religious life. This was initially taken up by E. Stanley Jones, a well-known Methodist missionary to India, as he explored the idea of a 'round table conference' where people of different faiths could gather to share their own religious experiences without confronting each other or trying to persuade others to change their convictions.[38]

Stanley Samartha, who became the first director of the sub-unit on dialogue at the World Council of Churches, articulated his theology of dialogue as an attempt to understand and express our own particularity not just in terms of our own heritage but also in relation to the spiritual heritage of our neighbours of other faiths.[39] His theology is based on his understanding of God's covenant with his people and also Christ's incarnation, both of which demonstrate the dialogical relationship between God and his people. A natural expansion of this understanding is that the relationship between different religious communities should be a form of mutual dialogue, and not at all confrontational. Samartha draws his theology from the Indian multireligious setting, from Indian philosophical approaches of finding truth by consensus and from an attitude of acknowledging others as partners on the way rather than imposing one's own truth claims on others. In his approach, mutual respect of one another's convictions is of crucial importance in dialogue, and this should take place in community, creating a 'community of communities'. He saw dialogue among world religions as the demand of our age and an opportunity to work together to discover new dimensions of religious truths.

This idea of a mutual search for the truth was taken up by the World Council of Churches and became a major plank of ecumenical theology, as explained in 'Guidelines on Dialogue with People of Living Faiths and Ideologies' (1979).[40] This document sets clear aims and

---

38 E. Stanley Jones, *The Christ of the Indian Road* (New York: Abingdon Press, 1925).

39 Samartha, *Courage for Dialogue*.

40 World Council of Churches (1979), 'Guidelines on Dialogue with People of Living Faiths and Ideologies', http://www.oikoumene.org/en/resources/documents/wcc-programmes/interreligious-dialogue-and-cooperation/interreligious-trust-and-respect/guidelines-on-dialogue-with-people-of-living-faiths-and-ideologies.html (accessed 17 Feb. 2011).

objectives of dialogue and gives some practical guidelines for Christians who are engaging in a multireligious situation. It states that dialogue is the responsibility of Christians and should be carried out with the spirit of reconciliation and hope provided by Christ. It emphasizes the vital importance of acknowledging that all communities seek a secure sense of identity and realizing that in this process a religious community may often become exclusive and absolutize its own religious and cultural identity. It also asserts that dialogue should be based on mutual trust and respect for the integrity of others, and therefore it is a vital part of Christian service in community as well as a means of living one's faith in Christ. 'Ecumenical Considerations for Dialogue and Relations with People of Other Religions' (2001)[41] takes account of the recent development of fundamentalism and reflects the rising concern for the relevance of dialogue in this context. It insists that the role of dialogue is not only to reconcile conflict between communities but also to prevent religion becoming the source of tension between communities in the first place. It also adds the importance of mutual empowerment in the common pursuit of the betterment of society and encourages religious communities to examine critically their own conduct in relation to other communities.[42]

Taking this theological notion of dialogue between different religious communities, in the case of Britain, we find an urgent need for critical dialogue between religious and secular groups, with the attitude of 'commitment to one's conviction and openness to that of other's with genuine respect'. In the course of the debate for or against the Racial and Religious Hatred Bill, British society exhibited its mature attitude by conducting open and frank discussions in public and, as I see it, the end result of the Bill reflected both sides of the argument. This process should be a beacon of democratic society where both the secular and religious identities are respected and also critically assessed.

---

41 World Council of Churches (2001), 'Ecumenical Considerations for Dialogue and Relations with People of Other Religions', http://www.oikoumene.org/en/resources/documents/wcc-programmes/interreligious-dialogue-and-cooperation/interreligious-trust-and-respect/ecumenical-considerations-for-dialogue-and-relations-with-people-of-other-religions.html (accessed 17 Feb. 2011).

42 For Catholic discussion on dialogue, see William Burrows (ed.), *Redemption and Dialogue: Reading Redemptoris Missio and Dialogue and Proclamation* (Maryknoll, NY: Orbis Books, 1993).

Conclusion

By engaging in dialogue, we are able to question secularism that does not respect faith, which is part and parcel of the identity of many individuals and communities, and to challenge religion that sets itself against the wider interests of society, which has often been the most disturbing element undermining secular identity. The question of identity in a secular and multireligious society lies not in whether one is right or not, nor in who is holding the moral high ground, but it is rather an acknowledgement of differences and respect of each other's differing identities. The notion of dialogue encourages us to continue to engage in conversation with each other, to exchange our views for mutual inspiration, without holding an attitude of forcefully attempting to change others or ignoring other views as something irrelevant. Religious and secular communities need to listen to each other, and prepare to be shaped by each other's differing views. Both 'respect for faith' and 'freedom of expression' are core values to form the identity of both communities as they uphold them at a great cost. This, however, should not be regarded as the absolute value and needs to be negotiated in the context of contemporary society by engaging in open and critical dialogue.

Epilogue

Duncan Forrester has reminded us that Christian theology should not cease to provide 'insights into the shape and grounding of human equality which are of continuing public significance', and that 'to withdraw them from public debate would result in its serious impoverishment'.[1] This book provides samples of doing public theology in various contexts – India, Korea, Latin America, Europe and the USA – and of theological responses to different issues – biblical interpretation, ecology, Church and society, exclusion, community identity, reconciliation, justice, equality and human dignity, peace-making, multicultural society, critical dialogue and the permeation of the gospel. This book is not a comprehensive or systematic treatment of the topic of public theology as a discourse, but rather a demonstration of theology in action in the public sphere. Public theology is theology engaging in conversation with the main bodies in the public sphere and the Church's attempt to contribute to the wider society. This takes place in many forms and contexts and this book highlights the wide range of the issues and the many ways to approach them.

The concept of the public sphere continues to be important to those who are engaged in doing public theology. As I have pointed out in Chapter 1, the 'public' is not to be understood as over against the domestic or private. It is not to do with the place of doing theology but with the openness of theology in relation to universal access, critical inquiry and open debate for all members of society. This means that the Church, while exercising its prophetic role in society with critical inquiry and open debate, has to be open to the wider society for public scrutiny. As M. M. Thomas (see Chapter 4) made clear, this does not mean a loss of the Church's spiritual and religious identity, but its becoming a catalyst for the permeation of gospel values into society. We need to reclaim the meaning of 'public philosophy', 'public Church' and 'secular fellowship' as the activity of the whole Church in the world. Although numerous individuals and groups are sacrificially involved in

---

1 Duncan B. Forrester, *On Human Worth: A Christian Vindication of Equality* (London: SCM Press, 2001), pp. 72–4.

sharing God's concern for the poor and marginalized, throughout the history of the Church much of the theological enterprise has been concentrated on activities within the Church and for church members, or even on establishing hegemony over other denominations or religious traditions. In particular, theology, unlike other academic disciplines, has been reduced to serving the particular constituency of church members and leaders, and its findings have a very limited audience. Public theology extends the concerns of Christians for human well-being, justice and community life into the wider public sphere.

This brings us to our next question of developing a methodology for engaging with each of the main bodies in the public sphere. I have suggested that there are six main bodies in the public sphere: the state, the market, the media, civil society, academies and religious communities. Further research should be carried out to make a comprehensive theory of engagement between these bodies. In particular, a systematic study of public theology has to address the methodology of interaction between theology, which sits in the academy and in the Church, and the other academic disciplines. Perhaps public theology has to be subdivided into different areas according to those who are engaged in it and the particular discipline used, for example, on ecological issues, media, or civil society respectively. There is no public theology as such, but many public theologies.

Theology has already been interacting with philosophy, history and religious studies in its development and needs to extend its conversation partners to wider disciplines. The difficult task, though, is that while theology is prepared to (or already has been) engaged with politics, economics, sociology and other subjects, the interest tends to be one-way and a key role of public theologians is to encourage other disciplines to interact with theology. My own involvement with the Ebor lecture series in York, the series of International Conferences on Peace and Reconciliation and the Symposium of Cosmopolitanism, Religion and the Public Sphere are just a few examples of the increasing tendency in academic circles towards interdisciplinary approaches, where scholars from various disciplines interact with each other to deal with contemporary national and international problems. As I have shown in this book, issues in the contemporary world are rarely just caused by one single problem of economy, politics, society, race, culture or religion, but are generally related to several or all of them; therefore the involvement of all the concerned disciplines is required.

How then can the diverse interpretations of the Bible and theological positions held by theologians and congregations help public discussion? And who should be the ones doing public theology? In my view, a variety of views and voices is not a problem, and in fact it is a hallmark of a healthy community that various interpretations exist. It is also the case in any other field that through competition, critical debate and negotiation the most appropriate solutions are found. In the examples I have given, and in numerous other historical and contemporary cases, the religious traditions have provided aspirations for hope, justice and peace, reconciliation and sharing of resources for people who otherwise lack the fullness of life. In particular, Christian theology could contribute to the other bodies in the public sphere in the areas of ethics, wisdom and spirituality. In order to do this, a vital aspect of public theology, as John de Gruchy has pointed out, is the public-ness of the subject of theological exploration in that it is not monopolized by theologians or church leaders. This requires the active involvement of the congregation in the areas of both theory and practice. Public theology should not remain within the circle of public theologians but constantly examine the implications and application of its findings in society. Reflections on this will, in turn, feed back into the articulation of authentic public theology. There is an ongoing call for those who are interested in the ethos of public theology to be part of this new venture by contributing research articles, interacting with others' contributions and applying the findings in various contexts to further encourage critical engagement with our contemporary society.

The Kairos Document from South Africa, which was quoted at the beginning of this book, well expresses the role of theology in the public sphere:

> Our present KAIROS calls for a response from Christians that is biblical, spiritual, pastoral and, above all, prophetic. It is not enough in these circumstances to repeat generalized Christian principles. We need a bold and incisive response that is prophetic because it speaks to the particular circumstances of this crisis, a response that does not give the impression of sitting on the fence but is clearly and unambiguously taking a stand.[2]

---

2 Kairos Document.

Bibliography

Books and articles

Abraham, K. C., 'A Theological Response to the Ecological Crisis', in David Hallman (ed.), *Ecotheology: Voices from South and North*, Geneva: World Council of Churches, 1994, pp. 65–78.

Adamo, David, 'The Use of Psalms in African Indigenous Churches in Nigeria', in Gerald O. West and Musa W. Dube (eds), *The Bible in Africa: Transactions, Trajectories, and Trends*, Boston: Brill, 2000, pp. 336–49.

Ahmad, Imtiaz, 'The Tamilnadu Conversions, Conversion Threats and the Anti-Reservation Campaign: Some Hypotheses', in Asghar Engineer (ed.), *Communal Riots in Post-Independence India*, Hyderabad: Sangam Books, 1984, pp. 118–29.

Ahn, Byung-Mu, 'Jesus and the Minjung in the Gospel of Mark', in CTC–CCA (eds), *Minjung Theology: People as the Subject of History*, 1981, pp. 138–52.

Ahn, Byung-Mu, *The Story of Minjung Theology*, Seoul: Korea Institute of Theology, 1990.

Aleaz, K. P., *Christian Thought through Advaita Vedānta*, Delhi: ISPCK, 1996, pp. 148–55.

Alev, Faith, 'The Cartoons Were the Last Straw', *Emel* (Mar. 2006), p. 44.

Allen, Roland, *Missionary Methods: St. Paul's or Ours?*, Grand Rapids, MI: Eerdmans, 1962 [first published 1912].

Amaladoss, Michael, 'Ashrams and Social Justice', in D. S. Amalorpavadass (ed.), *The Indian Church in the Struggle for a New Society*, Bangalore: NBCLC, 1981, pp. 370–8.

Anderson, Allan, *Zion and Pentecost: The Spirituality and Experience of Pentecostal and Zionist/Apostolic Churches in South Africa*, Pretoria: University of South Africa Press, 2000.

Annan, Kofi A., *Prevention of Armed Conflict: Report of the Secretary-General Kofi A. Annan*, New York: United Nations, 2002.

Aruldoss, J., 'Dalits and Salvation', in Andrew Wingate, Kevin Ward, Carrie Pemberton and Wilson Sitshebo (eds), *Anglicanism: A Global Communion*, London: Mowbray, 1998, pp. 294–300.

Atherton, John, *Public Theology for Changing Times*, London: SPCK, 2000.

Augustine, P. A., 'Conversion as Social Protest', *Religion and Society* XXVIII/4 (Dec. 1981), pp. 48–53.

Azariah, V. S., 'India and Christ', *International Review of Mission* XVII/65 (Jan. 1928), pp. 154–9.

Baago, Kaj, 'The Post-Colonial Crisis of Missions', *International Review of Mission* LV/219 (July 1966), pp. 322–32.

Baek, Nak-Chung, 'Who are Minjung?', in *Essays on Minjung*, Seoul: Korea Theological Study Institute, 1984, pp. 13–28.

Baillie, John, *What is Christian Civilization?*, London: Christophers, 1947.

Barnett, Paul, *The Message of 2 Corinthians*, The Bible Speaks Today Series, Leicester: InterVarsity Press, 1988.

Barton, Mukti, *Scripture as Empowerment for Liberation and Justice: The Experience of Christian and Muslim in Bangladesh*, Bristol: University of Bristol, 1999.

Baxter, M. J., 'John Courtney Murray', in Peter Scott and William T. Cavanaugh (eds), *The Blackwell Companion to Political Theology*, Oxford: Blackwell, 2004, pp. 150–64.

Bell, Daniel M., 'State and Civil Society', in Peter Scott and William T. Cavanaugh (eds), *The Blackwell Companion to Political Theology*, Oxford: Blackwell, 2004, pp. 423–38.

Bellagamba, Anthony, *Mission and Ministry in the Global Church*, Maryknoll, NY: Orbis Books, 1992.

Bellah, Robert, 'Public Philosophy and Public Theology', in Leroy Rouner (ed.), *Civil Religion and Political Theology*, Notre Dame, IN: Notre Dame University Press, 1986, pp. 79–97.

Benne, Robert, *The Paradoxical Vision: A Public Theology for the Twenty-First Century*, Minneapolis, MN: Fortress Press, 1995.

Bevans, Stephen B., *Models of Contextual Theology*, Maryknoll, NY: Orbis Books, 1992.

Bhargava, Rajeev (ed.), *Secularism and Its Critics*, Delhi: Oxford University Press, 1998.

Blair, William N. and Bruce Hunt, *The Korean Pentecost and the Sufferings which Followed*, Edinburgh: The Banner of Truth Trust, 1977.

Blewett, Jane, 'The Greening of Catholic Social Thought?', *Pro Mundo Vita Studies* 13 (Feb. 1990), pp. 22–32.

Boff, Leonardo, *Ecclesiogenesis: The Base Communities Reinvent the Church*, trans. Robert R. Barr, London: Collins, 1986.

Boff, Leonardo, 'Social Theology: Poverty and Misery', in David Hallman (ed.), *Ecotheology: Voices from South and North*, Geneva: World Council of Churches, 1994, pp. 235–47.

Bonino, José Miguez, *Doing Theology in a Revolutionary Situation*, Philadelphia, PA: Fortress Press, 1975, pp. 26–7.

Bosch, David J., *Transforming Mission: Paradigm Shifts in Theology of Mission*, Maryknoll, NY: Orbis Books, 1992.

Botman, H. R., 'Truth and Reconciliation: The South Africa Case', in Harold Coward and Gordon S. Smith (eds), *Religion and Peacebuilding*, Albany, NY: State University of New York Press, 2004, pp. 243–60.

Boyd, Robin, *An Introduction to Indian Christian Theology*, rev. edn, Delhi: ISPCK, 1975.

Breitenberg, E. Harold, 'To Tell the Truth: Will the Real Public Theology Please Stand Up?', *Journal of the Society of Christian Ethics* 23/2 (2003), pp. 55–96.

Breyfogle, Todd, 'Time and Transformation: A Conversation with Rowan Williams', *Cross Currents* (Fall 1995), pp. 293–311.

British Foreign Bible Society, *Report of British Foreign Bible Society* (1907).

Brown, Callum, *The Death of Christian Britain*, London and New York: Routledge, 2001.

Bruce, Steve, *Religion in Modern Britain*, Oxford: Oxford University Press, 1995.

Brun, Tony, 'Social Ecology: A Timely Paradigm for Reflection and Praxis for Life in Latin America', in David Hallman (ed.), *Ecotheology: Voices from South and North*, Geneva: World Council of Churches, 1994, pp. 79–91.

Burrows, William (ed.), *Redemption and Dialogue: Reading* Redemptoris Missio *and* Dialogue and Proclamation, Maryknoll, NY: Orbis Books, 1993.

Cady, Linell E., *Religion, Theology and American Public Life*, Albany, NY: State University of New York Press, 1993.

Cahill, Lisa S., *Love Your Enemies: Discipleship, Pacifism, and Just War Theory*, Minneapolis, MN: Fortress Press, 1994.

Calhoun, Craig (ed.), *Habermas and the Public Sphere*, Cambridge, MA: MIT Press, 1992.

Chaplin, Jonathan, 'Legal Monism and Religious Pluralism: Rowan Williams on Religion, Loyalty and Law', *International Journal of Public Theology* 2/4 (2008), pp. 418–41.

Chaturvedi, Benarsidas and Marjorie Sykes, *Charles Freer Andrews: A Narrative*, London: George Allen & Unwin Ltd, 1949.

Cho, Yonggi, *Threefold Blessing*, Seoul: Yongsan Publications, 1977.

Cho, Yonggi, *The Fourth Dimension*, Seoul: Seoul Word Publications, 1996.

Choi, Hyeung-Mook, 'Some Issues of Minjung Theology in 1990s', *Sidae ywa Minjung Theology* (1998), pp. 345–69.

Chopp, Rebecca, 'Latin American Liberation Theology', in David F. Ford (ed.), *The Modern Theologians: An Introduction to Christian Theology in the Twentieth Century*, 2nd edn, Oxford: Blackwell, 1997, pp. 409–25.

Chung, Hyun Kyung, 'Come, Holy Spirit – Renew the Whole Creation', in Michael Kinnamon (ed.), *Signs of the Spirit: The Official Report of the Seventh Assembly*, Geneva: World Council of Churches, 1991, pp. 37–47.

Chung, Hyun Kyung, '"Han-pu-ri": Doing Theology from Korean Women's Perspective', in R. S. Sugirtharajah (ed.), *Frontiers in Asian Christian Theology: Emerging Trends*, Maryknoll, NY: Orbis Books, 1994, pp. 52–62.

Chung, Hyun Kyung, 'Ecology, Feminism and African and Asian Spirituality: Towards a Spirituality of Eco-Feminism', in David Hallman (ed.), *Ecotheology: Voices from South and North*, Geneva: World Council of Churches, 1994, pp. 175–8.

Chung, Sung-Han, *A History of Unification Movements in Korean Churches*, Seoul: Grisim, 2003.

Clarke, Sathianathan, *Dalits and Christianity: Subaltern Religion and Liberation Theology in India*, New Delhi: Oxford University Press, 1999.

Clegg, Cecelia, 'Embracing a Threatening Other: Identity and Reconciliation in Northern Ireland', in S. Kim, P. Kollontai and G. Hoyland (eds), *Peace and Reconciliation: In Search of Shared Identity*, Aldershot: Ashgate, 2008, pp. 81–93.

Collet, Sophia D., *The Life and Letters of Raja Rammohun Roy*, Calcutta: Sadharan Brahmo Samaj, 1900.

Commission on World Mission and Evangelism, *Your Kingdom Come: Mission Perspectives*, Geneva: World Council of Churches, 1980.

Corbridge, Stuart (ed.), *Development Studies: A Reader*, London: Edward Arnold, 1995.

Coward, Harold (ed.), *Hindu–Christian Dialogue*, Maryknoll, NY: Orbis Books, 1989.

Coward, Harold and Gordon S. Smith (eds), *Religion and Peacebuilding*, Albany, NY: State University of New York Press, 2004.

Crossley, Nick and John Michael Roberts (eds), *After Habermas: New Perspectives on the Public Sphere*, Oxford: Blackwell, 2004.

D'sa, Francis, 'How Is It that We Hear, Each of Us, in Our Own Native Language', in Philip Wickeri (ed.), *Scripture, Community, and Mission*, Hong Kong: CCA, 2003, pp. 127–51.

Daly, Mary, *Beyond the Father: Toward a Philosophy of Women's Liberation*, London: The Women's Press, 1986.

Davie, Grace, *Europe – The Exceptional Case: Parameters of Faith in the Modern World*, London: Darton, Longman & Todd, 2002.

de Gruchy, John, *Reconciliation: Restoring Justice*, London: SCM Press, 2002.

de Gruchy, John, 'Public Theology as Christian Witness: Exploring the Genre', *International Journal of Public Theology* 1/1 (2007), pp. 26–41.

Dean, William, 'Forum', *Religion and American Culture* 10/1 (2000), pp. 1–8.

Deane-Drummond, Celia E., *The Ethics of Nature*, Oxford: Blackwell, 2004.

Deane-Drummond, Celia E., *Eco-Theology*, London: Darton, Longman & Todd, 2008.

Devasahyam, D. M. and A. N. Sunarisanam, *Rethinking Christianity in India*, Madras: Hogarth Press, 1938.

Dussel, Enrique, *A History of the Church in Latin America*, trans. Alan Neely, Grand Rapids, MI: Eerdmans, 1981.

Elliott, Charles, *Sword and Spirit: Christianity in a Divided World*, London: BBC Books, 1988.

Fenn, Eric, 'The Bible and the Missionary', in S. L. Greenslade (ed.), *The Cambridge History of the Bible*, Cambridge: Cambridge University Press, 1963, pp. 383–406.

Fernandes, Walter, 'Caste and Conversion Movements in India', *Social Action* 31 (Jul.–Sept. 1981), pp. 261–90.

Fernandes, Walter, 'Conversion, the Caste Factor and Dominant Reaction', *International Review of Mission* 6/4 (Oct. 1984), pp. 289–306.

Fiorenza, Elisabeth Schüssler, *In Memory of Her: A Feminist Theological Reconstruction of Christian Origins*, New York: Crossroad, 1983.

Forrester, Duncan B., *Caste and Christianity: Attitudes and Policies on Caste of Anglo-Saxon Protestant Missions in India*, London: Curzon, 1980.

Forrester, Duncan B., *Christian Justice and Public Policy*, Cambridge: Cambridge University Press, 1997.

Forrester, Duncan B., *On Human Worth: A Christian Vindication of Equality*, London: SCM Press, 2001.

Frame, Tom, 'Rowan Williams on War and Peace', in Matheson Russell (ed.), *On Rowan Williams: Critical Essays*, Eugene, OR: Cascade Books, 2009, pp. 163–85.

Freire, Paulo, *Pedagogy of the Oppressed*, trans. Myra Bergman Ramos, New York: Seabury Press, 1970.

Freston, Paul, *Evangelicals and Politics in Asia, Africa and Latin America*,

Cambridge: Cambridge University Press, 2001.

George, K. M., 'Integrity of Creation and the Church's Task', *National Council of Churches in India Review* CVIII/8 (Sept. 1988), pp. 475–84.

George, Koonthanam, 'Yahweh the Defender of the Dalits: A Reflection on Isaiah 3:12–15', in R. S. Sugirtharajah (ed.), *Voices from the Margin: Interpreting the Bible in the Third World*, London: SPCK, 1995, pp. 105–16.

Giddens, Anthony, *Modernity and Self-Identity: Self and Society in the Late Modern Age*, Cambridge: Polity Press, 1991.

Gispert-Sauch, George, 'Asian Theology', in David F. Ford (ed.), *The Modern Theologians: An Introduction to Christian Theology in the Twentieth Century*, 2nd edn, Oxford: Blackwell, 1997, pp. 460–1.

Gnanadason, Aruna, 'Towards a Feminist Eco-Theology for India', in Daniel D. Chetti (ed.), *Ecology and Development: Theological Perspectives*, Madras: Gurukul, 1991, pp. 26–37.

Gnanadason, Aruna, 'Women, Economy and Ecology', in David Hallman (ed.), *Ecotheology: Voices from South and North*, Geneva: World Council of Churches, 1994, pp. 179–85.

Goel, Sita Ram, *Catholic Ashrams: Sannyasins or Swindlers?*, 2nd edn, New Delhi: Voice of India, 1994.

Granberg-Michaelson, Wesley, 'Creation in Ecumenical Theology', in David Hallman (ed.), *Ecotheology: Voices from South and North*, Geneva: World Council of Churches, 1994, pp. 96–106.

Griffiths, Bede, *Christ in India: Essays Towards a Hindu–Christian Dialogue*, New York: Charles Scribner's Sons, 1966.

Gutiérrez, Gustavo, *A Theology of Liberation: History, Politics and Salvation*, rev. edn, London: SCM Press, 1973.

Gutiérrez, Gustavo, 'Towards the Fifth Centenary', in Leonardo Boff and Virgil Elizondo (eds), *1492–1992: The Voice of the Victims*, London: SCM Press, 1990, pp. 1–10.

Habermas, Jürgen, *The Structural Transformation of the Public Sphere: An Inquiry into a Category of Bourgeois Society*, trans. Thomas Burger, Cambridge: Polity Press, 1989 [original publication in German in 1962].

Hainsworth, Deirdre King and Scott R. Paeth (eds), *Public Theology for a Global Society: Essays in Honor of Max L. Stackhouse*, Grand Rapids, MI: Eerdmans, 2010.

Hallman, David (ed.), *Ecotheology: Voices from South and North*, Geneva: World Council of Churches, 1994.

Ham, Seok-Heon, 'The True Meaning of Ssi-al', in NCC (ed.), *Minjung and Korean Theology*, Seoul: Korea Theological Study Institute, 1982, pp. 9–13.

Hanson, Eric O., *Religion and Politics in the International System Today*, Cambridge: Cambridge University Press, 2006.

Hardy, Daniel, 'Theology through Philosophy', in David Ford (ed.), *The Modern Theologians: An Introduction to Christian Theology in the Twentieth Century*, vol. 2, Oxford: Blackwell, 1989, pp. 31–9.

Hastings, Adrian, 'Latin America', in Adrian Hastings (ed.), *A World History of Christianity*, London: Cassell, 1999, pp. 328–68.

Hehir, J. Bryan, 'Forum', *Religion and American Culture* 10/1 (2000), p. 20.

Hennelly, Alfred T. (ed.), *Liberation Theology: A Documentary History*, Maryknoll, NY: Orbis Books, 1990.

Henzell-Thomas, Jeremy, 'Cartoon Wars: The Challenge from Muslims in the West', *Emel* (March 2006), pp. 41–2.

Hewitt, Marsha Aileen, 'Critical Theory', in Peter Scott and William T. Cavanaugh (eds), *The Blackwell Companion to Political Theology*, Oxford: Blackwell, 2004, pp. 455–70.

Hewitt, Tom, 'Developing Countries: 1945 to 1990', in Tim Allen and Alan Thomas (eds), *Poverty and Development in the 1990s*, Oxford: Oxford University Press, 1992, pp. 223–34.

Heyd, David, 'Introduction', in David Heyd (ed.), *Toleration: An Elusive Virtue*, Princeton, NJ: Princeton University Press, 1996, pp. 11–17.

Higton, Mike, 'Rowan Williams and Sharia: Defending the Secular', *International Journal of Public Theology* 2/4 (2008), pp. 400–17.

Himes, Michael J. and Kenneth R. Himes, *Fullness of Faith: The Public Significance of Theology*, New York: Paulist Press, 1993.

Hoekendijk, J. C., 'The Church in Missionary Thinking', *International Review of Mission* XLI/163 (July 1952), pp. 334–5.

Hofmann, Murad, 'Sliding Towards the Clash', *Emel* (March 2006), p. 44.

Hogg, A. G., in John Mott (ed.), *Evangelism for the World Today: As Interpreted by Christian Leaders throughout the World*, New York: Harper Brothers, 1938, pp. 20–5.

Hogg, A. G., 'The Christian Attitude to Non-Christian Faith', in IMC, *The Authority of the Faith*, Oxford: Oxford University Press, 1939, pp. 102–25.

Hollenbach, David, 'Public Theology in America: Some Questions for Catholicism after John Courtney Murray', *Theological Studies* 37/2 (June 1976), pp. 290–303.

Hollenbach, David, *The Global Face of Public Faith: Politics, Human Rights, and Christian Ethics*, Washington, DC: Georgetown University Press, 2003.

IMC, *The World Mission of the Church*, London: IMC, 1939.

Institute of Korean Church History Studies, The, *A History of Korean Church* I, Seoul: Korean Literature Press, 1989.

Institute of Theological Studies, The, *Research on Socio-Political Consciousness of Korean Protestant Christians*, Seoul, 2004.

Jathanna, Origen Vasantha, *The Decisiveness of the Christ-Event and the Universality of Christianity in a World of Religious Plurality*, Berne: Peter Lang, 1981.

Jayakumar, Samuel, *Dalit Consciousness and Christian Conversion: Historical Resources for a Contemporary Debate*, Delhi: ISPCK, 1999.

Jenkins, Philip, *The Next Christendom: The Coming of Global Christianity*, Oxford: Oxford University Press, 2002.

John, T. K. (ed.), *Bread and Breath: Essays in Honor of Samuel Rayan*, Anand: Gujarat Sahitya Prakash, 1991.

Jones, E. Stanley, *The Christ of the Indian Road*, New York: Abingdon Press, 1925.

Jones, Kenneth W., *The New Cambridge History of India, III.1: Socio-Religious Reform Movements in British India*, Cambridge: Cambridge University Press, 1989.

Jung, Hoon-Taek, 'The "Blessed" in the New Testament', *Mockhea ywa Sinhack* (Dec. 1999), pp. 92–104.

Kalam, Mohammed A., 'Why the Harijan Convert to Islam Views Reservations with Reservation', *South Asia Research* 4/2 (Nov. 1984), pp. 153–67.

Kang, Chun-Mo, 'Korean Church under Kibock Sinang', *Pulbit Mockhea* (Sept. 1996), pp. 15–31.

Kang, Sa-Moon, 'The Problem of Application of Jubilee Law to 50th Anniversary of Liberation', in Korean Association for Christian Studies (ed.), *50th Anniversary of Liberation and Jubilee*, pp. 47–82.

Kang, Seung-Jae, 'Critique on Kibock Sinang', *Pulbit Mockhea* (Mar. 1990), pp. 82–98.

Khan, Mumtaz Ali, 'A Brief Summary of the Study on "Mass Conversions of Meenakshipuram: A Sociological Enquiry"', *Religion and Society* XXVIII/4 (4 Dec. 1981), pp. 37–50.

Kim, Byeung-Seo, 'Well Established Kibock Sinang', *Sinang Saekae* (Apr. 1989), pp. 34–9.

Kim, Chang Rak, 'Jubilee in the Bible and Jubilee in the Korean Peninsula', in Institute of Theological Studies, *People's Unification and Peace*, Seoul: The Institute of Theological Studies, 1995, pp. 157–215.

Kim, Chi Ha, *The Gold-Crowned Jesus & Other Writings*, Maryknoll, NY: Orbis Books, 1978.

Kim, Eun-Hong, 'Overcoming Family-Based Kibock Sinang', *Kidockyo Sasang* (Mar. 2000), pp. 138–42.

Kim, Jin-Ho and Lee Sook-jin, 'A Retrospect and Prospect on the Korean Modernity and Minjung Theology', *The Journal of Theologies and Cultures in Asia* (Feb. 2002), pp. 157–75.

Kim, Jin-Hong, 'The Shadow of Kibock Sinang in the Church', *Mockhea ywa Sinhack* (Dec. 1999), pp. 60–6.

Kim, Joon-Gon, 'Korea's Total Evangelization Movement', in Ro Bong-Rin and Marlin L. Nelson (eds), *Korean Church Growth Explosion*, Seoul: Word of Life Press, 1983, pp. 17–50.

Kim, Kirsteen, 'Gender Issues in Intercultural Theological Perspective', in Mark J. Cartledge and David Cheetham (eds), *Intercultural Theology: A Primer*, London: SCM Press, 2011, pp. 75–92.

Kim, Kirsteen, 'India', in John Parratt (ed.), *An Introduction to Third World Theology*, Cambridge: Cambridge University Press, 2004, pp. 44–73.

Kim, Sebastian and Kirsteen Kim, *Christianity as a World Religion*, London: Continuum, 2008.

Kim, Sun-Jae, 'Yesterday, Today and Tomorrow of *Minjung* Theology', *Shinhack Sasang* (Spring 1998), pp. 8–9.

Kim, Yong-Bock, 'Preface', in Korean Association for Christian Studies (ed.), *50th Anniversary of Liberation and Jubilee*, pp. 5–14.

Kim, Young Jae, 'The Relationship between Kibock Sinang of the Korean Church and the Church Growth', *Mockhea ywa Sinhack* (Dec. 1999), pp. 74–8.

Kinnamon, Michael (ed.), *Signs of the Spirit: The Official Report of the Seventh Assembly*, Geneva: World Council of Churches, 1991.

Kinuka, Hisako, 'The Syrophoenician Woman: Mark 7.24–30', in R. S. Sugirtharajah (ed.), *Voices from the Margin: Interpreting the Bible in the Third World*, London: SPCK, 1995, pp. 138–55.

Klausen, Jytte, *The Cartoons that Shook the World*, New Haven and London: Yale University Press, 2009.

Klausen, Jytte, *The Islamic Challenge: Politics and Religion in Western Europe*,

Oxford: Oxford University Press, 2005.

KNCC, 'Declaration of the Churches of Korea on National Reunification and Peace', 1988.

Koopman, Nico, 'Some Comments on Public Theology Today', *Journal of Theology for Southern Africa* 117 (Nov. 2003), pp. 3–19.

Kraemer, Hendrik, *The Christian Message in a Non-Christian World*, London: Edinburgh House, 1938.

Kunelius, Risto, Elisabeth Eide, Oliver Hahn and Ronald Schroeder (eds), *Reading the Muhammed Cartoons Controversy: An International Analysis of Press Discourses on Free Speech and Political Spin*, Bochum/ Freiburg: Projektverlag, 2007.

Küng, Hans, *On Being a Christian*, trans. Edward Quinn, London: Collins, 1977.

Lan, Kwok Pui, 'Discovering the Bible in the Non-biblical World', in R. S. Sugirtharajah (ed.), *Voices from the Margin: Interpreting the Bible in the Third World*, London: SPCK, 1995, pp. 289–305.

Lee, Archie, 'Theological Reading of Chinese Creation Stories of P'an Ku and Nu Kua', in John England and Archie Lee (eds), *Doing Theology with Asian Resources*, Auckland: PTCA, 1993, pp. 230–7.

Lee, Archie, 'The Chinese Creation Myth of Nu Kua and the Biblical Narrative in Genesis 1—2', in R. S. Sugirtharajah (ed.), *Voices from the Margin: Interpreting the Bible in the Third World*, London: SPCK, 1995, pp. 368–80.

Lee, Moon-Jang, 'What about Kibock Sinang of the Koreans?', *Mockhea ywa Sinhack* (Dec. 1999), pp. 52–9.

Lesser, R. H., 'Ecology and Spirituality', *In Christo* 29/1 (Jan. 1991), p. 24–33.

Liechty, Joseph and Cecelia Clegg, *Moving beyond Sectarianism: Religion, Conflict, and Reconciliation in Northern Ireland*, Dublin: Columba Press, 2001.

Lindsey, W. D., 'Public Theology as Civil Discourse: What are We Talking About?', *Horizons* 19/1 (1992), pp. 44–69.

Little, David (ed.), *Peacemakers in Action: Profiles of Religion in Conflict Resolution*, Cambridge: Cambridge University Press, 2007.

Little, David and L. Scott Appleby, 'A Moment of Opportunity? The Promise of Religious Peacebuilding in an Era of Religious and Ethnic Conflict', in Harold Coward and Gordon S. Smith (eds), *Religion and Peacebuilding*, Albany, NY: State University of New York Press, 2004, pp. 1–23.

Lochhead, David, 'The Liberation of the Bible', in Norman K. Gottwald (ed.), *The Bible and Liberation: Political and Social Hermeneutics*, Maryknoll, NY: Orbis Books, 1983, p. 133.

Luzbetak, Louis, *The Church and Cultures: New Perspectives in Missiological Anthropology*, 2nd edn, Maryknoll, NY: Orbis Books, 1988.

Martinez, Gaspar, *Confronting the Mystery of God: Political, Liberation, and Public Theologies*, London: Continuum, 2001.

Marty, Martin, 'Reinhold Niebuhr: Public Theology and the American Experience', *The Journal of Religion* 54/4 (Oct. 1974), pp. 332–59.

Marty, Martin, *Public Church: Mainline–Evangelical–Catholic*, New York: Crossroad, 1981.

Maryknoll Documentation, *Between Honesty and Hope*, Maryknoll, NY: Maryknoll Documentation Series, 1970.

Mataji, Vandana, *Gurus, Ashrams and Christians*, Delhi: ISPCK, 1978.

Mataji, Vandana, *Waters of Fire*, Bangalore: ATC, 1989.

Mataji, Vandana (ed.), *Christian Ashrams: A Movement with a Future?*, Delhi: ISPCK, 1993.

Mataji, Vandana, *Christian Ashrams: A Movement with a Future?*, Delhi: ISPCK, 1993.

Mathew, George, 'Politicisation of Religion: Conversions to Islam in Tamil Nadu', *Economic and Political Weekly* (19 and 26 June 1982), pp. 1032–3, 1068–9.

Mathews, Charles T., *A Theology of Public Life*, Cambridge: Cambridge University Press, 2007.

Mattam, Joseph and Sebastian Kim (eds), *Dimensions of Mission in India*, Bombay: St Pauls, 1995.

Mattam, Joseph and Sebastian C. H. Kim (eds), *Trends in Mission: Historical and Theological Perspectives*, Bombay: St Pauls, 1997.

Matthew, K. M., 'In Search of a Theology of the Environment: The Message of the Earth Summit II', *Vidyajyoti* LVII/4 (April 1993), pp. 216–29.

Mbiti, John, *Bible and Theology in African Christianity*, Oxford and Nairobi: Oxford University Press, 1986.

McKay, Stan, 'An Aboriginal Perspective on the Integrity of Creation', in David Hallman (ed.), *Ecotheology: Voices from South and North*, Geneva: World Council of Churches, 1994, pp. 213–17.

McLeod, Hugh, *Religion and the People of Western Europe 1789–1989*, Oxford and New York: Oxford University Press, 1997.

Meeks, M. Douglas, 'Global Economy and the Globalization of Theological Education: An Essay', in Alice Frazer Evans, Robert A. Evans and David A. Roozen (eds), *The Globalization of Theological Education*, Maryknoll, NY: Orbis Books, 1993.

Michael, S. M. (ed.), *Dalits in Modern India: Vision and Values*, New Delhi: Vistaar Publications, 1999.

Min, Jong-Ki, 'Let Us Remove Kibock Sinang from the Church', *Mockhea ywa Sinhack* (December 1999), pp. 67–73.

Min, Kyeung Bae, *History of Christian Church in Korea*, Seoul: Christian Literature Society of Korea, 1982.

Min, Kyeung Bae, *Korean Christianity and Reunification Movement*, Seoul: Korean Institute of Church History, 2001.

Min, Yong-Jin, *Peace, Unification and Jubilee*, Seoul: Christian Literature Society of Korea, 1995.

Minear, Paul S., *Images of the Church in the New Testament*, London: Lutterworth Press, 1961.

Mojola, Aloo Osotsi, 'How the Bible is Received in Communities: A Brief Overview with Particular Reference to East Africa', in Philip L. Wickeri (ed.), *Scripture, Community, and Mission*, Hong Kong: Christian Conference of Asia, 2002, pp. 46–69.

Moltmann, Jürgen, *God for a Secular Society: The Public Relevance of Theology*, London: SCM Press, 1999.

Moltmann, Jürgen, 'Public Theology in Germany after Auschwitz', in William Storrar and Andrew Morton (eds), *Public Theology for the 21st Century*, London and New York: T & T Clark, 2004, pp. 37–43.

Moon Ik-Hwan, *I Shall Go Even on Foot*, Seoul: Shilchun Munhacksa, 1990.

Moon, Cyris, 'A Korean Minjung Perspective: The Hebrews and the Exodus', in R. S. Sugirtharajah (ed.), *Voices from the Margin: Interpreting the Bible in the Third World*, London: SPCK, 1995, pp. 228–43.

Moon, Dong-Hwan, '21st Century and *Minjung* Theology', *Shinhack Sasang* (Summer 2000), pp. 30–54.

Mosala, Itumeleng, 'The Implications of the Text of Esther for African Women's Struggle for Liberation in South Africa', in R. S. Sugirtharajah (ed.), *Voices from the Margin: Interpreting the Bible in the Third World*, London: SPCK, 1995, pp. 168–78.

Mosse, David, 'The Politics of Religious Synthesis: Roman Catholicism and Hindu Village Society in Tamil Nadu, India', in Charles Stewart and Rosalind Shaw (eds), *Syncretism/Anti-Syncretism: The Politics of Religious Synthesis*, London: Routledge, 1994, pp. 87–92.

Murray, John Courtney, *We Hold these Truths: Catholic Reflections on the American Proposition*, New York: Sheed & Ward, 1960.

Na, Young-Hwan, 'Minjung Theology from the Evangelical Perspective', *Mockhea ywa Sinhack* (Aug. 1992), pp. 40–50.

Nag, Kalidas and Debajyoti Burman (eds), *The English Works of Raja Rammohun Roy*, Part II, Calcutta: Sadharan Brahmo Samaj, 1945.

Nandy, Ashis, 'The Politics of Secularism and the Recovery of Religious Tolerance', *Alternatives* XIII/2 (Apr. 1988), pp. 177–94.

National Bible Society of Scotland, *Report of National Bible Society of Scotland*, 1930.

Neill, Stephen, *A History of Christian Mission*, London: Penguin, 1963.

Neill, Stephen, *The Unfinished Task*, London: Edinburgh House, 1957.

Nereparampil, Lucius, 'An Eco-Theology Foreshadowed in the Gospel of John', *Bible Bhasyam* XIX/3 (1993), pp. 183–94.

Neuhaus, Richard John, *The Naked Public Square: Religion and Democracy in America*, 2nd edn, Grand Rapids, MI: Eerdmans, 1986.

Newbigin, Lesslie, 'Salvation and Humanisation – Book Review', *Religion and Society* XVIII/1 (Mar. 1971), pp. 71–80.

Newbigin, Lesslie, 'The Call to Mission – A Call to Unity?', in *The Church Crossing Frontiers*, Uppsala: Gleerup, 1969, pp. 254–65.

Nirmal, Arvind P., 'Ecology, Ecumenics and Economics in Relation: A New Theological Paradigm', in Daniel D. Chetti (ed.), *Ecology and Development: Theological Perspectives*, Madras: Gurukul, 1991, pp. 3–25.

Noll, Mark, 'Forum', *Religion and American Culture* 10/1 (2000), pp. 9–12.

Northcott, Michael, *A Moral Climate: The Ethics of Global Warming*, London: Darton, Longman & Todd, 2007.

Northcott, Michael, *Christianity and Environmental Ethics*, Cambridge: Cambridge University Press, 1996.

Padilla, C. Rene, *Mission between the Times: Essays on the Kingdom*, Grand Rapids, MI: Eerdmans, 1985.

Paik, Lak-Geoon George, *The History of Protestant Missions in Korea: 1832–1910*, Seoul: Yonsei University Press, 1929.

Panikkar, Raymond, *The Unknown Christ of Hinduism*, London: Darton, Longman & Todd, 1964.

Panikkar, Raimundo, *The Unknown Christ of Hinduism: Towards an Ecumenical*

Christophany, rev. edn, Maryknoll, NY: Orbis Books, 1981.

Parekh, Bhikhu, *Rethinking Multiculturalism: Cultural Diversity and Political Theory*, New York: Palgrave, 2000.

Parekh, Manilal, 'Keshub Chunder Sen: His Relation to Christianity', *International Review of Mission* XVII/65 (Jan. 1928), pp. 145–54.

Parekh, Manilal, 'The Spiritual Significance and Value of Baptism', *National Council of Churches in India Review* XLIV/9 (Sept. 1924), pp. 324–9.

Park, Jong Hwa, 'Theological and Political Task for Jubilee in the Church and People in Korea', in Korean Association for Christian Studies (ed.), *50th Anniversary of Liberation and Jubilee*, Seoul, 1995, pp. 25–44.

Park, Soon-Kyeung, *The Future of Unification Theology*, Seoul: Saknejul, 1997.

Park, Sung-Jun, 'Reflection on Minjung Theology in the Context of the 21st Century', *Shinhack Sasang* (Summer 2000), pp. 70–89.

Parratt, John, 'Recent Writing on Dalit Theology: A Bibliographical Essay', *International Review of Mission* 83/329 (1994), pp. 329–37.

Perkins, Harvey, Harry Daniel and Asal Simanjuntak, 'Let My People Go', in Gerald H. Anderson and Thomas F. Stransky (eds), *Mission Trends No 3: Third World Theologies*, New York: Paulist Press, 1976, pp. 192–210.

Pieris, Aloysius, 'Inculturation in Non-Semitic Asia', *The Month* 19/3 (Mar. 1986), pp. 83–7.

Pieris, Aloysius, *An Asian Theology of Liberation*, Maryknoll, NY: Orbis Books, 1988.

Pike, Frederick B., 'Latin America', in John McManners (ed.), *The Oxford History of Christianity*, Oxford: Oxford University Press, 2002, pp. 437–73.

Potts, E. Daniel, *British Baptist Missionaries in India, 1793–1837: The History of Serampore and its Missions*, Cambridge: Cambridge University Press, 1967.

Radhakrishnan, S., *The Hindu View of Life*, New Delhi: HarperCollins, 1927.

Radhakrishnan, S., *Eastern Religions and Western Thought*, 2nd edn, Oxford: Oxford University Press, 1940.

Radhakrishnan, S., 'Hinduism', in A. L. Basham (ed.), *A Cultural History of India*, Delhi: Oxford University Press, 1975, pp. 70–2.

Raj, S. Albones, 'Mass Religious Conversion as Protest Movement: A Framework', *Religion and Society* XXVIII/4 (Dec. 1981), pp. 59–64.

Rayan, Samuel, 'Theological Priorities in India Today', in Virginia Fabella and Sergio Torres (eds), *Irruption of the Third World – Challenge to Theology. Papers from the Fifth International Conference of the Ecumenical Association of Third World Theologians*, Maryknoll, NY: Orbis Books, 1983, pp. 30–41.

Rayan, Samuel, 'Caesar versus God' in Sebastian Kappen (ed.), *Jesus Today*, Madras: AICUF, 1985, pp. 88–97.

Rayan, Samuel, 'The Earth is the Lord's', in David Hallman (ed.), *Ecotheology: Voices from South and North*, Geneva: World Council of Churches, 1994, pp. 130–54.

Robinson, Rowena, *Christians of India*, New Delhi: Sage, 2003.

Ruether, Rosemary Radford, 'Spirit and Matter, Public and Private: The Challenge of Feminism to Traditional Dualisms', in Paula M. Cooey, Sharon A. Farmer and Mary Ellen Ross (eds), *Embodied Love: Sensuality and Relationship as Feminist Values*, San Francisco: Harper & Row, 1987, pp. 65–76.

Ruether, Rosemary Radford, 'Motherearth and the Megamachine: A Theology of Liberation in a Feminine, Somatic and Ecological Perspective', in Carol P. Christ and Judith Plaskow (eds), *Womanspirit Rising: A Feminist Reader in Religion*, San Francisco: Harper, 1992, pp. 43–52.

Ruether, Rosemary Radford, 'Eco-feminism and Theology', in David Hallman (ed.), *Ecotheology: Voices from South and North*, Geneva: World Council of Churches, 1994, pp. 199–204.

Samartha, Stanley J., 'Scripture and Scriptures', in R. S. Sugirtharajah (ed.), *Voices from the Margin: Interpreting the Bible in the Third World*, London: SPCK, 1995, pp. 9–36.

Samartha, Stanley J., *Courage for Dialogue: Ecumenical Issues in Inter-Religious Relationships*, Geneva: World Council of Churches, 1981.

Samuel, Vinay, 'Modernity, Mission and Non-Western Societies', in Philip Sampson (ed.), *Faith and Modernity*, Oxford: Regnum Lynx, 1994, p. 320.

Sauter, Gerhard, 'What does Common Identity cost – not only economically and politically, but also spiritually and mentally? Some German experiences and provoking questions', in S. Kim, P. Kollontai and G. Hoyland (eds), *Peace and Reconciliation: In Search of Shared Identity*, Aldershot: Ashgate, 2008, pp. 21–34.

Schmidt-Leukel, Perry (ed.), *War and Peace in World Religions: The Gerald Weisfeld Lectures 2003*, London: SCM Press, 1989.

Schreiter, Robert J., *Constructing Local Theologies*, Maryknoll, NY: Orbis Books, 1985.

Schreiter, Robert, 'Establishing a Shared Identity: The Role of the Healing of Memories and of Narrative', in S. Kim, P. Kollontai and G. Hoyland (eds), *Peace and Reconciliation: In Search of Shared Identity*, Aldershot: Ashgate, 2008, pp. 7–20.

Schreuder, Deryck and Geoffrey Oddie, 'What is "Conversion"? History, Christianity and Religious Change in Colonial Africa and South Asia', *The Journal of Religious History* 15/4 (Dec. 1989), pp. 512–13.

Scott, David C., 'Some Reflections on "A Theological Response to Ecological Crisis"', *Bangalore Theological Forum* XXV/1 (Mar. 1993), pp. 21–2.

Sebastian, Joseph, *God As Feminine: Hindu and Christian Visions in Dialogue*, Tiruchirapalli: St Paul's Seminary, 1995, pp. 167–233.

Segundo, Juan Luis, *The Liberation of Theology*, trans. John Drury, Maryknoll, NY: Orbis Books, 1976.

Selvanayagam, Israel (ed.), *Moving Forms of Theology: Faith Talk's Changing Contexts*, Delhi: ISPCK, 2002.

Senior, Donald and Carroll Stuhlmueller, *The Biblical Foundations for Mission*, London: SCM Press, 1983.

Sharpe, Eric J., *Faith Meets Faith: Some Christian Attitudes to Hinduism in the Nineteenth and Twentieth Centuries*, London: SCM Press, 1977.

Shorter, Aylward, *Toward a Theology of Inculturation*, Maryknoll, NY: Orbis Books, 1988.

Sivard, Ruth Leger, with Arlette Brauer and Milton I. Roemer, *World Military and Social Expenditures*, Washington, DC: World Priorities, 1989.

Smith-Christopher, Daniel L. (ed.), *Subverting Hatred: The Challenge of Non-violence in Religious Traditions*, Maryknoll, NY: Orbis Books, 1998.

Soares-Prabhu, George, 'From Alienation to Inculturation: Some Reflections on Doing Theology in India Today', in T. K. John (ed.), *Bread and Breath: Essays in Honour of Samuel Rayan, S. J.*, Anand: Gujarat Sahitya Prakash, 1991.

Sobrino, Jon, 'The Crucified Peoples: Yahweh's Suffering Servant Today', in Leonardo Boff and Virgil Elizondo (eds), *1492–1992: The Voice of the Victims*, London: SCM Press, 1990, pp. 120–9.

Song, C. S., *Third-Eye Theology: Theology in Formation in Asian Settings*, London: SCM Press, 1980.

Song, Jae-Keun, 'The Danger of Kibock Sinang from the Perspective of Covenant Theology', *Mockhea ywa Sinhack* (Dec. 1999), pp. 79–91.

Stackhouse, Max, *Public Theology and Political Economy: Christian Stewardship in Modern Society*, Lanham, MD: University Press of America, 1991.

Stackhouse, Max, 'Public Theology and Ethical Judgement', *Theology Today* 54/2 (1997), pp. 165–79.

Stackhouse, Max, *Globalization and Grace: A Christian Public Theology for a Global Future*, New York: Continuum, 2007.

Staffner, Hans, 'Conversion to Christianity, Seen from the Hindu Point of View', in Joseph Pathrapankal (ed.), *Service and Salvation: Nagpur Theological Conference on Evangelization*, Bangalore: Theological Publications in India, 1973, pp. 235–48.

Staffner, Hans, *The Significance of Jesus Christ in Asia*, Anand: Gujarat Sahitya Prakash, 1985.

Staffner, Hans, *Jesus Christ and the Hindu Community: Is a Synthesis of Hinduism and Christianity Possible?*, Anand: Gujarat Sahitya Prakash, 1988.

Storrar, William and Andrew Morton (eds), *Public Theology for the 21st Century*, London and New York: T & T Clark, 2004.

Sugirtharajah, R. S., *Voices from the Margin: Interpreting the Bible in the Third World*, London: SPCK, 1995.

Sugirtharajah, R. S. and Cecil Hargreaves (eds), *Readings in Indian Christian Theology I*, Delhi: ISPCK, 1993.

Sugirtharajah, R. S., *The Bible and the Third World*, Cambridge: Cambridge University Press, 2001.

Suh, David Kwang-sun, *The Korean Minjung in Christ*, Hong Kong: CCA, 1991.

Suh, Nam-Dong, 'Toward a Theology of Han', in Kim Yong Bock (ed.), *Minjung Theology: People as the Subjects of History*, Maryknoll, NY: Orbis Books, 1983, pp. 51–65.

Sumithra, Sunand, *Christian Theology from an Indian Perspective*, Bangalore: Theological Book Trust, 1990.

Taylor, John V., *The Go-Between God: The Holy Spirit and the Christian Mission*, London: SCM Press, 1972.

Taylor, Richard W., 'Christian Ashrams as a Style of Mission in India', *International Review of Mission* LXVIII/271 (July 1979), pp. 281–93.

Therukattil, George, 'Towards a Biblical Eco-Theology', *Jeevadhara*, XXI/126 (Nov. 1991), pp. 475–84.

Thiemann, Ronald F., *Constructing a Public Theology: The Church in a Pluralistic Culture*, Louisville, KY: John Knox Press, 1991.

Thistelton, Anthony, *New Horizons of Hermeneutics*, London: HarperCollins, 1992.

Thomas, M. M., 'The Struggle for Human Dignity as a Preparation for the Gospel', *National Council of Churches in India Review* LXXXVI/9 (Sept. 1966), pp. 356–9.

Thomas, M. M., *Salvation and Humanisation: Some Critical Issues of the Theology of Mission in Contemporary India*, Madras: CLS, 1971.

Thomas, M. M., 'The Post-Colonial Crisis in Mission – A Comment', *Religion and Society* XVIII/1 (Mar. 1971), pp. 64–70.

Thomas, M. M., 'Baptism, the Church and *Koinonia*', *Religion and Society* XIX/1 (Mar. 1972), pp. 69–90.

Thomas, M. M., *The Acknowledged Christ of the Indian Renaissance*, 3rd edn, Madras: The Senate of Serampore College, 1991.

Thompson, Henry O., *World Religions in War and Peace*, London: McFarland, 1988.

Tipton, Steven M., 'Public Theology', in Robert Wuthnow (ed.), *The Encyclopedia of Politics and Religion*, Washington, DC: Congressional Quarterly Inc., 1998, pp. 624–5.

Tracy, David, *The Analogical Imagination: Christian Theology and the Culture of Pluralism*, New York: Crossroad, 1981.

Tutu, Desmond, *No Future Without Forgiveness*, London: Rider, 1999.

Ukpong, Justin, 'Developments in Biblical Interpretation in Africa', in Gerald O. West and Musa W. Dube (eds), *The Bible in Africa: Transactions, Trajectories, and Trends*, Boston: Brill, 2000, p. 24.

Vajpeyi, Dhirendra, 'Muslim Fundamentalism in India: A Crisis of Identity in a Secular State', in Dhirendra Vajpeyi and Yogendra K. Malik (eds), *Religious and Ethnic Minority Politics in South Asia*, New Delhi: Manohar, 1989, pp. 66–7.

Valentin, Benjamin, *Mapping Public Theology: Beyond Culture, Identity, and Difference*, London: Continuum, 2002.

Van Elderen, Marlin, 'Integrity of Creation', *National Council of Churches in India Review* CVIII/8 (Sept. 1988), pp. 487–92.

Veeraraj, Anand, 'Eco-Spirituality and the Religious Community', *National Council of Churches in India Review* CX/9 (Oct. 1990), pp. 535–44.

Verkuyl, Johannes, *Contemporary Missiology: An Introduction*, Grand Rapids, MI: Eerdmans, 1978.

Wallis, Jim, 'Disarm Iraq ... Without War', *Sojourners Magazine* (Nov./Dec. 2002).

Wallis, Jim and John Bryson, 'There is a Third Way', *Washington Post*, 14 March 2003.

Wallis, Jim, *God's Politics: Why the Right Gets It Wrong and the Left Doesn't Get It*, New York: HarperSanFrancisco, 2005.

Warrior, Robert, 'A Native American Perspective: Canaanites, Cowboys, and Indians', in R. S. Sugirtharajah (ed.), *Voices from the Margin: Interpreting the Bible in the Third World*, London: SPCK, 1995, pp. 277–85.

Weigel, George, 'Moral Clarity in a Time of War', *First Things* (Dec. 2002).

Weigel, George, 'Reality of Terrorism Calls for Fresh Look at Just-War Tradition', *The Catholic Difference*, 20 September 2001.

Weigel, George, 'What is the Just War Tradition For?', *The Catholic Difference*, 4 December 2002.

West, Gerald O. and Musa W. Dube (eds), *The Bible in Africa: Transactions, Trajectories, and Trends*, Boston: Brill, 2000.

Wilfred, Felix, 'Understanding Conversion in India Today', *International Review of Mission* 5/1 (Jan. 1983), pp. 61–73.

Wilfred, Felix, 'Towards a Better Understanding of Asian Theology: Some Basic Issues', *Vidyajyoti* 62/12 (1998), pp. 890–915.

Williams, Bernard, 'Toleration: An Impossible Virtue?', in David Heyd (ed.), *Toleration: An Elusive Virtue*, Princeton, NJ: Princeton University Press, 1996, pp. 18–27.

Williams, Rowan, 'Presidential Address', *Church Times*, 15 February 2008.

Wilson, Frederick R. (ed.), *The San Antonio Report – Your Will be Done: Mission in Christ's Way*, Geneva: World Council of Churches, 1990.

Wilson, Frederick R. (ed.), *The San Antonio Report*, Geneva: World Council of Churches, 1990.

Wingate, Andrew, 'A Study of Conversion from Christianity to Islam in Two Tamil Villages', *Religion and Society* XXVIII/4 (Dec. 1981), pp. 32–4.

Wingate, Andrew, *The Church and Conversion: A Study of Recent Conversions to and from Christianity in the Tamil Area of South India*, New Delhi: ISPCK, 1997.

Yates, Timothy, *Christian Mission in the Twentieth Century*, Cambridge: Cambridge University Press, 1994.

Yi, Mahn-Yol, *A Study of History of the Reception of Christianity in Korea*, Seoul: Durae Sidae, 1998.

Yi, Mahn-Yol, *Korean Christianity and Unification Movement*, Seoul: Institute of Korean Church History, 2001.

Yoo, Dong-Sik, *The Mineral Vein of Korean Theology*, Seoul: Jun Mang Sa, 1984.

Websites

'Declaration on Behalf of Muslim Leaders' (official translation), http://www.guidancemedia.com/downloads/articles/declaration.pdf (accessed 29 Apr. 2006).

'Environment and Climate Change Link', http://www.ctbi.org.uk/BAA/67/#christian (accessed 15 Oct. 2010).

'Letter from the Danish Government', 23 January 2006. http://www.um.dk/NR/rdonlyres/00D9E6F7-32DC-4C5A-8E24-F0C96E813C06/0/060123final.pdf (accessed 26 Mar. 2006).

'Letter from the Prime Minister to the Ambassadors', 21 October 2005, http://gfx-master.tv2.dk/images/Nyhederne/Pdf/side3.pdf (accessed 28 Apr. 2006).

'Scriptural Reasoning', http://www.scripturalreasoning.org/ (accessed 6 Mar. 2011).

Adlerstein, Yitzchok, and Michael Broyde, 'There Can Only Be One Law of the Land', Forward: The Jewish Daily, 20 February 2008, http://www.forward.com/articles/12733/ (accessed 20 Feb. 2010).

Association of Muslim Lawyers (UK), 'Submissions to the House of Lords', October 2002, http://www.muslim-lawyers.net/news/index.php3?aktion=show&number=168 (accessed 31 Aug. 2005).

BBC, 'BBC's Dilemma Over Cartoons', 3 February 2006, http://news.bbc.co.uk/newswatch/ukfs/hi/newsid_4670000/newsid_4678100/4678186.stm (accessed 26 Mar. 2006).

BBC, 'Bush's UN speech: Full text', 13 September 2002, http://news.bbc.co.uk/1/hi/world/middle_east/2254712.stm (accessed 25 July 2010).

BBC, 'Full Text: Tony Blair's Speech', 18 March 2003, http://www.guardian.co.uk/politics/2003/mar/18/foreignpolicy.iraq1 (accessed 25 July 2010).

BBC, 'Millions Join Global Anti-war Protests', 17 February 2003, http://news.bbc.co.uk/1/hi/world/europe/2765215.stm (accessed 25 Mar. 2009).

Beattie, Tina, 'Rowan Williams and Sharia Law', 12 February 2008, http://www.opendemocracy.net/article/faith_ideas/europe_islam/sharia_law_uk (accessed 12 Feb. 2010).

Benedict XVI, *Caritas in Veritate*, 29 June 2009, http://www.vatican.va/holy_father/benedict_xvi/encyclicals/documents/hf_ben-xvi_enc_20090629_caritas-in-veritate_en.html (accessed 15 Oct. 2010).

Brown, Andrew, 'Misjudgment That Made Martyrs of Others', *Guardian*, 9 February 2008, http://www.guardian.co.uk/politics/2008/feb/09/uk.religion3 (accessed 22 July 2010).

Cardinale, Gianni, 'The Catechism in a Post-Christian World: Interview with Cardinal Ratzinger', April 2003, http://www.30giorni.it/us/articolo.asp?id=775 (accessed 22 July 2010).

Catholic Education Resource Centre, 'Father Richard Neuhaus on the Iraqi Crisis', *ZENIT*, 10 March 2003, http://www.catholiceducation.org/articles/religion/re0627.html (accessed 20 July 2010).

Church of England Archbishop's Council, 'Evaluating the Threat of Military Action against Iraq: Briefing Paper', 20 March 2002, www.casi.org.uk/info/churcheng/020320coewar.pdf (accessed 23 Mar. 2010).

Church of England, 'Case for War Yet to Be Made, Warns House of Bishops', 14 January 2003, http://www.churchofengland.org/media-centre/news/2003/01/case_for_war_yet_to_be_made,_warns_house_of_bishops.aspx (accessed 22 July 2010).

Church of England, 'Church Leaders meet Foreign Secretary', http://www.cofe.anglican.org/news/church_leaders_meet_foreign_secretary.html (accessed 22 July 2010).

Church of England, 'The Church of England's Seven-Year Plan on Climate Change and Environment', October 2009, http://www.shrinkingthefootprint.cofe.anglican.org/misc_lib/14.pdf (accessed 15 Oct. 2010).

Daily Mail, 'Two of the Most Powerful Clergy in Britain Launch Stinging Attack on Archbishop Over Sharia Row', 10 February 2008, http://www.dailymail.co.uk/news/article-513351/Two-powerful-clergy-Britain-launch-stinging-attack-Archbishop-sharia-row.html (accessed 20 Feb. 2010).

Deen, Thalif, 'Pontifical Council on Climate Change and Development, 26–27 April 2007', http://www.religiousconsultation.org/News_Tracker/pontifical_council_on_climate_change.htm (accessed 15 Oct. 2010).

Ekklesia, 'Incitement to Religious Hatred: Growing Disagreement between Christians', 18 January 2005, http://www.ekklesia.co.uk/content/news_syndication/article_050118hatred.shtml (accessed 10 June 2005).

European Evangelical Alliance, 'Publication of Danish Cartoons', 8 February 2006, http://www.europeanea.org/documents/PublicationofDanishCartoonsFeb2006.doc (accessed 25 Apr. 2006).

Evangelical Climate Initiative, 'The Evangelical Climate Initiative', http://christiansandclimate.org/ (accessed 15 Oct. 2010).

Forum Against Islamophobia & Racism (FAIR), 'The Religious Offences Bill 2002: A Response', October 2002, www.fairuk.org/docs/rof2002.pdf (accessed 31 Aug. 2005).

Goddard, Andrew, 'Islamic Law and the Anglican Communion: Is there a Common Vision?' http://www.fulcrum-anglican.org.uk/page.cfm?ID=274 (accessed 20 Feb. 2010).

Goddard, Andrew, 'Prudence and Jurisprudence: Reflections on the Archbishop's Interview and Lecture', http://www.fulcrum-anglican.org.uk/page.cfm?ID=275 (accessed 25 Mar. 2010).

Guardian, 'Interview: Rowan Williams', 21 March 2006, http://www.guardian.co.uk/world/2006/mar/21/religion.uk (accessed 15 Mar. 2010).

Hobson, Theo, 'Rowan Williams: Sharia Furore, Anglican Future', 13 February 2008, http://www.opendemocracy.net/article/rowan_williams_sharia_furore_anglican_future (accessed 25 Mar. 2010).

Home Office, 'Government Reply to the Report from the Religious Offences Committee', December 2003, http://www.archive2.official-documents.co.uk/document/cm60/6091/6091.pdf (accessed 31 Oct. 2006).

Home Office, 'Racial and Religious Hatred Bill – Frequently Asked Questions', http://www.publications.parliament.uk/pa/cm200506/cmbills/011/en/060 11x--.htm (accessed 26 Aug. 2005). See also http://old.homeoffice.gov.uk/docs/racerel1.html (accessed 19 Aug. 2005).

Home Office, 'Racial and Religious Hatred Bill', 9 June 2005, http://www.publications.parliament.uk/pa/cm200506/cmbills/011/2006011.pdf (accessed 20 Oct. 2005).

House of Commons, 'Anti-Terrorism, Crime and Security Bill', 12 November 2001, http://www.publications.parliament.uk/pa/cm200102/cmbills/049/2002049.htm (accessed 18 Aug. 2005).

House of Lords, 'Racial and Religious Hatred Bill: Amendment', 20 October 2005, http://www.publications.parliament.uk/pa/ld200506/ldbills/015/amend/amo15-e.htm (accessed 3 Nov. 2005).

House of Lords, 'Religious Offences in England and Wales – First Report', 10 April 2003, http://www.publications.parliament.uk/pa/ld200203/ldselect/ldrelof/95/9501.htm (accessed 10 June 2005).

House of Lords, 'Religious Offences in England and Wales – First Report', 10 April 2003, http://www.publications.parliament.uk/pa/ld200203/ldselect/ldrelof/95/9501.htm (accessed 10 June 2005).

John Paul II, 'Address of His Holiness John Paul II to the Diplomatic Corps', 13 January 2003, http://www.vatican.va/holy_father/john_paul_ii/speeches/2003/january/documents/hf_jp-ii_spe_20030113_diplomatic-corps_en.html (accessed 22 July 2010).

John Paul II, 'Angelus', 16 March 2003, http://www.vatican.va/holy_father/john_paul_ii/angelus/2003/documents/hf_jp-ii_ang_20030316_en.html (accessed 22 July 2010).

Laghi, Pio Cardinal, 'Statement' following meeting with George Bush, 5 March 2003, http://www.cm-ngo.net/PapalEnvoyvisitsPresidentBush.html (accessed 22 July 2010).

Land, Richard, 'Letter to George W. Bush', 3 October 2002. So-called 'Land Letter', http://erlc.com/article/the-so-called-land-letter/ (accessed 25 Mar. 2010).

Lord Philips, Lord Chief Justice, 'Equality before the Law', 3 July 2008, http://www.judiciary.gov.uk/docs/speeches/lcj_equality_before_the_law_030708.pdf (accessed 13 July 2008).

Methodist Church, 'Peacemaking: A Christian Vocation', http://www.methodist.org.uk/index.cfm?fuseaction=opentogod.content&cmid=1866 (accessed 25 July 2010).

Methodist Church, 'Statement Regarding Offensive Cartoons and Inter-faith Relations', 6 February 2006, http://www.methodist.org.uk/index.cfm?fuseaction=news.newsDetail&newsid=108 (accessed 20 Mar. 2006).

Modood, Tariq, 'Multicultural Citizenship and the Anti-Sharia Storm', 14 February 2008, http://www.opendemocracy.net/article/faith_ideas/europe_islam/anti_sharia_storm (accessed 15 Mar. 2010).

National Archives, 'Racial and Religious Hatred Act 2006', http://www.opsi.gov.uk/acts/acts2006/20060001.htm (accessed 4 Feb. 2007).

National Council of Churches in the Philippines (NCCP), 'Let Not the Flame of Peace Be Extinguished', 20 March 2003, http://www.ncccusa.org/iraq/iraqstatements2.html (accessed 22 July 2010).

National Council of Churches USA, 'Statements in Response to the War on Iraq', 20 March 2003, http://www.ncccusa.org/iraq/iraqstatements2.html (accessed 22 July 2010).

NCCCUSA, 'Church Leaders United Against War in Iraq: Statement Adopted in Berlin, Germany, February 5, 2003', http://www.ncccusa.org/news/03news6.html (accessed 22 July 2010).

Office for National Statistics, 'Religion: 7 in 10 Identify as White Christian', 21 March 2005, http://www.statistics.gov.uk/CCI/nugget.asp?ID=460&Pos=1&ColRank=1&Rank=326 (accessed 20 Oct. 2005).

Pew Forum, 'Religious Groups Issue Statements on War with Iraq', 19 March 2003, http://pewforum.org/PublicationPage.aspx?id=616 (accessed 19 Mar. 2009).

Scruton, Roger, 'Islamic Law in a Secular World', 14 February 2008, http://www.opendemocracy.net/article/faith_ideas/europe_islam/secular_world (accessed 25 Mar. 2010).

Stiltner, Brian, 'The Justice of War on Iraq', http://www.elca.org/What-We-Believe/Social-Issues/Journal-of-Lutheran-Ethics/Issues/March-2003/The-Justice-of-War-on-Iraq.aspx (accessed 25 March 2010).

UN Special Rapporteurs, 23 January 2006, http://www.ambdamaskus.um.dk/NR/rdonlyres/337D2B4D-A68A-4832-AFB0-7A6BF6779E7B/0/PMsNewYearAddress2006.pdf (accessed 28 Apr. 2006).

United for Peace and Justice, 'Disarm Iraq Without War: A Statement from Religious Leaders in the US and UK', http://www.unitedforpeace.org/article.php?id=2837 (accessed 19 Mar. 2009).

United States Conference of Catholic Bishops, 'Statement on Iraq', 13 November 2002, http://www.nccbuscc.org/bishops/iraq.shtml (accessed 22 July 2010).

WCC, 'A sign of hope for the future for people of good will', 18 December 2009, http://www.oikoumene.org/gr/resources/documents/wcc-programmes/justice-diakonia-and-responsibility-for-creation/climate-change-water/statement-to-cop15-un-climate-conference-copenhagen.html (accessed 15 Oct. 2010).

WCC, 'Statement Against Military Action in Iraq', 21 February 2003, http://www.oikoumene.org/resources/documents/wcc-commissions/international-affairs/regional-concerns/middle-east/statement-against-military-action-in-iraq.html (accessed 22 July 2010).

Williams, Rowan, http://www.archbishopofcanterbury.org/852 (accessed 22 July 2010).

Williams, Rowan, 'Civil and Religious Law in England: A Religious Perspective', http://www.archbishopofcanterbury.org/1575 (accessed 12 Feb. 2010).

Williams, Rowan, 'The Media: Public Interest and Common Good', http://www.archbishopofcanterbury.org/992 (accessed 20 Mar. 2010).

Williams, Rowan, http://www.archbishopofcanterbury.org/73 (accessed 30 Mar. 2010).

Williams, Rowan, http://www.archbishopofcanterbury.org/745 (accessed 20 Feb. 2010).

World Council of Churches, 'Ecumenical Considerations for Dialogue and Relations with People of Other Religions' (2001), http://www.oikoumene. org/en/resources/documents/wcc-programmes/interreligious-dialogue-and-cooperation/interreligious-trust-and-respect/ecumenical-considerations-for-dialogue-and-relations-with-people-of-other-religions.html (accessed 17 Feb. 2011).

World Council of Churches, 'Guidelines on Dialogue with People of Living Faiths and Ideologies' (1979), http://www.oikoumene.org/en/resources/documents/ wcc-programmes/interreligious-dialogue-and-cooperation/interreligious-trust-and-respect/guidelines-on-dialogue-with-people-of-living-faiths-and-ideologies.html (accessed 17 Feb. 2011).

Wright, Tom, 'Letter to Durham Clergy on Law and Public Life', http://www. fulcrum-anglican.org.uk/page.cfm?ID=277 (accessed 20 Feb. 2010).

Zubaida, Sami, 'Sharia: Practice of Faith, Politics of Modernity', 22 February 2008, http://www.opendemocracy.net/article/faith_ideas/europe_islam/sharia_politics_of_modernity (accessed 30 Mar. 2010).

Index of Subjects and Names